G20 数字普惠金融高级原则
——基本原理

《G20数字普惠金融高级原则》(以下简称《原则》)旨在促使G20领导人采取行动运用数字方法实现普惠金融目标，以及实现包容性发展和提高妇女经济活动参与度等G20相关目标。《原则》认为，迫切需要为无法获得金融服务或缺乏金融服务的群体提供高质量、合适的金融产品和服务，同时也认为在可能的情况下需要利用数字技术实现该目标。缺乏金融服务的群体(通常包括穷人、妇女、年轻人和农村地区人口，有时也包括少数族群)需要得到特别关注，同时也需要关注移民、老年人和残疾人等弱势群体。此外，无法获得金融服务的弱势群体中可能存在一部分人无法获得数字金融服务或者不愿意接受数字金融服务，我们应切实管理和解决这种风险。

"数字普惠金融"还处于不断发展阶段，并没有统一的定义。本《原则》采用2016年G20普惠金融全球合作伙伴(GPFI)报告《全球标准制定机构与普惠金融：不断变化发展的格局》(GPFI白皮书)中的概念，即"'数字普惠金融'泛指一切通过使用数字金融服务以促进普惠金融的行动。它包括运用数字技术为无法获得金融服务或缺乏金融服务的群体提供一系列正规金融服务，其所提供的金融服务能够满足他们的需求，并且是以负责任的、成本可负担的方式提供，同时对服务提供商而言是可持续的。"[1]

"数字普惠金融"涵盖各类金融产品和服务(如支付、转账、储蓄、信贷、保险、证券、财务规划和银行对账单服务等)，通过数字化或电子化技术进行交易，如电子货币(通过线上或者移动电话发起)、支付卡和常规银行账户。[2]

本《原则》基于2010年《G20创新性普惠金融原则》[3]并对其进行了补充。这些原则体现着不断发展变化的数字金融服务，整合了自2010年起G20、GPFI以及国际标准制定机构提出的重要指引中的核心内容。更重要的是，《原则》意识到了仅靠金融服务的可得性不足以达成普惠目标；而且促进负责任的数字金融服务的广泛使用和理解，事关个人、国家和全世界的福祉。《原则》还指出，必须认识到并且积极地平衡好数字创新与快速发展的技术所带来的新风险。

落实《原则》的一个有效途径是在充分考虑本国国情的基础上，制定可实施的国家战略、相关的国家行动计划并采取国家层面的行动。

G20数字普惠金融高级原则
——具体行动

原则一
倡导利用数字技术推动普惠金融发展

促进数字金融服务是推动包容性金融体系发展的重点，它包括采用协调一致、可监测和可评估的国家战略和行动计划。

贯穿于政府部门和私人部门的政策指引与合作是发展普惠金融的关键因素。有效扩大广泛的金融服务的可得性、所有权和使用度进而实现普惠金融目标，需要通过树立榜样和主动促进创新性数字技术的使用，以惠及无法获得金融服务和缺乏金融服务的群体。[4]这一目标可通过制定国家战略实现，该战略应具有明确的愿景和具体的行动计划，它应在磋商中形成，具有协调一致性且能够被严格监测和评估，并且反映出政府与私人部门等所有利益相关者在其中发挥的作用。正如摘要中提到的，对利益相关者而言，认清如下事实十分重要，即无法获得金融服务的弱势群体中可能存在一部分人无法获得数字金融服务或者不愿意接受数字金融服务，我们应切实管理和解决这种风险。

“政府与私人部门行动”是支付与市场基础设施委员会（CPMI）和世界银行集团（WBG）联合发布的2016年《普惠金融支付领域报告》[5]（PAFI报告）中的七项指导性原则（PAFI指导性原则）的首项。它强调需要积极的、有足够资源支持的和协调一致的行动，促使原来通过现金和支票支付的付款方式向数字支付转变。2014年GPFI报告《数字化支付机遇》[6]和2015年GPFI报告《提高妇女经济参与度的数字金融方案》[7]都强调了在促进数字金融服务方面需要政府积极引导和采取相关行动。

促进数字普惠金融的关键行动包括但不限于：

● 根据具体国情，确保相关国家战略和行动计划能够反映实现数字普惠金融政策目标的新型数字商业模式，能够推广使用这些战略和行动计划，能够以证据为基础，目标具体、结果可测以及责任明确。

• 有效加强政策制定者、中央银行、金融监管者、相关监管机构、金融纠纷处理专员和其他负有数字金融服务方面职责的机构（如通信、竞争和消费者保护等管理机构）的合作。

• 积极促进所有重要利益相关者（包括政府、私人部门和民间团体）之间有关数字普惠金融方面的对话和合作，确保他们对数字普惠金融目标和市场行为预期的理解一致。

• 在可行条件下，政府机构向消费者和小型企业做出的大额经常性支付应数字化，进一步促进和激励以非现金数字方式（如以更低的手续费为激励）[8]与政府进行款项收付。

• 鼓励和加强私人部门营利或非营利组织大额经常性支出的非现金化和数字化（比如，与薪金、转移支付和人道主义援助，以及汇款等方面有关的大额经常性支出）[9]。

• 倡导金融行业：(1) 接受以客户为中心的产品设计理念，该理念关注客户的需求、偏好、行为并且促进无法获得和缺乏金融服务的群体获取和使用数字金融服务；(2) 为无法获得金融服务的群体提供低成本的基础性交易账户，此账户能够用于数字支付并提供安全存储。这种倡导应当包括为缺乏金融服务的群体（如年轻人）提供针对此类账户所具有的法律灵活性和可适用性方面的清晰指引。[10]

• 消除数字金融服务发展与数字金融服务获取的障碍，包括：让无法获得金融服务的群体（尤其是贫困人口、女性和年轻人）易于获得和使用移动电话和网络装置；改革阻碍广泛获取新技术的税收制度和进口限制。

• 为促进数字普惠金融，与其他国家监管机构合作消除跨境金融服务障碍，为跨境金融服务提供便利。

原则二
平衡好数字普惠金融发展中的创新与风险

在实现数字普惠金融的过程中平衡好鼓励创新与识别、评估、监测和管理新风险之间的关系。

过去几年，数字金融服务方面的创新（包括金融技术创新，也称“金融科技”[11]）速度惊人，拓展了金融服务群体，拓宽了金融服务空间，改进了金融服务设计和提供渠道，并具有显著降低金融服务成本的潜力。政策制定者应鼓励和培育此类创新，利用其所产生的利益惠及大众，尤其是缺乏金融服务的群体，同时政策制定者也要认识到迅速发展的数字创新也带来了许多个别的和系统性新风险，需要及时有效地识别和处理这些风险。应推动金融市场网络复原能力建设，并致力于保护金融体系免受非法活动侵扰，认识到这一点很有必要。[12]

PAFI报告、GPFI白皮书和其他国际标准设定机构的指引都承认在使用数字技术的过程中主要风险会不断发展变化和增加，并且应该有效地评估与管理这些风险。[13]数字金融风险有许多形式，可能来自于已有的和新型金融服务提供商的组合；可能来自新技术的运用；可能来自对代理商网络的过度依赖；可能来自多个服务提供商的新产品绑定；更有可能来自消费者金融素养不足。数字技术风险在整个数字金融服务与市场价值链上都有可能出现，如运行、清算、流动性、信贷、消费和反洗钱/反恐融资等层面。数字技术还有助于产生和分析大量的消费者和交易数据（“大数据”），其所带来的风险和收益需要妥善管理。

平衡好数字普惠金融中的创新与风险的关键行动包括但不限于：

● 通过以市场为导向的激励和公私部门的合作，鼓励数字创新，特别是以此惠及无法获得正规金融服务和缺乏金融服务的群体。

● 鼓励金融行业为数字金融服务研发安全简单的使用界面，使其更易于使用，降低错误交易和冒用的风险，特别是要考虑到弱势群体的需求。[14]

- 与行业和风险管理专家合作，研究、识别和评估在使用新数字技术过程中出现的风险，并且确保有效地监测和管理这些风险。
- 在监管者和服务提供商之间建立常规的信息分享机制以及畅通的交流渠道。
- 鼓励监管者与行业制定风险管理战略，该战略要反映不同司法辖区的特定条件和法律框架，如符合当地情况的“了解你的客户”规则，通过该手段可有效管理和减轻已经识别的风险，而不是规避此类消费者与账户。监管指引也应强调普惠金融作为反洗钱和反恐融资监管中有利因素的重要性，并包含对相关监管规则灵活性的明确建议，包括以运用风险导向监管方法为目的的建议。
- 鼓励服务提供商更好地使用数字数据中的多种资源，在适当的安全保障下评估消费者和中小企业信用状况，同时促进完善此类数据并且公平、非歧视地使用此类数据。这些可供选择的数据资源包括移动电话的使用、公用事业缴费、企业注册数据信息和其他能够对传统贷款偿还数据或者保险相关数据进行补充的数据。
- 与金融行业合作，探索发行数字法定货币对普惠金融的益处。
- 探索识别新兴技术风险的新方法，如针对潜在网络犯罪的压力测试。

原则三
构建恰当的数字普惠金融法律和监管框架

针对数字普惠金融，充分参考G20和国际标准制定机构的相关标准和指引，构建恰当的数字普惠金融法律和监管框架。

如果数字普惠金融市场能够持续地发展和扩大，那么服务提供商和其他市场参与主体就需要一个可预测的、以风险为导向的、公平的法律监管框架，它允许有新进入者，而不过度增加非风险导向的合规成本。特别是该框架应能够从市场、服务提供商和消费者的角度反映出对相关风险的认真评估；能够提供明确的市场参与规则；能够为市场参与主体建立一个公平、公开、平等的竞争环境，并确保在基本的监管能力和资源范围内受到有效监管。[15]如果没有这种恰当的法律和监管框架，创新和投资的意愿将被削弱，无法获得金融服务或缺乏金融服务的群体获取金融服务的潜在机会也将被剥夺。此外，风险可能无法得到充分控制。

整体政策环境和监管框架应该反映适当的、可行的监管方法。这对各国充分实现各自的数字普惠金融目标，以及相关的经济增长是必要的。[16]近期的GPFI白皮书介绍了所涉及的适当性方法，如“……根据监管者和被监管机构的监管成本，平衡好风险和收益”[17]。然而，就像GPFI白皮书所指出的，国际标准制定机构对“适当性”的定义是多样的。[18]

法律和监管框架也应反映如下普遍认识：“普惠金融、稳定性、诚信和消费者保护之间不仅相互兼容，还会相互促进。”（2014年《G20普惠金融行动计划》）。由于新型商业模式、产品、销售渠道和数字技术的快速发展，因此对数字普惠金融来说，这些目标之间的相互协调尤为重要。[19]

同样重要的是，数字普惠金融法律和监管框架的监管者需具备技能、能力和资源以有效监管相关主体和整个市场。这应当包括理解数字技术和数字金融服务市场创新的能力，以及识别不断变化的风险和市场的能力。监管者也应当能够利用新技术有效、高效地开展监管行动。[20]为达到适度监管目标，需要运用以风险为导向的合规监管方法。

构建恰当的法律和监管框架的关键行动包括但不限于[21]：

• 构建一个数字普惠金融法律框架，规定市场参与门槛（包括准入要求），合适的审慎性条件（如资本和流动性），市场行为和诚信，消费者保护，反洗钱/反恐融资保障机制和破产机制等。该框架应该是技术中性并且足够灵活，能够覆盖新的和现有的服务提供商和产品创新（例如，对受监管的数字金融提供商及其服务进行宽泛定义，随着时间推移，可以对这一定义进行修改）。

• 此框架应该允许尝试创新性的服务提供渠道、产品、服务和商业模式，在试验性项目开展早期不需完全遵守所有的监管要求，但必须确保公平、均衡的监督机制和与国际标准接轨的反洗钱/反恐融资的义务要求，并确保没有参与者在试点中获得不当的优势。此框架还应平衡好数字普惠金融风险和监管合规成本。

• 确保不论何种机构使用何种技术，同样类型的数字金融服务供应商应拥有同等的权利和义务；对于市场参与门槛（包括新准入机构和外国准入机构）和特定类型数字金融服务的提供都有明确一致的标准；并且确保对同类风险采用相同的监管方法；完善以风险为导向的适当的监管方法，以此促进竞争并促成公平、开放、公平的竞争环境，实现普惠金融。

• 评估国际国内法律中有关数字普惠金融的所有内容，辨别和处理重叠或矛盾的部分以及准入过程中的差距、阻碍或其他障碍。这些部分可能包括：金融服务；支付系统；通信；竞争；歧视；身份；无法获得正规金融服务的群体获取数字金融服务的障碍；代理商和雇员的义务等。

• 确保在有关数字金融服务和总体的数字普惠金融的法律和监管框架中，对监管者的职责有清晰描述。

• 提升数字普惠金融法律和监管框架中的监管者能力，使其能更好地理解数字技术（如通过国内或国际培训和同业学习项目），并且鼓励根据需要利用数字技术改进他们的监管流程和能力。

• 制定简单易懂的数字普惠金融法律、法规和指引，同时使金融行业和消费者易于获得这些法律法规（如通过可公开访问的网站和其他可获得的交流渠道）。

• 在G20成员之间建立可持续的关于数字普惠金融法律和监管框架、监管方法的定期交流和信息交换机制，包括与风险管理策略和经验相关的内容。

原则四
扩展数字金融服务基础设施生态系统

扩展数字金融服务生态系统，包括加快金融和信息通信基础设施建设，用安全、可信和低成本的方法为所有相关地域提供数字金融服务，尤其是农村和缺乏金融服务的地区。

政策制定者应当与私营部门合作，将优先发展数字基础设施作为经济与社会发展计划的一项基础性工作。[22]政府部门和私营部门越来越依赖于数字网络传递重要的公共服务和私人服务（从医疗教育到通信和金融服务）。建立数字金融服务生态系统的重点在于：加快稳健、安全、高效且广泛可得的零售支付和信息通信基础设施建设，为所有用户提供便捷、可靠的服务网点，使用户可以在服务网点内收支款项并获得其他数字金融服务。这些基础设施应在最大程度上打通农村地区金融服务的“最后一公里”，并服务主要城市地区和重要的交通走廊。PAFI 报告的第三项原则讨论了对这些基础设施的需求（包括支持这些系统的移动数据连接和电力供应等）。[23]

数字支付平台具有即时性，且所有服务提供商都能够进行访问。使用数字支付平台有可能大幅降低服务提供商和消费者的数字交易成本。这些平台能够持续处理那些在世界金融交易中占主导地位的小额交易。因此，平台能够通过鼓励市场创新和引入更多市场参与者，动态地改变业务状况。开放的数字平台能够扩展消费者和服务提供商用以进行交易和提供存取款服务的网络，提高平台间的互通性并给消费者带来更多选择。这些服务网点不仅包括分支机构和代理商，也包括 ATM、POS 设备、移动电话和网络应用等。

扩展国家数字金融服务生态系统的关键行动包括但不限于：

- 在有需要的地方，各政府机构通力合作，保障支持数字普惠金融的基础设施，包括电信和电力设施。

• 通过政策机制，如创新性公私伙伴关系、共享基础设施项目的激励机制和有针对性的采购政策，使宽带网络/数据覆盖延伸到金融服务匮乏的地区。

• 推动零售支付系统基础设施的现代化，并扩展该基础设施，建立开放的支付平台。该平台与国家支付清算系统相连接，并向银行、非银行金融机构和新兴支付服务提供商开放，通过采取适当的风险管理和保障措施，使上述主体能够安全、高效地进行访问。[24]

• 鼓励服务提供商推动服务网点及渠道的互通性，并进一步扩大消费者服务网点的覆盖范围、提高使用交易账户的整体便利性。

• 利用广泛的政府渠道（如在合适情况下可通过邮局）协助提供数字金融服务。

• 在充分考虑适当的风险缓释措施和安全保障的前提下，与行业合作探索分布式账本技术在提高批发和零售金融基础设施透明度、有效性、安全性和可得性方面的潜力。[25]

• 在考虑多种抵押物类型的基础上推动完善动产抵押登记系统，更好地反映用户的日常生活，更好地拓宽稳健的中小企业融资部门的基础。[26]

• 根据国际征信委员会（International Committee on Credif Reporting,IC-CR）提出的最佳方案，推动建立和负责任地使用灵活的、动态的信用记录报告机制模型，模型应包括相关的、准确的、及时的和丰富的数据，采用系统性的方法从所有可靠、正当、可获得的资源中搜集数据，并且长时间地保存这些数据。[27]信用记录报告的整个法律和监管框架应该是清楚的、可预测的、非歧视性的、适当的，并支持消费者数据保护和隐私规则。

• 支持消费者数据保护和隐私规则，鼓励在信用记录报告机制中使用创新性数据来源，如公用事业缴费、手机话费充值，以及电子钱包或者电子货币账户和电子商务交易数据等。此项原则可以由原则七中提及的客户身份识别系统协助实施。

原则五
采取负责任的数字金融措施保护消费者

创立一种综合性的消费者和数据保护方法，重点关注与数字金融服务相关的具体问题。

负责任的数字金融措施的必要性已得到广泛认可。[28]在获取和持续使用数字金融服务的过程中，健全的消费者和数据保护框架对构建消费者信任和信心必不可少，尤其是对于那些金融素养不高或承担损失能力有限的消费者。就数字普惠金融环境而言，技术、服务、供应商、销售渠道的快速革新以及个人数据处理的数量、速度和种类尤为重要，它们在提高消费者金融服务可得性的同时也带来了风险。

涉及数字金融服务的消费者风险多种多样，尤其当消费者为无法获得金融服务或缺乏金融服务的群体时。这些风险包括：作为非审慎监管对象的供应商所保有的消费者资金缺乏安全保障；有关费用、条款和条件（如使用移动电话的条款和条件）的信息披露不全；代理商流动性不足和代理商欺诈；使用具有误导性的用户界面增加错误交易风险；系统安全性不足；通过数字方式不负责任地提供贷款；系统崩溃导致资金无法获取；不明晰的或限制性的损失追索制度；以及无法维护个人数据保密性和安全性等。同时，对金融服务不足群体的歧视也存在重大风险。

为实现数字普惠金融的目标和价值，消费者保护框架必须充分考虑个人数据使用和处理的数量、种类和速度，其中包括身份识别、交易、账户、手机话费充值和互联网社交平台数据。这些数据能够提高金融可得性并改善产品和消费者服务，同时也能够提供有关普惠金融水平的公共信息，但使用这些数据也可能对消费者造成损害（包括将消费者排斥在金融体系之外）。

采取负责任的数字金融措施保护消费者并解决相关监管和行业自律问题的关键行动包括但不限于：

• 设计数字金融服务消费者保护框架。该框架可以解决数字环境的特定风险，并可以反映统计和行为证据以及直接的消费者信息（如来自免费消费者热线、网上论坛和投诉的数据）。

• 构建稳定的法律框架以保障不受审慎监管的服务提供商所持有的客户资金的安全（如通过信托账户、引入存款保险机制和追加保险要求）。同时，结合针对弱势群体的项目，进一步严格执行反数字金融服务欺诈行为的有关规则并建立合理的追索机制。

• 确保投诉解决机制便于消费者使用。该机制应易于理解、高效、免费且能远程访问和操作（如通过呼叫中心、网站或互联网社交平台），并由服务提供商和专门处理纠纷的第三方（如金融纠纷处理专员）负责提供。

• 针对数字金融服务，对服务提供商提出适当的要求。例如：(1) 披露条款、费用和佣金等信息，且表述明晰、简洁，内容具有可比性；(2) 定期提交反映交易和费用明细的账户报表；(3) 开通免费客服热线；(4) 明确未经授权交易、错误交易和系统中断的处理流程和责任；(5) 规范贷款和债务催收行为；(6) 引导消费者正确使用数字金融服务，有效防止个人数据被滥用、泄露、篡改和损毁；(7) 提供用于消费者咨询的官方联系方式（如电话号码和网站)。所有消费者信息都能以数字方式提供（包括通过移动电话）并被保存。

• 要求数字金融服务提供商对其代理商及雇员进行培训，培训内容应涉及产品特征、监管职责、公平对待缺乏金融服务的群体和弱势群体、追索流程及应客户要求或在语言障碍情形下对信息披露文件进行解释。

• 鼓励服务提供商定期提交有关数字金融服务投诉数据的报告，数据应按主要目标群体划分。

• 鼓励数字金融服务提供商采用高于通行法律要求的自律标准（如通过可执行的行业行为准则）。

• 明确“个人数据”的定义，该定义需对综合各类信息以进行个体识别的能力加以考虑。

• 确保数字金融服务消费者能够对个人数据进行有意识的选择和控制，包括通过基于相应语言文本的，明晰、简洁、全面、与年龄相符且简短的隐私政策披露的知情同意权；透明、可负担和便利的访问权和更正权，这些权利可通过远程和互联网访问实施，如移动电话、网站或24小时呼叫中心。

● 禁止以不公平歧视性方式使用数字金融服务相关数据。例如：在通过数字服务提供信贷或保险时歧视女性。

● 制定指引以保障数据的准确性和安全性，其中，数据涉及：账户和交易、销售中的数字金融服务及针对无法获得金融服务或缺乏金融服务的消费者开展的信用评分。该指引应包括传统数据形式和创新性数据形式，如公用事业缴费、手机话费充值、数字钱包或电子账户[29]使用及互联网社交平台或电子商务交易数据。

原则六
重视消费者数字技术基础知识和金融知识的普及

根据数字金融服务和渠道的特性、优势及风险，鼓励开展提升消费者数字技术基础知识和金融素养的项目并对项目开展评估。

对政策制定者和服务提供商而言，金融素养方面的缺陷依然是他们向无法获得金融服务或缺乏金融服务的群体推广金融服务的重大挑战。[30]金融服务供给的数字化变革给那些没接触过或极少使用数字工具（无论是移动的还是在线的）的新用户增加了新一层的复杂性。政策制定者、监管机构及服务提供商必须通力合作，确保用户能够拥有并充分认识数字金融工具，确保有简易指引告知用户如何操作，确保用户能够明晰如何获取更多信息，以及用户在即时、非面对面[31]的新交易环境中对任意错误享有追索权。更加广泛和深入的金融知识可以补充和加强对如何使用特定金融工具的理解。否则，数字技术可能在金融服务可得性和使用度方面导致更广泛的不公平现象。同样重要的是，商家（特别是小企业）应认识到通过数字方式进行支付和转账可带来诸多好处。

急需提升消费者和商家的数字技术基础知识和金融素养已得到普遍认可，尤其当消费者为无法获得金融服务或缺乏金融服务的群体（包括属于弱势群体的人群）时。具体例子包括：PAFI报告有关金融素养的第六项指导性原则，2014年数字支付机遇报告《引导数字金融服务提供商对消费者和小企业开展教育，提升其信心、技能和接收度》[32]的第五条建议以及2015年的报告《为妇女推出数字金融解决方案》[33]中涉及女性金融技能的核心发现。G20国家领导人在2012年签署的OECD/INFE《金融教育国家战略高级原则》为制定有效的金融教育国家战略提供了国际指引和政策选择。[34]

提升消费者数字技术基础知识和金融素养的关键行动包括但不限于：

• 明确因金融服务数字化和多元化带来的金融素养方面的新要求（例如：通过移动电话获取小额信贷和小额保险，使用创新数据源进行信用评分以及将保险和信贷产品加以组合）。

• 鼓励开发、评估实用度高、可得性强并着重于数字化的金融素养和金融意识项目，尤其是针对无法获得金融服务或缺乏金融服务的群体的项目，需要帮助消费者理解数字金融服务的特征、好处、风险和成本，以及保护个人账户和信息安全的必要性。此外，鼓励业界将这些项目的详情、结果及适用数据分享给监管者。

• 利用新兴的高质量数字工具开发数字技术基础知识和金融知识普及项目，为消费者提供使用数字金融服务所需的知识，使消费者能够理解数字金融服务并对其产生信心。例如：在消费者需要做决定或需要向消费者提示其储蓄目标时及时发送的短信问题和信息；线上工具（如帮助家长教育孩子理财的各类游戏）；监测收入和花销的数字工具包；小企业在线财务管理项目以及互动教育项目。在“可教育时刻”，进行金融知识普及的有效性更高。如消费者在开始新工作、退休或孩子出生等人生重大时刻，往往需要做出具有重大财务影响的决策，此时进行金融知识普及，消费者特别易于接受信息和建议。

• 促使小企业充分意识到通过数字方式进行支付和转账的好处以及当前可获得的数字金融服务的特性。

• 推进由雇主和服务提供商赞助的公正的数字金融能力评估。该评估针对当前无法获得金融服务或缺乏金融服务的群体。随着数字化的推进，这些群体可能成为金融服务的首次使用者。

• 鼓励通过支持开发相关工具（如价格比对网站），使消费者能够对比相似的数字金融产品和服务，从而做出明智选择。

原则七
促进数字金融服务的客户身份识别

通过开发客户身份识别系统，提高数字金融服务的可得性，该系统应可访问、可负担、可验证，并能适应以基于风险的方法开展客户尽职调查的各种需求和各种风险等级。

各国政府普遍认可身份证明作为日常生活基本必需品的重要性。全世界约有15亿人口（绝大多数居住在亚洲和非洲）因为无法认证官方身份而无法获取基本服务，无法享受应有权利，并在经济活动中被逐渐边缘化。相关证据表明，没有官方身份证明的群体通常是最贫穷国家中最弱势的人群。[35]由于各国越来越依赖于数字网络提供重要的公共和私人服务，消费者通过身份识别远程获取服务的能力变得尤为重要。

获取可靠的身份数据对于实现普惠金融目标至关重要。[36]更简易的客户身份验证促使监管机构和服务提供商在满足反洗钱和反恐融资要求的同时采取措施提高客户登记效率。鉴于可以在线获取身份信息并对其进行验证，服务提供商可以简化获取客户的流程并降低相应成本。数字技术（包括生物识别技术和其他方式）为构建稳定、高效的身份识别系统带来了特有的机会，与传统纸质身份识别方式相比，该系统是一个巨大的进步，覆盖面之广前所未有。当然，这种数字身份识别系统的安全性和保密性也十分重要。

促进数字金融服务的客户身份识别的关键行动包括但不限于：

- 确保出生登记以及其他基础身份系统的普适性和可负担性。同时，对禁止或阻碍金融服务不足群体（如已婚妇女）进行数字身份识别登记的法律法规进行修订。
- 确保政府身份数据库（如出生登记和税务登记号码）在经过客户同意的前提

下（如果数据保护法有相关要求）能够被政府其他部门合理、安全地访问。

● 在必要且可行的情形下，建立一个互通的、技术中性的国家数据库系统，与相关民事登记和身份系统关联，并在经客户同意的前提下（如果数据保护法有相关要求）向被授权方开放，被授权方（如金融服务提供商）可以合理、安全地进行访问。

● 必要时，开发和推进新的身份登记和验证方式（如数字生物身份识别产品和在线身份验证服务），尤其针对那些目前还无法通过任何方式进行身份识别的人。同时，设立可被接受的开放性标准以管理身份、交易和账户风险。

● 执行基于风险的客户身份识别和验证要求，促进低风险数字金融服务的获取以实现普惠金融目标。例如：通过客户尽职调查分层框架，授权从一个或多个状态验证源进行身份识别；同时，清楚地说明可以用于身份验证的数据来源，并满足反洗钱金融行动特别工作组（FATF）对“可靠、独立的源文件、数据或信息”的相关要求。[37]

● 构建保护身份数据隐私和安全的法律框架，明确只有在知情同意的前提下才能使用、披露该数据。同时，建立稳定的追索机制，使个体在知情权等权利或隐私被侵犯时能够获得救济。

● 加强与非政府利益相关者，如人道主义机构和其他相关非政府组织的合作，推进针对被金融排斥群体的身份识别项目及有关普惠金融和其他目标的身份识别项目。

● 针对公共机构和私人机构在身份管理中担任的角色和承担的责任，建立明确的问责机制并保障其透明度。

● 鼓励开发安全可靠的数字签名系统，它有利于推进身份验证，尤其是针对缺乏金融服务的群体的身份验证。

原则八
监测数字普惠金融发展进程

通过全面、可靠的数据测量评估系统来监测数字普惠金融的进展。该系统应利用新的数字数据来源，使利益相关者能够分析和监测数字金融服务的供给和需求，并能够评估核心项目和改革的影响。

有效利用数字技术实现普惠金融目标需要一个全面的监测评估系统来追踪进展、识别障碍（包括短板）和展示国家层面及项目层面的成果。国家监测评估系统应与新兴数字模式相适应，具有如下三个核心要素：具有核心指标和相应目标的成果评估框架；采集供需方数据所需的数据基础设施；针对核心项目和变革的评估行动。这些要素可用于量化和衡量数字普惠金融重点议题的进展情况，深入分析普惠金融的发展趋势和障碍（尤其在目标群体中[38]），以及提供有关改革和项目效率、效力及影响的可靠见解。PAFI报告的第五部分指出了监测普惠金融目标进展情况的重要性，并提供了相关指引。

监测数字普惠金融进展的关键行动包括但不限于：

• 与关键利益相关者（包括私营部门）进行磋商，设立国家核心绩效指标，并在适当情况下设立获取、使用数字金融产品和服务的目标。

• 建立健全普惠金融数据采集系统以覆盖新的数字金融提供商和产品。例如，可以使用个人和公司金融服务需求方调查，金融服务供应方报告（如通过非现场监管报告模板）及新的数字化数据源。

• 与数字金融服务提供商通力合作，使数据采集系统适于提供按人口统计主要标准进行分解的数据，如按性别、收入、年龄和地域进行分类。

• 在收集数字金融服务提供商数据的各监管当局之间建立谅解备忘录，以确保高效、开放的信息交换。

• 建立在线数据门户和（或）发布定期报告，提供有关获取和使用数字金融服务的公开数据，以及进一步向国际机构提供有关获取和使用数字金融服务的报告，在合理可行的范围内监测普惠金融数据。

- 资助有关数字普惠金融的核心项目和改革，并鼓励对其影响力进行评估。
- 监测《原则》各方面的实施进展情况。

尾注

1.见2016年GPFI报告《全球标准制定主体与普惠金融：不断变化发展的格局》（2016年3月，第46页）。（http：//www.gpfi.org/publications/global-standard-setting-bodies-and-financial-inclusion-evolving-landscape ）。也可参照框8中的数字普惠金融模型核心要素（第46页）。（http：//www.gpfi.org/sites/default/files/documents/GPFI_WhitePaper_Mar2016.pdf）。

2.“数字金融服务”的描述来自2014年GPFI《有关数字普惠金融及其对消费者、监管者和标准制定主体的影响》的议题报告（第1、2页）。（http：//www.gpfi.org/sites/default/files/documents/Issues%20Paper%20for%20GPFI%20BIS%20Confe-ence%20on%20Digital%20Financial%20Inclusion.pdf ）。也可参照CPMI和世界银行2016年《普惠金融支付领域的报告》（PAFI报告，第13页第47段）。（http：//www.bis.org/cpmi/publ/d144.htm）。

3.

G20数字普惠金融高级原则（HLPs）	2010年G20创新性普惠金融原则（2010年G20原则）
原则一：倡导利用数字技术推动普惠金融发展	一、以2010年G20原则的第一项原则——“指引”和第六项原则——“合作”为基础。
原则二：平衡好数字普惠金融发展中的创新与风险	二、以2010年G20原则的第一项原则——“指引”、第三项原则——“创新”和第四项原则——“保护”为基础。
原则三：构建恰当的数字普惠金融法律和监管框架	三、以2010年G20原则的第四项原则——“保护”、第八项原则——“适当性”和第九项原则——“框架”为基础。
原则四：扩展数字金融服务基础设施生态系统	四、以2010年G20原则的第九项原则——“框架”为基础。
原则五：采取负责任的数字金融措施保护消费者	五、以2010年G20原则的第四项原则——“保护”和第五项原则——“赋权”为基础。
原则六：重视消费者数字技术基础知识和金融知识的普及	六、以2010年G20原则的第五项原则——“赋权”为基础。
原则七：促进数字金融服务的客户身份识别	七、以2010年G20原则的第一项原则——“指引”和第六项原则——“合作”为基础。
原则八：监测数字普惠金融发展进程	八、以2010年G20原则的第七项原则——“知识”为基础。

4.个人持有账户对扩大女性普惠金融尤其重要，这在2015年G20/GPFI关于《提高妇女参与度的数字金融方案》（如第1.1部分）的报告中被提出。http：//gpfi.org/sites/default/files/documents/03-Digital%20Financial%20Solution%20to%20Advance%20Women....pdf。

5.http：//www.bis.org/cpmi/publ/d133.pdf.

6.http：//gpfi.org/sites/default/files/documents/FINAL_The%20Opportunities%20of%20Digitizing%20Payments.pdf.

7.http：//gpfi.org/sites/default/files/documents/03-Digital%20Financial%20Solution%20to%20Advance%20Women....pdf.

8.PAFI指导性原则7：大额经常性支付。

9.PAFI指导性原则7：大额经常性支付。

10.为PAFI指导性原则1（公共部门与私人部门的义务）设计的核心行动建议为所有人的交易账户开发一个贯穿始末且可评估阶段性成果的明确战略。也可参照PAFI报告第3.2.1.2部分（“交易账户和支付产品特点”）。

11.FSB主席在向G20财长和央行行长的信件（2016年2月22日）中提议，FSB将支持2016年中国任G20主席国期间的“评估数字技术创新的系统性影响和源于业务中断的系统性风险”的相关目标（第1页）。(http：//www.fsb.org/wp-content/uploads/FSB-Chair-letter-to-G20-Ministers-and-Governors-February-2016.pdf)。

12.见支付和市场基础设施委员会（CPMI）和国际证监会组织（IOSCO）于2016年6月发布的《金融市场基础设施的网络复原能力指引》(http：//www.bis.org/cpmi/publ/d146.htm）和支付，与结算体系委员会（现CPMI）和国际证监会组织（IOSCO）技术委员会于2012年发布的《金融市场基础设施原则》(http：//www.bis.org/cpmi/publ/d101.htm)。

13.见PAFI指导性原则2和GPFI白皮书IVA部分“数字普惠金融——机遇与风险”。

14.见修订版2012年FATF建议中涉及新技术的建议15。http：//www.fatf-gafi.org/media/fatf/documents/recommendations/pdfs/FATF_Recommendations.pdf。

15.见国际清算银行巴塞尔银行监管委员会公布的咨询报告（《有效银行监管核心原则在普惠金融机构监管上的运用指引》）的原则2、8、9和25。

16.见GPFI白皮书建议12-18，VIA和VIB部分，以及PAFI指导性原则2“法律监管框架”。

17.GPFI白皮书，第二部分D节脚注16。也可参照建议6、7。

18.国际标准制定者使用过各种适当性方法，包括在修订的2012年《巴塞尔有效银行监管核心原则》中能够评估核心原则履行情况的适当性方法，即监管程度与银行的风险状况和系统重要性相匹配。2012年的FATF建议也提出强化的尽职调查措施需要与有关风险相匹配；有效的、适当的和具有劝诫性的制裁以及监管者之间的信息交换都应当与他们的需求相匹配。FSB呼吁在对影子银行进行监管时采用适当性方法，它既能识别相关风险，也能识别银行获得的收益。(见《将影子银行转变为有弹性的市场化融资：2015年进展和路线图概述》)。http：//www.fsb.org/wp-content/uploads/Progress-Report-on-Transforming-Shadow-Banking-into-Resilient-Market-Based-Financing.pdf。

19.FSB《全球影子银行监测报告》(巴塞尔，2014)和《针对其他影子银行主体的FSB政策框架实施情况的主题性同行审议：总结的参考条款》(巴塞尔，2015)。巴塞尔核心银行原则1强调金融系统的安全性和稳定性是最重要的，同时也意识到金融监管者需要承担其他不相冲突的责任(如普惠金融和消费者保护)。

20.GPFI白皮书建议31–35和VIB部分。

21.这些要素大多数被纳入GPFI白皮书第6部分的建议中或PAFI报告中。

22.PAFI报告第3.1.3部分讨论了金融和ICT基础设施；PAFI报告第3.2.2部分讨论了服务点和网络连接渠道。

23.见PAFI指导性原则3：金融和ICT基础设施。

24.见PAFI指导性原则3：为作进一步指导的金融和ICT基础设施。

25.FSB已将分布式分类技术作为评估主要金融技术创新领域的一部分。(http：//www.fsb.org/2016/03/meeting-of-the-financial-stability-board-in-tokyo-on-30-31-march/)。国际清算银行支付与市场基础设施委员会也考虑了分布式分类技术：见2015年关于数字货币的报告。https：//www.bis.org/cpmi/publ/d137.pdf.

26.见PAFI指导性原则3：作为进一步指导的金融和ICT基础设施。

27.背景可参照世界银行关于有效破产和债权人/债务人权利的原则(2015年，原则A4和A5)。http：//www.fsb.org/2011/09/cos_110907/。

28.主要例子包括PAFI指导性原则2“法律监管框架”和原则6“意识和金融素

养"；GPFI白皮书建议19-24和IVB部分；G20金融消费者保护高级原则。http：//www.oecd.org/daf/fin/financial-markets/48892010.pdf。

29.见2004年国际清算银行支付与结算体系委员会《电子货币和网络移动支付发展调查》（第2.1部分）中有关"电子货币"的定义。http：//www.bis.org/cpmi/publ/d62.pdf。

30."金融素养"这个术语在OECD/INFE《金融教育国家战略高级原则》（2012年由G20国家领导人签署）中被定义为："'做出稳健财务决定和最终实现个人金融福祉所需的金融意识、知识、技能、态度和行为的综合要素'：见Atkinson和Messy（2012）"（脚注4）。（http：//www.oecd.org/daf/fin/financial-education/OECD-INFE-Principles-National-Strategies-Financial-Education.pdf）。

更广义的术语"金融能力"在2016巴塞尔银行监管委员会有关银行业监管的咨询报告（《有效银行监管核心原则在普惠金融机构监管上的运用指引》）中被定义为："世界银行（2013年）将'金融能力'定义为：根据社会经济环境，能够产生最优经济效益的内在能力，它包含知识、态度、技能、消费者理解、选择和使用金融服务的行为以及获得适合自身需求金融服务的能力。"（脚注79）。

金融能力被视为产品质量和服务传递的一部分。根据国际清算银行有关《普惠金融相关监管和监管机构实践》报告（第3.2部分）的主题调查，服务传递是普惠金融的主要组成部分。

31.2015年G20关于《促进女性经济参与的数字金融解决方案》的报告由优于现金联盟提供。

32.2014年G20关于《数字化支付所带来的机遇》的报告由世界银行发展研究小组、优于现金联盟和盖茨基金会提供。

33.https：//www.betterthancash.org/tools-research/reports/digital-financial-solutions-to-advance-women-s-economic-participation

34.http：//www.oecd.org/daf/fin/financial-education/OECD-INFE-Principles-National-Strategies-Financial-Education.pdf. 见原则6：国家战略路线图：重点议题、目标受众、影响力评估和资源。

35.可持续发展目标中的目标16.9提及"到2030年，为所有人提供合法身份证明，包括出生登记"。

36.PAFI报告第115-117段、指导性原则3“金融和ICT基础设施”以及GPFI白皮书IVD部分和建议26。也可参照2015年GPFI《关于涉及政府行为和数字身份识别系统开发的促进女性经济参与的数字金融解决方案的报告》的主要发现。

37.修订的2012年FATF建议对采用风险为本的客户身份识别要求进行了授权。见FATF建议10和相关注释。http://www.fatf-gafi.org/media/fatf/documents/recommendations/pdfs/FATF_Recommendations.pdf。

38.见2013年《G20妇女和金融进展报告》优先行动第5项。http://www.g20australia.org/sites/default/files/g20_resources/library/G20_Women_and_Finance_Progress_report_WB_and_OECD.pdf。

二十国集团（G20）普惠金融全球合作伙伴（GPFI）

报告二

数字普惠金融：新兴政策与方法

致谢

本报告是在德国担任G20主席国期间，应主席国要求撰写的。本报告由世界银行集团（金融和市场全球实践部门）负责，得到了GPFI执行伙伴的大力支持。这些执行伙伴包括：扶贫协商小组（CGAP），普惠金融联盟（AFI），以及优于现金联盟（BTCA）。

来自世界银行集团的核心起草团队成员包括：Douglas Pearce，Loretta Michaels（顾问），Nomsa Kachingwe，以及Sheirin Iravantchi。

其他对本报告作出贡献和提出意见或建议的人员包括：

- **普惠金融联盟**：Charles Marwa
- **阿根廷中央银行**：Anabela Gómez
- **法兰西银行**：Luc Jacolin
- **优于现金联盟**：Ruth Goodwin-Groen
- **比尔及梅琳达·盖茨基金会**：SungAh Lee
- **德国联邦经济合作与发展部（BMZ）**：Volker Hey
- **德意志联邦银行**：Jelena Stapf，Franziska Schobert
- **扶贫协商小组（CGAP）**：Xavier Faz，Gerhard Coetzee，Ivo Jenik，Louis de Koker（顾问），Anand Raman（顾问）
- **澳大利亚外交与贸易部**：Jayne Harries
- **欧盟委员会**：Sirpa Tulla
- **英国金融行为监管局（FCA）**：Thomas Ward
- **德国国际合作机构（GIZ）**：Albert Joscha，Wolfgang Buecker，Judith Frickenstein
- **意大利国际经济与关系委员会**：Ricardo Settimo
- **阿根廷财政部**：Estefania Campaniello

- **中国人民银行**：汪天都
- **中小企业融资论坛**：Matthew Gamser
- **英国国际发展部**：Francesca Brown
- **美国国际开发署（USAID）**：Matt Homer
- **世界银行集团**：Sebastian Molineus，Harish Natarajan，Massimo Cirasino，Jennifer Chien，Vyjayanti Desai，Lin Huang，Emile J. M. Van der Does de Willebois，Fredesvinda Montes Herraiz， Dorothee Delort，Timothy Kelly

（原注：如无荷兰外交部的慷慨资助，本报告不可能完成。）

目录

概要

数字金融服务，若辅之以有效监管，可以扩大金融服务的规模、范围和半径，能够在消弭现有普惠金融服务供需缺口方面发挥重要作用。数字技术还为个人、家庭和企业提供了可负担的便捷的储蓄、支付、信贷和保险服务。2016年，二十国集团（G20）全球普惠金融合作伙伴（GPFI）发布《G20数字普惠金融高级原则》[①]（简称《原则》），旨在促进各国政府采取行动，注重利用数字技术推动普惠金融发展。报告介绍了一些案例，对一些国家采取的符合《原则》精神的做法进行了总结。报告的结构对应《原则》的前四项原则。

原则一倡导将促进数字金融服务作为推动包容性金融体系发展的重点，包括采用协调一致的国家战略和行动计划。它强调，政策引导及公私部门协调是发展普惠金融的关键因素，它同时强调了在推进数字解决方案方面率先示范的重要性。报告中讨论的方法来自印度、中国及其他国家，这些内容广泛、涉及多个方面的方法，被用于推进所在国家的数字普惠金融发展。特别是，印度在建设数字基础设施提高金融服务可得性方面做出了巨大努力，包括唯一身份证明计划（unique ID scheme）和数字印度项目（digital India program）。在行业发展的早期阶段，中国大力鼓励非银行支付机构成长，尤其是考虑到其对于新兴的电子商务的重要意义；中国也已明确，数字金融将对传统金融产生积极影响。另一个为这些国家及其他国家采用的、用以推动数字普惠金融发展的常见方法，是数字化政府对个人（G2P）支付，该方法为巴西、土耳其（及越来越多国家）所采用。

原则二强调的是，尽管金融服务创新对发展普惠金融非常重要，但它也产生了一些（个别的和系统性）新风险，需要及时有效识别和处理这些风险。政策制定者正致力于在创新/风险之间取得平衡，他们采取的行动包括：加强监管机构和私人部门之间的相互学习和信息共享，如通过“边试边学”的试点方法，引入创新型服

① https://www.gpfi.org/publications/g20-high-level-principles-digital-financial-inclusion

务；了解行业及消费者的新模式，以及更好地理解消费者有关新数字分销渠道体验的努力。报告介绍了英国、美国和肯尼亚“边试边学”方法案例，也介绍了保险监管者如何看待诸如移动电话等新兴分销渠道。

原则三指出，为了数字金融服务的繁荣壮大，需要一个可预测的、基于风险的、公平的法律和监管框架。该框架应允许新提供者进入市场，它应是技术中性的；同时，该框架还应免于实施任何非必需的、不是基于风险的合规成本。政策制定者和监管者应确保，该框架在基本的监管能力和资源范围内受到有效监管。存在两个关键主题：其一是，基于风险的监管方法越来越多地得到运用，包括以反洗钱和反恐融资（AML/CFT）为目的的风险为本的客户尽职调查（CDD）方法。其二是，日益认识到报告和监测系统有必要更加复杂化，应更加注重与金融机构信息系统的直接联系，也应更加注重实时监测能力和适当的隐私及数据保护。我们介绍了中国、墨西哥和坦桑尼亚的分类监管和客户尽职调查制度，还介绍了奥地利和卢旺达的自动数据报告系统。

原则四强调，政策制定者需与业界共同努力，建成强大、开放和高效的数字基础设施（包括广泛可得的零售支付系统和信息通信技术基础设施）。国家有关部门特别关注的领域包括零售和在线支付基础设施，即与各种各样POS机、ATM机和代理网络连接的可互通的平台、缴费平台、征信系统、数字资产（尤其是动产）登记，在某些情况下还包括支持这些系统的底层通信基础设施。报告强调了秘鲁和坦桑尼亚所采用的不同的互通方式，以及中国和墨西哥征信系统的案例。报告还探讨了肯尼亚的利益相关者在零售商中推广数字支付工具所做的努力。一些监管者也在研究发行用于数字金融服务生态系统的数字法定货币的潜在收益、成本和风险。

从报告中所介绍的众多案例可以看出，金融业数字技术的创新及应用的步伐在不断加快，复杂度也日益提升，这意味着政策和监管方法也必须与时俱进，并符合各国国情。尽管没有任何两个国家的方法或者特定的市场情况相同，但我们仍可从报告介绍的案例中提炼出若干论断。

●积极主动的领导力和政治意愿是全局性的成功因素，这包括政府相关部门间的整合及协作，以解决利用数字技术方面的众多问题。

●数字工具方面尚需取得更大进步，从而帮助监管者做好监管工作。由于数字创新正在重新定义人们对金融服务提供者的认识，金融监管者须采用更积极主动的、数据驱动的方法，以加深对行业的理解。身处交易量日益增加且更多使用快速或实时支付交易的时代，监管数字金融服务提供商需要能提供实时监控和分析的更复杂、自动化程度更高的系统。

●推动互联互通、开放的数字金融服务技术平台有助于建立一个广泛的生态系统，从而使私人实体和政府机构更好地服务消费者，并最终提高其金融生活质量。实现互联互通的方法和时机可能会变化，但政策制定者需要清楚互联互通是未来趋势。

●数字身份识别是公共数字基础设施的重要基石，也为获取经济中的各种服务（不只是金融服务业）提供了机会。各国政府需要将数字身份证明的可获得性置于优先地位；数字身份证明应是强大及易于验证的，无论它是基于生物统计学的，或基于其他数据类型的，它都应能用于促进数字金融服务的获得。人们对隐私权和公民自由权问题的担忧是有根据的，这些担忧有待解决。关于有效监管诸如数据安全、服务质量，以及网络的可靠性等问题，也出现了一些新案例。

1.引言

认识到新技术和新商业模式对于发展普惠金融的重要意义，二十国集团（G20）制定了《2010年创新性普惠金融原则》（2010 Principles for Innovative Financial Inclusion），该原则鼓励政策行动及国家层面的努力，从而促进金融服务创新。基于《2010年创新性普惠金融原则》，G20普惠金融全球合作伙伴（GPFI）[①]制定了《G20数字普惠金融高级原则》（G20 High Level Principles for Digital Financial Inclusion（HLPs），以下简称《原则》），目的在于使各国政府行动起来，注重利用数字技术促进普惠金融发展，并为各国根据自己的实际国情制订国别行动计划和倡议提供基础（详见专栏1关于《原则》的简要介绍）。

《原则》向各国推荐了推进数字普惠金融的具体行动。许多国家正采取符合《原则》精神的措施，包括制定国家战略增加数字金融服务的使用，也包括采用"边试边学"（test-and-learn）方法促进创新并管理潜在的风险，还包括扩展数字基础设施（如互联互通的服务平台和信息数据库）等。

报告围绕此类行动，密切关注《原则》前四项所强调的政策制定者和监管者的角色。《原则》第5~8项由其他跨部门的GPFI执行伙伴项目负责，例如负责任金融论坛（Responsible Finance Forum）[②]，促进发展身份证明倡议（Identity for Development，ID4D）[③]等，因此没有在报告中进行讨论。报告对所选案例进行了思考和总结，也指出了在落实上仍存在明显不足。我们希望国别案例和相关分析能在G20和非G20国家政策制定者中起到激发灵感、促进对话和信息共享的作用。

鉴于数字技术在普惠金融中的应用发展迅速，因此报告中所列案例不一定就是所谓的"最佳实践"。报告中简要介绍的许多案例反映了若干项高级原则推荐的行动建议。这

① www.gpfi.org
② https://responsiblefinanceforum.org/
③ http://www.worldbank.org/en/programs/id4d

些行动建议表明，利用数字技术发展普惠金融的机遇及其面临的约束呈现出内容广泛的特性。因此，并不存在“放之四海而皆准”的方法，但从报告所选案例中可以归纳出一些共同主题。

根据《原则》，GPFI执行伙伴积极支持借助新技术提升金融服务可得性和使用体验的各类举措。支持各国政府进行政策改革和采取其他举措的GPFI执行伙伴有世界银行集团（世界银行和国际金融公司（IFC））、扶贫协商小组（CGAP）、中小企业融资论坛（SME Finance Forum）、普惠金融联盟（AFI）[①]，以及设在联合国的优于现金联盟（BTCA）。联合国秘书长普惠金融特别代表马克西玛王后陛下是GPFI的代言人（patron），也是一位具有广泛影响的《原则》建议行动的倡导者。在世界银行[②]和GPFI的支持下，全球标准制定机构（SSB）正在提供越来越多的指导和原则，以帮助各国的金融监管者安全地运用创新与技术[③]。

专栏1：2016年《数字普惠金融高级原则》

原则一：倡导利用数字技术推动普惠金融发展

促进数字金融服务成为推动包容性金融体系发展的重点，它包括采用协调一致、可监测和可评估的国家战略和行动计划。

原则二：平衡好数字普惠金融发展中的创新与风险

在实现数字普惠金融的过程中，平衡好鼓励创新与识别、评估、监测和管理新风险之间的关系。

原则三：构建恰当的数字普惠金融法律和监管框架

针对数字普惠金融，充分参考G20和国际标准制定机构的相关标准和指引，构建恰当的数字普惠金融法律和监管框架。

原则四：扩展数字金融服务基础设施生态系统

扩展数字金融服务生态系统，包括加快金融和信息通信基础设施建设，用安全、可信和低成本的方法为所有相关地域提供数字金融服务，尤其是农村和缺乏

① http://www.afi-global.org/working-groups/digital-financial-services-working-group

② http://www.worldbank.org/en/topic/paymentsystemsremittances/brief/pafi-task-force-and-report

③ 由世界银行和支付与市场基础设施委员会（CPMI）共同担任主席的金融监管者专门工作组于2016年发布了“普惠金融支付”框架和指导原则。GPFI2016年发布的一份报告概述了其他标准制定机构的倡议：http://www.gpfi.org/sites/default/files/documents/GPFI_WhitePaper_Mar2016.pdf。

金融服务的地区。

原则五：采取负责任的数字金融措施保护消费者

创立一种综合性的消费者和数据保护方法，重点关注与数字金融服务相关的具体问题。

原则六：重视消费者数字技术基础知识和金融知识的普及

根据数字金融服务和渠道的特性、优势及风险，鼓励开展提升消费者数字技术基础知识和金融素养的项目并对项目开展评估。

原则七：促进数字金融服务的客户身份识别

通过开发客户身份识别系统，提高数字金融服务的可得性，该系统应可访问、可负担、可验证，并能适应以基于风险的方法开展客户尽职调查的各种需求和各种风险等级。

原则八：监测数字普惠金融进展

通过全面、可靠的数据测量评估系统来监测数字普惠金融的进展。

2.普惠金融新兴政策与监管方法

普惠金融涉及很多利益相关方，从政策制定者和金融监管者，到包括雇主、教育系统、社区和个人在内的私人部门。正如《原则》所指出的，政策制定者和监管者在此背景下的责任，是在保护好消费者权益的同时，构建一个开放有利的金融服务环境，既包括可预见的法律和监管规则，也包括建设可靠而便捷的物理基础设施。

2.1 原则一：倡导利用数字技术推动普惠金融发展

原则一倡导将促进数字金融服务作为推动包容性金融体系发展的重点，包括采用协调一致、可监测的国家战略和行动计划。它强调加强公共和私营部门间的政策领导和协调，以此作为推动普惠金融发展的关键要素，它同时强调了在推动数字解决方案中率先尝试的重要性。

对于数字化金融服务（包括推进普惠金融发展）的重要性，全球已形成了广泛共识，全球层面和国家层面政策制定者的努力和公开声明也证明了这一点。越来越多的国家将数字金融技术使用作为其普惠金融国家战略的重点（参见专栏2）。《玛雅宣言进展报告（2016年）》表明，在撒哈拉以南非洲和亚洲的普惠金融联盟成员所做出的目标和承诺中，“数字金融服务”在前三大主题中占据重要地位。[①]越来越多的国家和大型机构承诺将其大规模政府支出流予以数字化。[②]

专栏2：以数字化为重点的普惠金融国家战略

巴基斯坦2015年发布了普惠金融国家战略（NFIS），旨在确保个人和企业可以获得和使用一系列高质量的支付、储蓄、信贷和保险服务，以公正、有尊严地

① 《玛雅宣言进展报告（2016年）》。参见：http://www.afi-global.org/publications/2359/The-2016-Maya-Declaration-Report。

② 据优于现金联盟统计，截至2016年末，有54家成员对BTCA的数字支付原则做出了承诺。https://www.betterthancash.org/news/newsletters#filters。

满足其需求。其中强调，“努力实现正规账户普及的愿景，正规账户不再局限于简单的传统储蓄和支票账户，也包括数字交易账户（DTAs），比如无网点银行账户”。此外，巴基斯坦NFIS行动框架将数字交易账户作为推动普惠金融的核心驱动因素，明确了行动要点，包括通过政府支付数字化的方式来推动数字交易账户的使用、扩大数字交易账户的规模及提高其可行性。①

坦桑尼亚2014年发布的普惠金融国家战略指出，要建设“强大的电子支付平台”和“强大的、包含个人、企业基本信息、信贷记录和抵押物情况的电子信息基础设施”，这些基础设施是普惠金融发展的核心驱动要素。②建设这些驱动要素的相关措施有许多，其中包括制定移动金融服务的监管规则、支持市场实现支付互通性的努力，以及实施风险为本的“客户尽职调查”（将在2.3节进一步讨论）。

在菲律宾，2015年发布的普惠金融国家战略也关注技术和其他创新在服务金融排斥群体方面所起的作用。该国NFIS还涉及监管战略、促进以技术为基础的（零售支付和政府对个人转移支付）解决方案的互通性。③

在中国，2015年末出台的《推进普惠金融发展规划（2016—2020年）》设定了宏伟目标，旨在全面提高金融产品和服务的覆盖率、可得性和质量，并且明确指出要重视数字技术的运用。它鼓励金融产品和服务的数字创新，鼓励金融机构运用新兴技术（例如大数据和云计算），并将互联网作为实现金融服务可获得性和可负担性的重要工具。④

在墨西哥，《国家普惠金融政策》2016年6月由国家普惠金融委员会批准，其主要目标之一是建立鼓励创新并促进金融体系稳健运行的监管框架，为金融体系利用技术创造条件，进而将低收入人群纳入其服务范围。在这方面，《国家普惠金融政策》设定了一套行动计划，旨在运用技术创新推进普惠金融发展。行动计划包括，对现行监管框架进行全面修订和更新，使新兴金融服务提供者得以进入，

---

① 《巴基斯坦普惠金融国家战略（2015年）》。来源：http://pubdocs.worldbank.org/en/232671435258828008/Pakistan-National-Financial-Inclusion-Strategy-2015.pdf。

② 《坦桑尼亚普惠金融国家战略（2014-2016年）》。来源：http://www.afiglobal.org/sites/default/files/publications/tanzania-national-financial-inclusion-framework-2014-2016.pdf。

③ 《菲律宾普惠金融国家战略（2016年）》。来源：http://www.bsp.gov.ph/downloads/publications/2015/PhilippinesNSFIBooklet.pdf。

④ http://pubdocs.worldbank.org/en/911391453407695993/CHINESE-Advancing-Financial-Inclusion-in-China-Five-Year-Plan-2016-2020.pdf; http://www.cbrc.gov.cn/EngdocView.do?docID=14667AC65F6444079F404024229CD810

并使金融服务能通过新渠道提供；推动相关机制建设以降低现金使用，并增加数字金融产品和服务的使用；促进数字金融服务的互联互通。①

其他普惠金融国家战略也认识到技术和数字金融服务在覆盖无法获得金融服务或金融服务不足群体方面的重要作用，还有一些国家（如赞比亚、牙买加）也将数字普惠金融内容融入其正在编制的国家战略中。

公共战略和承诺，当然需要辅之以具体行动，以激励服务提供者创新，提供适当的产品，同时这些产品能被用户更快、更便捷、更安全地接受。这样的政策措施不仅应能提高使用体验，也应当有助于消除或减弱影响金融服务可得性的问题。印度和中国近些年来已经采取了广泛的行动，不但为本节、也为本报告贡献了重要案例。为促进数字普惠金融发展，各国政府所采取的、符合原则一建议的通用方法是政府对个人支付（G2P）的数字化，这一点为巴西、土耳其（而且也为更多的国家）的经验所证实。

本节的案例表明，为确保监管框架和基础设施生态系统能有利于数字普惠金融发展，需要横跨多个利益相关方的强有力的政策统筹和有效协调，包括金融监管和政策制定部门、信息通信技术（ICT）监管部门、国家身份证管理部门、支付服务提供者及其他利益相关方。通过发布数字普惠金融指导意见或制定数字普惠金融战略，明确发展数字金融服务的优先政策及方法，能有效促进并影响众多利益相关方的行动。

印度数字平台：一个多方参与的数字普惠金融方案

印度在落实所有原则尤其是原则一方面成效突出。2015年7月，印度正式启动“数字印度项目”。作为该项目的一部分，印度政府采取了若干举措致力于推动数字经济发展，包括促进数字普惠金融发展。②观察者把许多由政府和非政府利益相关者采用的技术措施的总和，包括那些“数字印度项目”启动前的技术措施，称为“印度数字平台（India Stack）”（详见专栏3）。平台的核心要素在于提升政府对个人社会转移支付（如补贴和社会资金转移）的交付效率，以及消除影响金融可得

① 《墨西哥国家普惠金融政策（2016年）》。来源（西班牙语）:http://www.gob.mx/cms/uploads/attachment/file/110408/PNIF_ver_1jul2016CONAIF_vfinal.pdf。

② 数字印度项目基于20世纪90年代推行的电子治理倡议以及2006年启动的《国家电子治理计划》。http://digitalindia.gov.in。

性的各种障碍，包括难以获取正式身份证明文件、难以获得银行分支机构或其代理商的服务，也包括中小微企业融资方面的障碍。

专栏3：印度数字平台的要素

印度数字平台是一个开放式数字基础设施平台，它运用开放应用程序编程接口[①]，推动不同经济领域的各项服务实现“去现场化、无纸化和去现金化交付”。[②]印度数字平台以如下四个技术层面为基础：

• 去现场化（presence less）层面，利用印度Aadhaar唯一身份证明和验证系统实现对个人和企业的远程实时身份证明和验证。

• 无纸化（paper less）层面，由“数字锁”和“数字签名”（或电子签名）构成，实现主体间资料共享，以及实施数字化和远程化签约。

• 去现金化（cash less）层面，以最新研发的“统一支付界面”为基础，实现所有银行账户和手机钱包之间的实时、互联互通支付。在此情境下，交易能被储存，交易记录能够共享。例如，共享给信贷提供者使其据以生成替代性信用评分模型。

• 知情同意层面，虽然尚不完备，但将会实现由个人自主决定所要共享的数据，或者仅在个人知情同意的情形下，允许其他人在特定时间内通过身份验证方式访问其数据。

虽然印度数字平台本身是一个能够提升数字金融服务可得性的创新性平台方法，但它基于由若干政府部门、其他公共机构和非政府利益相关者共同推出的各项举措之上。政府部门及其他公共机构推出的具体举措包括：

• 2009年，印度唯一身份证明管理局（UIDAI）启动Aadhaar身份证明项目，该项目已为超过十亿人口提供了唯一生物身份证。身份证明项目采集个人生物信息，包括虹膜扫描和十指指纹，并向每个居民配发唯一的12位身份证号码。[③]印度身份证明管理局基于Aadhaar身份证明数据库开发了一个“了解你的客户”电子平台。

• 2014年，印度政府启动“国民普惠金融使命”项目（PMJDY），该项目不仅

---

① 应用程序编程接口（API）是一组用来构建软件应用程序的例程、协议和工具。一个应用程序编程接口详细说明了软件组成部分应如何互相作用。一个开放应用程序编程接口允许厂商无偏地使用技术平台。

② http://indiastack.org/about/

③ https://uidai.gov.in/new/

为所有年满10周岁的印度人提供基本银行账户（主要用于发放福利），[①]还帮助民众获取更广泛的金融服务。截至2017年2月，“国民普惠金融使命”项目已注册2.739亿个银行账户。[②]

- 2015年，隶属于印度电子和信息技术部的认证管理局（CCA）推出电子签名，使Aadhaar身份证持有人能够采用数字化方式签署文件。[③]
- 2015年，印度储备银行（RBI）批准成立新型金融机构，即支付银行和小额融资银行，进一步提高交易账户可得性。
- 2016年，隶属于印度电子和信息技术部的全国电子治理委员会推出数字锁（DigiLocker）平台，旨在推动文件的数字发行和验证。[④]
- 2016年，印度财政部签发了一份内阁备忘录，为银行卡和数字支付发展提供指导原则，并协调政府推出的、旨在鼓励数字交易的各项措施。[⑤]印度政府还成立了数字支付委员会（也被称为“瓦塔尔委员会”（Watal Committee）），[⑥]研究和审视印度的数字支付框架，并提出推动数字支付发展的建议。[⑦]

非政府利益相关者采取的、对印度数字平台发展起支持作用的举措，也有助于数字普惠金融发展。这些举措包括：

- 2011年，印度国民支付公司（NPCI）推出Aadhaar支付桥和基于Aadhaar的支付系统，该系统应用Aadhaar身份证，为通过电子渠道发放政府福利和补贴提供了关键支持。[⑧]
- 印度软件产品行业圆桌会议（iSPIRT）成立于2013年，是一个旨在发展印度软件业的非政府性机构，在促进应用程序编程接口和印度数字平台支持系统发展方面起到了重要作用。

印度采取的、奠定数字平台基础的跨政府统筹协调方法，不仅使获得上述数字交易账户和其他金融服务[⑨]的人数有了大幅增长，还使政府得以用数字化方式

---

① http://pmjandhanyojana.co.in/
② https://www.pmjdy.gov.in/account
③ http://cca.gov.in/cca/?q=eSign.html
④ https://digilocker.gov.in/
⑤ http://dea.gov.in/sites/default/files/Promo_PaymentsMeans_Card_Digital_0.pdf
⑥ http://dea.gov.in/sites/default/files/Constitution_Committee_digitalpayments.pdf
⑦ http://www.finmin.nic.in/reports/watal_report271216.pdf
⑧ http://www.npci.org.in/
⑨ 借助PJMDY账户，印度政府也提供个人保险和养老金服务。

发放补贴和社会福利。据估计，截至2016年12月可节省费用近500亿卢比（7.5亿美元）。[①]

当然，印度政府在借助数字平台推进普惠金融中仍然面临着挑战。例如，将金融服务提供给农村或偏远地区时仍面临着打通“最后一公里”的挑战，在这些地区，银行的代理人或代理机构网络密度依然偏低。[②]同时，在代理商网络业务转型方面，新批准设立的由移动网络运营商主导的支付银行也面临着挑战，因为其代理网络长期以来主要提供通话和用户身份识别卡（SIM）注册服务，而现在则要提供金融服务。[③]

中国：发展数字金融服务

中国十分重视推动数字普惠金融发展，中国的数字金融近年来发展迅速。中国监管部门为新兴产业的创新和发展预留了较大空间，所以才有了中国银联、阿里巴巴，以及批发商敦煌网等电子支付和电子商务企业及行业的先期发展，电子支付和电子商务的发展又把商户纳入一个广泛的数字生态系统中。直到2010年，即支付宝上线6年后，中国人民银行才出台针对非银行支付服务的重要管理办法，规定了取得业务许可证的要求和程序，包含了注册资本最低限额要求和出资人要求等相关内容。5年之后的2015年7月，中国的四家金融监管部门（“一行三会”）、财政部和其他相关部委联合发布了《关于促进互联网金融健康发展的指导意见》（简称《指导意见》），[④]提出互联网金融（数字金融）[⑤]领域的六大发展目标：

- 积极鼓励互联网金融平台、产品和服务创新，鼓励现有金融机构采用新技术；
- 支持各类金融机构与科技企业开展合作；
- 促进风险资本投入、中小企业融资和公开上市，拓宽互联网金融企业融资渠道；
- 坚持简政放权，创造有利的发展条件及监管环境；

---

① https://dbtbharat.gov.in/
② http://indiabudget.nic.in/es2015-16/echapvol1-03.pdf
③ http://www.cgap.org/blog/how-india%E2%80%99s-new-payments-banks-stack
④ http://www.pbc.gov.cn/goutongjiaoliu/113456/113469/2813898/index.html（中文）。
⑤ 中国使用互联网金融一词，包含数字金融服务。

- 完善从业机构税收政策，使小企业受益，并促进新兴技术领域的投资；
- 鼓励互联网金融公司参与国家信用信息基础设施建设。

通过上述举措，中国政府明确了自身在互联网金融发展中的立场，即推动新兴金融技术发展能对传统金融产生积极影响。中国也注重数字金融均衡发展，出台了防控新兴风险（如欺诈、洗钱、非法集资，以及未经授权泄露客户个人信息）的新准则。这些准则进一步厘清了不同金融监管部门在互联网金融中的监管职责。中国人民银行负责监管互联网支付业务，中国银监会负责监管网络借贷业务、互联网信托业务和互联网消费金融业务，中国证监会负责监管股权众筹融资业务和互联网基金销售业务，中国保监会负责监管互联网保险业务。①

紧随着《指导意见》的发布，中国人民银行于2015年12月针对互联网支付行业起草了《非银行支付机构网络支付业务管理办法》并征求公众意见，在客户身份识别、在线支付、单日支付上限、验证方式与交易限额、信息披露等方面提出了新要求。该办法自2016年7月起施行（见原则三）。

在《指导意见》和互联网金融新规出台之前，中国已努力拓展农村地区的数字服务点。2010年，中国人民银行启动了助农取款服务试点，探索农民使用银行卡和POS终端取款服务，并在2014年增加了汇款和缴费服务。为了在农村地区推广电子支付和电子商务，中国人民银行也鼓励助农取款服务点和农村电子商务服务点之间的资源共享。截至2016年末，全国共有助农取款服务点98.34万个，覆盖了超过50万个行政村（覆盖率超过90%）。2016年共办理支付业务2.55亿笔，交易总金额达1 200亿元人民币。

<u>政府对个人支付数字化：巴西、墨西哥及其他国家</u>

政府对个人（G2P）支付方式迅速向数字化转变（尤其是在社会保障或福利支付方面），不但影响深远而且具有示范意义。当前，许多国家都采取措施运用电子手段实现G2P支付，在这方面有许多国别案例。②例如，在巴西，2003年发起的有条件的现金转移项目（即Bolsa Familia），通过电子福利卡发放补贴，覆盖了将

① 中国人民银行-世界银行联合报告（待发布）：《全球视野下的中国普惠金融：实践、经验与挑战》。（该报告已于2008年2月正式发布——译者注。）

② 即将出台的二十国集团普惠金融全球合作伙伴文件（Guidance Note on Building Inclusive Digital Payments Ecosystems）很有价值，可供进一步参考。

近1 400万家庭；[①]在墨西哥，联邦政府集中处理支付，并提高了通过交易账户发放的数字化支付的份额，包括某些社会福利的发放。[②]其他国家也已开始，或正处于从以现金方式发放个人转移支付向以电子方式发放个人转移支付的过程中，这些国家有巴基斯坦、南非、肯尼亚、乌干达、印度、尼泊尔、海地、哥伦比亚、孟加拉国，以及其他一些国家。

政府转移支付数字化是数字金融服务的催化剂，然而它也是一项涉及多方面的、需要认真筹划的工程。在上述举措已经取得成功的案例中，政策执行者都付出了巨大努力，与非政府组织、捐赠者和私人部门服务提供者共同采取协调一致的行动。从巴西、墨西哥等国采取的行之有效的措施中，我们可以得到如下启示：

• 要数字化、集中化处理政府转移支付，促进经济中电子支付的使用，成功的G2P措施通常是更宏大计划的一个必备要素；

• 即使不能提前建成，至少应当在启动数字G2P支付项目时，同步建设管理社会福利项目的内部自动化系统；

• 应有合乎需要的产品设计，方便受益人使用这些产品接受G2P转移支付，良好的设计对于受益人积极使用数字设备、运用其账户中所收到的资金进行收付款、转账至关重要，而不仅仅是在收到这些资金时将其取出；

• 建立延伸至用户生活、工作地点的数字生态系统（包括ATM、POS终端），以及激励商户接受数字支付（包括在线支付），是关键之举；

• 协调采取行动提升用户金融意识和能力，为补贴受益人（尤其是那些没有自己的移动电话的妇女）赋权，使其在接受G2P支付之外还能使用新的数字金融服务。

---

① 参见IDB (2015). How Does Bolsa Familia Work? Best Practices in the Implementation of Conditional Cash Transfer Program in Latin America and the Caribbean. 链接：https://publications.iadb.org/bitstream/handle/11319/7210/How_does_Bolsa_Familia_Work.pdf?sequence=

② 例如，该国主要有条件现金转移项目的所有注册受益人（PROSPERA，旧称Progresa和Oportunidades项目）在登记时都开设了银行账户，截至2017年4月，大约有81%的人收到了与项目相关的借记卡。该借记卡功能有限，只能用作身份证明工具，从政府代理机构以现金方式接收相应的转移支付。剩下的19%的人确实收到了功能齐全的借记卡，使用该卡，他们可以以通行方式动用其项目相关的存款，比如进行支付或取款。同样，大约有50%的老年转移支付受益人完全以现金方式接受其补贴，其余50%的老年受益人则通过普通银行账户接受补贴，他们能够借助通常的借记卡使用这笔资金。

2.2 原则二：平衡好数字普惠金融发展中的创新与风险

原则二强调的是，金融服务创新对发展普惠金融必不可少，同时它也带来了一些个别的和系统性的新风险，需要及时有效地识别和处理这些风险。政策制定者应鼓励和培育创新，利用其所产生的益处惠及大众，尤其是对那些无法获得或缺乏金融服务的群体。他们也应当认识到，创新必然会产生新的风险，新的风险和旧的风险均需防范和化解。但要认识到，并非所有的风险都能被消除。随着全球的政策制定者更加关注金融市场网络复原能力（cyber resilience）建设，并致力于保护金融体系免受非法活动侵扰，这一认识也就越发显得重要。

政策制定者平衡好创新和风险的行为包括：在监管者之间建立学习和信息共享机制，发展供监管者使用的数字监管工具，与私营部门的创新者建立密切联系，以及探索与行业和消费者沟通的新模式。

监管者与行业合作设计的新工具和新流程的情况已经出现。这些工具和流程不仅简化了公司的合规要求，而且从本质上重新设计了监管者收集和监测数据的方式（更详细的讨论见原则三）。更为常见的是，许多监管者正在根据服务提供商所使用的新数字分销渠道来重新审视如何管理某些金融服务，或者通过改变现有的规则，或者针对一些新服务类别，在做出任何监管决定前允许开展某些尝试。

数字金融服务的快速增长要求监管者和政策制定者主动与行业合作，确保当新的创新将金融服务的覆盖范围通过新渠道扩展到新的市场领域时，威胁消费者保护、金融包容、市场诚信与投资者信心、金融稳定等的潜在风险均已得到充分解决。

本节中的案例特别强调，监管者能够采用多种多样的方法来平衡数字普惠金融创新的风险和收益。欧盟等一些地区正在开展公共咨询，并成立工作组探索如何解决这一问题。[①]其他地区则决定创设一个试验框架。不论是通过现存监管机制，构建新的结构性边试边学环境，还是非正式参与方法，试验框架都能在控制潜在风险的同时，促进能够满足消费者需求的数字金融服务的发展。

---

① https://ec.europa.eu/info/files/consumer-financial-services-action-plan-better-products-more-choice_en

肯尼亚、美国和英国的“边试边学”方法

在新的数字环境下，金融监管者面临的最大的变化之一是怎样与受其监管的金融业互动，与金融业所服务的消费者互动。不论是在产品设计方面，还是在新兴参与者的数量和类型方面，金融服务快速创新都会产生风险，给传统金融监管方法带来挑战，使之难以实现金融稳定、金融诚信、消费者保护、金融包容等关键监管目标。

监管试点因其允许创新和测试新型金融服务（包括那些可能不在传统监管范畴内的金融服务），故而成为监管者如何应对新型数字金融服务创新方面的一个突出范例。金融监管者允许进行这种“尝试”，总体而言并不是一个全新概念。尤其是，早在2007年，肯尼亚中央银行（CBK）在尚未确立监管框架的情况下，允许移动运营商Safaricom公司推出M-Pesa移动支付服务。

许多国家正在数字金融领域尝试运用“边试边学”理念。英国金融行为监管局（FCA）在“项目创新”计划支持下创建了“监管沙箱”，该沙箱并非是为了规避或否定监管，而是为金融机构尝试创新性产品、服务、商业模型和交付机制提供一个安全空间，同时又能确保消费者得到充分保护。

在FCA启动“项目创新”计划的同时，美国消费者金融保护局（CFPB）正着手推出类似项目。CFPB的“项目催化剂”，为创新者提供了难得的参与机会，从而能够“鼓励金融消费产品和服务市场中消费者友好型创新”。[①]比如，CFPB定期实行非正式“办公时间”，最近宣布了一项有关替代性信贷数据的公众调查，[②]目的在于提高金融服务不足客户的信贷可得性。CFPB还允许创新者在类似沙箱的环境下运行试点项目，以便政府机构和公司可以共同研究满足监管或者信息披露要求的新方法。

对于CFPB而言，试点项目是一个有用的学习机制。试点的部分内容即是提供大量数据。由于提升了CFPB对金融消费者行为和金融创新的理解（包括金融创新是否能够或金融创新的哪些方面可以提升某些消费者群体的福祉），数据的获得能

① http://www.consumerfinance.gov/about-us/project-catalyst/

② https://www.consumerfinance.gov/about-us/newsroom/cfpb-explores-impact-alternative-data-credit-access-consumerswho-are-credit-invisible/

够对其他政策产生溢出效应。美国另一个监管机构货币监理署（OCC）2016年提出了“负责任创新”倡议，并透露他们将出台许多支持创新的举措，包括考虑允许金融科技公司获得全国性（而非州一级的）银行牌照。①

自从英国和美国宣布启动测试框架以来，许多国家或地区要么提出自己的行动计划（澳大利亚、马来西亚、新加坡、泰国、阿拉伯联合酋长国、以及中国香港），要么宣布很快将采用该方法（印度尼西亚、肯尼亚和瑞士）。中低收入国家同样正在建立类似沙箱的项目，着力促进金融科技创新，且通常与推进普惠金融的目标相结合（特别是在缺乏金融服务的农村地区）。而且，不只是银行监管者在考虑这一理念，保险监管者也在考虑边试边学方法。例如，加纳全国保险委员会（NIC）允许以个案方式尝试运用移动保险产品，NIC预先审查移动网络运营商(MNO)、技术服务提供商和保险公司之间缔结的商业协议，并在此后密切监控其活动。

尽管这些边试边学方法的名字和设计不尽相同，但是大多数方法有一个相似目标，即在一个小范围的、可控的环境下建立试验和创新框架，促进（创新性）金融部门发展及竞争力的提高，从而让消费者受益。这些“边试边学”的方法有两大共同属性：

- 金融监管机构和在边试边学环境中运营的企业（有时被称为“沙箱实体”）进行结构性交流，借助这种交流，金融监管机构向沙箱实体提出法律和监管要求方面的建议，并在某些情况下给予临时豁免；
- 在可控环境下对创新测试进行监测。

监管者适当监管创新项目的能力将是关键因素。在确保金融稳定、金融诚信、金融消费者保护的前提下，平衡创新和风险（以促进数字普惠金融发展）的能力对金融监管者至关重要。因此，那些考虑实施“监管沙箱”或“温室计划”的金融监管机构应该仔细考虑所有可用的方法，对比其成本和总体收益，考量其与现有法律和监管框架的相容性，以及自身的实施能力。在使用这些方法大力鼓励金融创新时，金融监管机构也要注意避免易造成市场扭曲的、过多的“先发优势”。提前对试点阶段设置适时的限制，或许有助于抑制这些扭曲效应。

① https://www.occ.treas.gov/topics/bank-operations/innovation/index-innovation.html

专栏4：英国金融行为监管局的监管沙箱

为推动更有效的竞争，英国金融行为监管局（FCA）希望鼓励金融服务领域的创新。因此，它要鼓励企业在一个降低了监管要求的可控环境下尝试创新性解决方案。FCA认为，如果不对试点活动在监管上给予某种程度的官方准许，行业参与者将不会投入研发创新服务所需要的时间和资源。安全测试环境或“沙箱”，给新的创新服务提供了边试边学的方法，但又处于经批准的测试参数范围、监督和信息共享框架之内，这既提供了灵活性又限定了风险。在设计项目时，FCA设法解决两个主要挑战：如何在现有的监管框架下，提供一个能够降低测试障碍的沙箱；如何确保测试新方案所产生的风险不会转嫁给消费者。

由此产生的沙箱项目既是针对那些在测试其服务之前需要授权的“未经授权的”（即未受监管的）企业，同时也针对已获授权企业在对某个明显不适用于现存管理框架的理念进行测试之前，寻求对可适用规则的明确解释。未经授权的企业能够获得仅允许测试其想法的限制性授权。这些企业仍然需要申请授权并满足门槛条件，但只能参与有限目的的沙箱测试。[①]对授权企业而言，监管沙箱有三种工具：个别指导；豁免或修改那些过于繁苛的FCA规则（但不豁免国家或国际性的法律法规）；以及在特定情况下，出具无执行行动承诺函（NALs）。只有在FCA认为不能个别指导或豁免，但又认为有足够的理由考虑到不同沙箱测试的具体情况和特征时，才会发出此类函件。该函件只在沙箱测试期内有效，且仅适用于FCA的纪律惩罚，企业依然要承担对消费者应尽的责任。

FCA制定了具体的标准作为企业申请沙箱测试必须满足的先决条件：

- 真正的创新。新的解决方案是否真的新颖，或者明显不同于现有的产品和服务？
- 消费者受益。消费者有切实受益的良好前景吗？这一标准在为期6个月的测试期内自始自终必须得到满足。
- 公司在适当的范围内吗？新的解决方案是为了金融服务行业而设计的吗？对金融服务行业有帮助吗？
- 沙箱测试的必要性。是否真的有在沙箱框架下进行测试的需求？

① https://www.handbook.fca.org.uk/handbook/COND.pdf

- 做好测试准备。是否做好充分的准备，能够保证现场测试？

2016年11月，FCA宣布69个申请企业中有24家第一批入选沙箱项目。选中的24家金融科技公司来自不同的国家（包括新加坡、丹麦、美国和加拿大），涵盖现有的和新的参与者，并且广泛覆盖支付和区块链，零售银行，抵押贷款和保险，顾问，信息收集披露，国际公共产品和服务，以及数字身份等领域。

通过数字渠道提高保险服务可得性

人们对利用数字技术提高保险服务可得性潜力的关注度越来越高，包括利用移动网络运营商（MNOs）等替代性数字渠道。对于大多数移动网络运营商提供的产品而言，提供保险通常只是一种吸引新客户以及培养客户忠诚度的手段，尽管许多产品正从作为增加客户忠诚度的手段向免费增值和付费模式转变。尤其在非洲，通过上述渠道提供的产品已有显著增长，2011年到2014年期间发售的高成长性产品，有5/7是通过MNOs分销出去的。就本报告中我们关注的非G20国家的具体产品而言，人寿保险、意外事故保险和微型健康保险是市场主流产品，虽然存在地区差异（如在亚洲，寿险和人身意外险占主导地位，而在拉丁美洲，信用寿险长期占主导地位）。[①]大多数早期的移动保险产品一开始不过是简单的人寿保险和人身意外事故保险，但随着时间推移，产品线变得日益多样化，一些产品方案现在还包括个人意外事故保险、农业险、住院险等，通常作为捆绑销售的保险产品。

虽然MNOs在供给微型保险产品方面的作用越来越重要，但它们目前总体上仍是作为分销渠道，通常与BIMA及MicroEnsure这样的技术服务提供商（TSPs）合作，而让商业保险公司成为主要的风险承担者。TSPs在移动保险的合作中扮演着重要角色，在保险价值链中发挥着关键作用。在一些情形下，除承保（与保险公司合作）外的所有功能都外包给了技术服务商。在这种情况下，由于涉及多个参与者，保险监管机构努力增进与电信监管机构的协作，从而加强监管。

例如，在加纳，德国国际合作机构（GIZ）代表德国联邦经济合作与发展部（BMZ），支持全国保险委员会（保险监管机构）对移动保险的整体情况进行深入的风险评估，并提出一套完善移动保险产品监管指导原则的风险框架。作为评估的结

① 更详细的信息请见 https://a2ii.org/sites/default/files/field/uploads/lessons_from_a_decade_of_microinsurance_regulation_a2ii_nov_2016.pdf

果，全国保险委员会（保险监管机构）最近与加纳银行（中央银行）、全国通信管理局（电信监管机构）签订了一份谅解备忘录（MOU），批准MNOs和保险机构之间签订的微型保险分销协议。[①]而且，全国保险委员会还起草了《保险公司及代理机构市场行为规则》，这份文件对监管市场发展以保护保单持有人和移动网络用户利益，与维护有益的市场发展激励二者做出权衡。然而，在一些市场中，MNOs正努力获取自己的微型保险许可证，有时与技术服务商合作，有时直接与保险服务提供者合作：[②]柬埔寨的移动网络运营商BIMA-Milvik和南非的移动网络运营商Vodacom SA，均是以提供微型保险而建立的商业保险公司。[③]这类机构的参与是近来的一个市场现象。与MNOs仅充当分销角色相比，MNOs和监管机构是否更青睐这种方式——对此问题进行观察将会非常有趣。

2.3 原则三：构建适当的法律和监管框架

原则三指出，为促进数字金融服务蓬勃发展，这需要一个可预测的、以风险为导向的、公平的法律和监管框架。该框架允许新参与者进入市场，是技术中性的，但不增加过度的、不是以风险为导向的合规成本。政策制定者和监管人员还应确保，在具备必要的监管能力和监管资源的情况下，该框架能够有效实施。

通过制定鼓励创新以及使新兴非银行机构发挥更大作用的监管规定，可扩大对无法获得银行服务者金融服务的广度和范围。以此为方向的努力，近年来取得了许多积极进展。例如，在数字支付、代理银行以及从支付分离出来的独立中介等方面，可以观察到这些发展变化。许多观察家将这些发展称之为“功能”监管方法，即要关注所讨论的服务，而不是提供服务的机构类型（即“机构”监管方法）。

《欧盟支付服务指令》（PSD）是该方法出现初期的一个典型案例。2007年欧盟通过了PSD，2015年将其升级为PSD2。PSD2旨在放宽新兴支付机构的市场准入，提

① http://www.ghananewsagency.org/economics/care-international-focuses-on-improving-financial-inclusion--110343

② https://a2ii.org/sites/default/files/field/uploads/lessons_from_a_decade_of_microinsurance_regulation_a2ii_nov_2016.pdf

③ BMZ 2015, Wiedmaier-Pfister and Leach

高透明度，协调欧盟各成员的法规，以进一步促进竞争和创新（其途径是向新兴金融科技公司开放欧盟零售支付市场），并改善消费者保护。[①]尤其是，为在充分保护消费者的同时支持创新，PSD2根据业务规模和风险程度对支付机构进行分级，并提出相应要求。

监管方面，另一个旨在扩大金融服务覆盖面的进展，是金融行动特别工作组(FATF)采用的风险为本方法，该方法要求准确评估反洗钱/反恐怖融资监管、合规及监督措施，以消除由服务提供者、顾客、产品和服务所产生的实际风险。尽管风险为本方法还有很多方面，在普惠金融框架下采用风险为本方法的一个共同方面是，应用分层级的客户尽职调查（CDD）机制。这个机制要求，随着产品和服务功能增加，相应提升客户尽职调查水平。反过来，也可以通过余额上限、交易限额以及使用限制的方式对功能进行控制。

此外，随着非银行支付服务提供商扩展其活动，监管者们正在重新考虑如何监督、监管这些机构。非银行数字支付服务本身已经不是新的事物了，因为用途有限的储值卡由来已久，诸如PayPal这样的支付公司在1998年就已出现。但这些早期的电子支付服务要么由闭环系统支持，如商店储值卡或交通运输系统支付卡，要么依赖和银行账户的直接关联，如PayPal那样。而新的方面是，对非银行支付机构运用数字方法提供开环支付和交易账户服务的广泛接受和认可。通用的、可以重复充值的预付卡正在快速地增长（特别是在美国），以及在世界很多地区（尤其是非洲）开始使用移动货币系统，已经向监管者们证明，人们对使用简单、低成本、易于操作而不需要用户开立传统银行账户的交易账户，存在大量的、未经开发的需求。这也逐渐引发了反思，怎样让游离于银行体系外的人群进入正规的金融服务市场，从传统上关注小额信贷和团队储蓄，转变到提供使用电子资金或者“电子货币”的个人交易账户上来。在过去的十年间一些国家制定了关于电子货币使用的指导原则，而这一趋势无疑将继续下去。

两个关键主题在兴起，一个是越来越多的监管机构采用风险为本的监管方法(包括风险为木的客户尽职调查方法)，另一个是人们越来越认识到，报告和监测系统应该变得更为复杂精密，除实时监控能力和适当的隐私和数据保护外，还需要更

① https://ec.europa.eu/info/business-economy-euro/banking-and-finance/consumer-finance-and-payments/paymentservices_en

加重视与金融机构信息系统的直接连接（如可行的话）。

对数字金融服务进行新的风险为本监管的一个例子是中国人民银行最近出台的一系列举措。2015年底，中国人民银行针对非银行机构网络支付颁布新规定，即《非银行支付机构网络支付业务管理办法》。

专栏5：分层监管与行业自律

中国的新规则从2016年7月起生效。新规则提高了对非银行支付机构客户尽职调查要求，设定三个层级，包括要求所有账户实名登记，随交易量增加相应提高审查等级。新规则中最有趣的地方可能是对支付平台的分层监管理念。对于平台所适用的身份验证方法有更严格的审查，平台所适用的方法越严格，越有可能被中国人民银行授予更高的评级。中国人民银行将会基于平台自身的分析和分类机制对各家支付平台进行评级，平台评级越高，受到的限制也越少，而评级较低的平台将面临来自监管者额外的审查。评级较高平台的另一个优势是，平台用户的单日限额最多可以增加到监管规定标准限额的两倍（分层规定里的年度限额仍然不变）。

除发布数字支付提供商的新规则外，中国人民银行还支持建立中国互联网金融协会（NIFA），推进行业自律。该协会由中国人民银行指导，是在民政部登记的“国家一级协会”，该协会有408个成员机构，包括银行、证券公司、基金公司、保险公司、信托公司、金融消费公司和非银行支付机构，以及其他相关机构，如担保公司、信用服务公司和互联网P2P公司。该协会的章程包括按照业态建立细分的行业标准和业务规范，促进行业内的信息共享和沟通，制定自律内容和惩罚机制，以及加强行业的法律及合规文化。2016年9月，中国互联网金融协会也推出了信用信息共享平台，收集和共享客户数据，但没有共享个人客户基本信息。当系统接收到一个请求时，它会将查询请求转发给所有成员并核对数据，不泄露数据的来源，从而保护竞争性信息。

分层级客户尽职调查机制

正如以上所述，对于数字普惠金融而言，以风险为本方法的重要表现之一就是分层级的客户尽职调查（CDD）机制。[①]客户识别机制是对进行金融交易的个人和企业身份识别和验证的过程，以查出可能涉及非法金融活动的交易，如洗钱和恐怖主义融资。有关国家机构日益认识到适当和适度的客户尽职调查机制是一个延缓“去风险”趋势的重要因素。

虽然有效的客户识别机制的极端重要性确定无疑，但也得承认，严格的客户识别机制有时会阻碍穷人和农村用户使用正规金融服务。根据传统规定，开立新的存款账户往往需要一些条件，而穷人常常难以满足这些要求（例如，需要验证身份，提供证明或地址和来源）。此外，客户识别要求成本可能过高，尤其是涉及利润率较低的客户时（比如，在这种情况下金融机构需要处理纸质表格，进行个人访谈，或使用昂贵的交易监控软件）。政策制定者和监管者现在认识到，低风险交易（如小额支付）可以应用简化的客户识别规则，而不会妨碍反洗钱、反恐融资（AML/CFT）目标。运用分层的方法，随着产品功能的增加，客户尽职调查的要求也相应增加，这既有助于有效缓释风险，又能将低收入消费者纳入正规金融部门。[②]

虽然监管层反复考虑合适的简化客户尽职调查机制有很长时间了（南非的分层方法可以追溯到2002年通过的第17条豁免条款（Exemption 17），即允许银行在为客户开立有限功能基本账户时，可以免除地址证明相关要求），[③]但标准制定机构（SSB）正式认可的概念仅可以追溯到2011年6月，当时金融行动特别工作组（FATF）发布了其第一份普惠金融指导文件，[④]并在2013年予以修订。[⑤]之后，一些国家（普惠金融联盟（AFI）称有42个成员）[⑥]开始采用正式的分层客户尽职调查机制。

正式建立分层尽职调查机制的两个著名例子是墨西哥和坦桑尼亚。2011年8月，墨西哥批准在信贷机构开立存款账户的分层方案。该方案提供了一个机构间协

① 实践中，了解你的客户（KYC）和客户尽职调查（CDD）这两个名词常常交换使用，尽管FATF建议使用CDD。

② http://www.fatf-gafi.org/media/fatf/documents/reports/AML_CFT_Measures_and_Financial_Inclusion_2013.pdf

③ http://www.cgap.org/sites/default/files/CGAP-Focus-Note-AML-CFT-Strengthening-Financial-Inclusion-and-IntegrityAug-2009.pdf

④ FATF Anti-Money Laundering and Terrorist Financing Measures and Financial Inclusion (June 2011)。http://www.fatfgafi.org/media/fatf/content/images/AML%20CFT%20measures%20and%20financial%20inclusion.pdf

⑤ FATF, Forty Recommendations。http://www.fatfgafi.org/media/fatf/documents/recommendations/pdfs/FATF_Recommendations.pdf

⑥ www.afi-dataportal.org

调的模式，因为它涉及中央银行，财政部以及银行监管机构等的相关部门。该方案包括4个层次——3个低风险账户和传统的活期账户，同时为小额、低风险账户提供了灵活的账户开设要求，随着交易额增加，要求也逐步提高。也许当时最著名的举措是“一类账户”规定的出台，在低风险的前提下免除开户的身份验证要求，允许以非面对面方式开立小额的、以借记卡为基础的电子钱包。尽管用户身份没有被验证，但可疑活动交易仍被严密监控。该方案还允许将一些客户尽职调查工作外包给第三方，也允许无纸化保存记录。在新规则出台后的两年内，新账户开立数量超过1 000万，其中大多数最初注册为一类账户（level 1 accounts）。①

在2015年，经过反复协商后，坦桑尼亚对移动货币业务建立了自己的分层客户尽职调查机制，共包括三个层级：层级一，基本的电子注册账户，只需要一个注册的电话号码；层级二，同时需要注册的电话号码和面对面确认，以及一份可接受的国家身份证明文件复印件；层级三，针对中小型企业，不仅包括完整的层级二客户尽职调查要求，除营业执照号外，还要有税号、增值税登记号。虽然新制度被认为是推广移动货币的好方法，但是，坦桑尼亚银行部门继续执行着他们传统的、更严格的客户尽职调查要求。鉴于移动货币与传统银行部门的不断趋同，以及银行对建立简化基本账户的兴趣与日俱增，坦桑尼亚简化的客户尽职调查制度需要协调一致。

这几个例子表明：监管机制出现了哪些不断增强的趋势。监管机制调整变化的目的是让金融机构在为之前的金融排斥群体开立账户时更为容易，这部分群体的风险非常低。然而，金融监管者也日益认识到，低效的（或根本不存在）的官方身份系统成为金融服务所有社会成员的重大障碍。因而，其中一些监管机构正通过推行特殊目的身份系统等措施来解决这个问题，特殊目的身份系统能在全民覆盖身份系统完成前的过渡期中发挥作用。

ID（身份证明）——促进数字普惠金融的关键因素

全球范围内的政策制定者、捐赠者及其他利益相关方都逐渐认识到，有必要建设综合性身份证明项目，以促进金融服务及其他各类服务的获得、使用。《可持续

① 到2016年末，全国有1 470万一类账户，1 950万二类账户，40万三类账户；有9 440万传统活期账户（Banco de México, 2017）。当时，15岁及以上人口估计约为9 000万（CONAPO）。

发展身份证明原则》[①]——由世界银行支持的“促进发展身份证明倡议”（或ID4D）[②]发布并得到了包括开发机构、智库及产业团体在内的15个以上国际组织[③]的支持，《可持续发展身份证明原则》提出了指导意见，推动建立强大的、包容性的数字身份证明系统。

数字身份证明系统具有提升金融服务可得性的巨大潜能，这方面的成功案例包括巴基斯坦的E身份证明系统及印度的Aadhaar系统（2.1节进行过讨论）。在巴基斯坦，全国数据库和登记局（NADRA）开发了国家计算机化身份证（CNIC），该身份证包含了生物信息，可为每位公民提供一个唯一的身份证号码。大约99%的巴基斯坦成年人拥有CNIC身份证。巴基斯坦几年前就开始采取措施，将CNIC与金融服务相融合，包括与初级交易账户、社会福利支付、电子信用信息局相连接，近来开始与电子支付设施相链接。[④]

在全国性身份证明系统尚未充分覆盖的国家，金融服务行业内部采取了许多临时方法，建立“特殊用途”身份证明系统。这方面的一个例子是尼日利亚的银行验证号码（BVN）。尼日利亚并没有在公民出生时就为其配发唯一的身份证号码，而是设法为公民提供一个唯一的全国性编号。公民可以获得三种官方身份证明中的一种，即护照、驾照或投票卡，但这些系统使用了不同的登记形式，而且因为系统没有统一或集中验证，使得人们可以在不同的系统使用不同的名字，甚至开立多个身份账户。

因为这种情况，同时也因为完全纠正这种情形可能需要许多年的时间，所以尼日利亚中央银行（CBN）决定与银行业一起建立BVN系统。要获得BVN，个人可以去包括所有银行网点在内的BVN注册中心免费注册，注册需提交个人的十指指纹，面部照片，姓名和家庭住址，这些信息随后被提交给中央匹配系统。一旦个人生物特征识别通过了核实，使之无法开立多个账户，这个人随后就被赋予一个与生物信息对应的11位数字号码。

---

① “Principles on Identification for Sustainable Development: Toward the Digital Age”,2017.(http://documents.worldbank.org/curatcd/cn/213581486378184357/pdf/112614-REVISED-PUBLIC-web-final-ID4DIdentificationPrinciples.pdf)

② http://www.worldbank.org/en/programs/id4d

③ 支持该倡议的国际组织的完整名单参见 “Principles on Identification for Sustainable Development: Toward the Digital Age” 报告第2页。

④ “Leveraging ID Systems for Financial Sector Development”,2017.海波龙咨询公司（Consult Hyperion）提交给世界银行集团ID4D倡议，及金融与市场全球实践部门的报告。

到目前为止，BVN已经被证明是金融行业行之有效的（虽说也有限）身份证明形式。公民不必开立账户就可以有BVN，但不能在没有BVN的情况下开设银行账户。BVN也开始在农业补贴等非银行服务领域应用。该系统仍处于发展完善中，尼日利亚的政策制定者们已着手将BVN数据库与尼日利亚的社会保障系统（NIMC）相连接，这样人们一旦获得一个BVN，就不必在社会保障系统再次登记。他们还准备将征信机构和诸如微型金融银行等非银行金融机构相连接，部分通过一个应用程序编程接口（API）提供直接接口或进行验证。虽然目前对非银行金融机构使用BVN没有要求，但是尼日利亚中央银行正在制定强制使用BVN的指导原则。

另一个中央银行在金融业建立身份证明系统的例子是乌干达。乌干达有一套特殊身份认证系统，与金融部门的信用数据相匹配，但这套特殊系统最终将被一项力求实现全覆盖的全国性身份证明方案所取代。乌干达银行正逐渐放弃使用最初的金融卡系统（FCS），因为乌干达的国家身份证明和登记局（NIRA）正推出全国性的身份证。到目前为止，NIRA已经发放了超过2 000万张身份证，而FCS智能卡只发行了140万张。FCS智能卡不会完全消失，因为FCS卡的供应商正在与NIRA一起努力，使FCS卡号码与新的全国性身份证号码相匹配，但全国性身份证号码最终会成为金融部门交易的关键标识符。

上述尼日利亚和乌干达的案例是这两个国家的金融监管当局在全国性身份证明系统不健全或完全缺失情况下进行的创新，并不是针对解决全国性身份证明问题所给的建议——注意到这一点很重要。正如原则七所指出的，政策制定者出于多种原因（不只是从普惠金融角度考虑）需要建立强大的全国性身份证明系统。像尼日利亚和乌干达所采用的基于部门的方法，可能能够实现有限的目标，但从全国性身份证明项目的总体背景下看则可能是无效的——除非各方能够就标准达成一致，从而使这些局部方案能够逐步发展并融入全国性身份证明方案之中。

利用技术增强监管能力：奥地利和卢旺达

开发和/或更新报告及监测系统是监管者日益关注的一个主题，特别是在监管要求不断提高和数字金融服务不断发展的背景下。虽然所有中央银行都采用某种信息系统，与其银行客户相连接，但是中央银行系统开发及其跟踪和监督非银行参与者（如数字支付提供商）的能力往往落后于行业发展步伐。在许多情况下，监管机构仍然依赖于行业自我报告，或偶尔的纸质/Excel报告。这种相对初级的监管方法，无法有效监管当今支付行业大量的数字交易，也无法赶上产品、交付机制和提供商的变革创新步伐。

实现数据收集、汇总和分析过程自动化的一个关键要素，是使用标准化报告格式。这些格式易于在系统之间扩展和移植，并能够利用明确定义的分类和元数据。全球范围内，消息和数据的交换有向可扩展标记语言（XML）转变的趋势。可扩展商业报告语言（XBRL）用于向资本市场监管机构和市场数据提供商报告经营结果、公司公告和资产负债表数据。可扩展商业报告语言现已被银行业监管机构广泛采用。

发达经济体的许多监管机构已经更新（或正在更新）其市场监测系统，在许多情况下与行业密切合作开发监管技术（或“RegTech”）系统，用于改进报告质量和合规性。RegTech[①]也有助于监管机构收集、分析和监测市场数据，以及确定消费者痛点。可以肯定的是，发达国家的监管机构仍然在改进传统的监管系统，而新兴市场报告和监测系统现代化步伐往往落后于实践发展需求（新兴市场数字金融服务提供商快速涌现），但也有一些明显的例外（详见专栏6）。

专栏6：自动化监管报告和监督

一些中央银行已开始采取措施，努力加强监管报告和非现场监管的内部系统和流程，试图从基于模板的方法向实时的、以输入为主（input-based）的方法转变，后者在收集银行和非银行金融机构的数据和信息方面更有效率。“以输入为主”的方法利用新技术（或“监管科技”），使监管者能够获取有关金融活动更高数据粒度的数据，这些金融活动包括市场新进入者的经营活动，新的数字化交付机制及产品相关活动，同时也减轻了来自被监管机构的报告负担。[②]

例如，奥地利中央银行，即奥地利国家银行（Oesterreiche Nationalbank，OeNB）与银行业合作，推出了一个新的软件平台，以改进奥地利商业银行的数据和监管报告报送流程。被称为“Aurep”的软件平台在奥地利央行和商业

① Regtech在此处指数据收集、分析和使用的技术支持解决方案的设计和运用，包括：1）提高市场监管水平；2）降低合规成本；3）推动更智能、适当、基于风险的监管；4）增加消费者信任、财务健康，及对金融系统的参与。

② BearingPoint Institute (2015) https://www.bearingpointinstitute.com/en/regulatory-reporting-are-we-headed-real-time

银行的IT系统之间提供了直接接口，使奥地利央行能够通过该平台自动获取商业银行的粒度数据。重要的是，Aurep平台还充当奥地利央行和商业银行之间的缓冲区，使得银行可以将由奥地利央行规定的标准化数据集（基本数据立方体）上传到平台上，但又保持了对商业敏感信息的控制。尔后平台可以将基本数据集转换为奥地利央行各部门所需的格式。这种新的报告系统大大减轻了受监管银行机构的合规负担，并且确保了在奥地利央行内部发送的数据有更大的一致性和更高的质量。奥地利央行是否打算拓展该平台并将非银行金融机构纳入其中，尚需观察。

在卢旺达，卢旺达国民银行（BNR）正在建设一个自动化金融报告和监督系统，以收集、分析和传送受监管银行和非银行金融机构报送的数据。该系统不仅力求改进数据收集流程，降低金融机构监管报告负担，而且还力争向BNR提供更多、具有更高数据粒度的数据，以监测普惠金融进展。该系统允许BNR自动从金融机构的核心管理信息系统（MIS）（对拥有该系统的机构而言）中提取数据，从而提高非现场报告数据的准确性、完整性和及时性。

在世界银行的支持下，卢旺达国民银行设计了新的报告模板，以改善数据的范围、一致性和质量，包括金融普惠性指标，例如目标市场群体、性别、地理位置等。所有持牌银行都已连接到系统上，而一些微型金融机构则以Excel格式提交新模板。卢旺达央行正在进行相关改革，在储蓄与信贷合作社（SACCO）建立核心管理信息系统，以确保它们也能够加入到上述新系统中。

本节所举例子说明，有必要建立一个法律和监管框架，该框架是适当的、以风险为导向的，同时能够创造有利于数字普惠金融发展的环境。例如，分层的客户尽职调查（CDD）制度可以降低个人消费者面临的合同文本障碍，以及降低金融服务提供者的合规成本，进而提高金融服务的可获得性。随着数字金融服务和交付机制变得越来越复杂，提升充分监管市场的能力也变得更为重要。监管者可以利用技术，在跟上市场发展变化步伐的同时，又能使自己更好地监测和监管市场。

2.4 原则四：扩展数字金融服务基础设施生态系统

原则四强调，需构建一个强大、开放和高效的数字基础设施，该数字基础设施包括广泛可得的零售支付系统和信息通信技术（ICT）基础设施，以便大范围地提供数字金融服务。这项原则要求政策制定者与私营部门密切合作，以确保整个数字金融服务生态系统能够平稳、连贯运行，生态系统既包括语音和数据网络（包含消费者依赖的各种数字服务点，例如POS机和ATM），也包括支撑这些网络的电力和传输系统。由于整个数字金融生态系统的提供必然由公共部门和私人部门共同参与完成，其所有权也必然属于这两个部门，政策制定者必须在各种选择之间做好平衡，即在仅仅依赖私人投资，在必要时运用公共支出于基础设施，在需要时进行精准补贴，和/或为了增进公共利益而对服务提供者进行法律授权等选择之间进行权衡取舍。

零售和在线支付基础设施是各国政策制定者特别关注的一个领域，包括有各种POS机和ATM相连的具有互通性的平台、代理网络、账单支付平台、征信系统、数字资产（尤其是动产）登记机构，以及在某些情况下支持所有这些系统的底层通信基础设施。一些监管机构还在探索发行可用于数字金融服务生态系统的数字法定货币的潜在收益、成本和风险，并将私人虚拟货币的好处与中央银行作为发行人所能提供的稳定性及对消费者的保护相结合。

本节所列举的例子强调，推动数字普惠金融发展需要监管者及政策制定者与私人部门的利益相关者合作，开发一个强大的数字基础设施生态系统，该系统包括ICT基础设施、信用信息基础设施和支付系统基础设施，该生态系统具有可得性，其各基础设施之间具有互通性。例如，在秘鲁和赞比亚，ICT基础设施方面的公共投资对夯实数字普惠金融发展基础有很大作用。此外，通过改革支付系统，促进电子支付的使用，并促使商户接受数字支付以及拓宽农村和偏远地区的使用渠道，将有助于推动数字金融服务的使用。

支付基础设施和征信系统：中国

一些国家正在采取广泛的国家举措来扩大其金融基础设施生态系统，如之前讨论过的印度。另一个计划则来自中国，实施该计划的部分原因是中国快速增长的电子商务部门。近年来，中国注重城乡协调发展，努力加强国家金融基础设施的建设，这是其在推进数字普惠金融方面取得进展的主要原因。[①]中国人民银行与有关利益相关者合作，建立了全面的、强大的国家支付系统基础设施。同时，政府优先考虑在农村地区建立和维持健全的支付基础设施，以此促进物理服务网络的增长，提高支付产品的多样性和效率，并促进政府对个人转移支付的数字化。该计划的关键要素如下：

- 2002年起，中国人民银行开发了多个银行间同业清算系统，包括中国现代化支付系统（CNAPS），中国境内外币支付系统和本地清算系统，以支持流通票据、支付卡和其他支付工具的使用。
- 中国银联（同样于2002年成立）的职责是开发和运营银行卡信息交换系统，并促进银行卡的互联互通。银联现在成为代理机构和支付卡互联互通的基础，也为支付宝和其他在线支付平台运行提供了基础。
- 中国人民银行运营网上支付跨行清算系统（IBPS），为通过网上银行发起的交易提供接近实时的跨行直接贷记和借记转账。农村信用社（和其他农村金融机构）以及城市商业银行为其各自的成员建立了清算系统，这些系统与中国人民银行的系统相连，从而使农村地区的银行和其他全国银行性之间的交易成为可能。
- 2011年，成立中国支付清算协会，加强了中国支付系统基础设施的协调性。
- 2014年8月，中国人民银行正式发布《全面推进深化农村支付服务环境建设的指导意见》，进一步扩大支付服务体系的覆盖面。

中国人民银行还建设了中国信用信息基础数据库，成立了中国人民银行征信中心，征信中心是一个公共征信机构，它从各类金融机构收集数据，包括银行，农村信用社，信托公司，消费金融公司，汽车金融公司和微型金融机构，融资担保公司，金融租赁公司，保险公司，证券公司等。

---

① 中国人民银行—世界银行联合报告（待发布）：《全球视野下的中国普惠金融：实践、经验与挑战》（Towards Universal Financial Inclusion in China: Models, Challenges, and Global Lessons）。该报告已于2018年2月正式发布——译者注。

专栏7：中国人民银行征信中心（CCRC）

设立征信中心的想法始于2006年，CCRC的职责是建立、运营和维护全国统一的企业和消费者征信系统。金融机构能够从系统中获取记录。除金融数据外，该系统也补充了一些公共信息，包括社会保障支付，住房公积金支付，行政处罚和环保奖励，税款拖欠，法院判决和无效率行为等信息和数据。

截至2016年年末，CCRC覆盖了9.1亿自然人[①]和2 210万家法人机构，其中4.3亿自然人和636万家机构有借款记录。征信中心收集所有相关信贷产品的信息，无论该产品价值多少，无论信息是正面还是负面。它不仅从传统来源（如正规的贷款机构和公共领域）中收集数据，还从替代性数据资源中收集数据，如公用事业、电信等。

中国人民银行持续推动中国征信体系建设，加强征信中心与其他征信机构的合作。这进一步促进了中国征信体系发展，目前年度查询量约5亿次，居世界首位。

互联互通：坦桑尼亚和秘鲁

在有助于促进数字金融服务的金融基础设施方面，政策制定者更加重视的一个问题是服务提供商和服务点（包括代理商）之间的服务互联互通。[②]这个问题对于在全国层面上积极采取措施，运用数字技术和交付机制，将金融服务范围拓展到之前缺乏金融服务的地区（通常是农村地区）至关重要。为农村地区客户提供服务背后的经济分析表明，所有服务提供商在所有地区设立代理机构是不切实际的，但同时政策制定者希望在金融服务领域保有一定程度的竞争，希望客户对金融服务有一定的选择权。推动金融服务提供商的互联互通有助于实现该目标，这将使得客户得以与他们需要接触的其他客户或商家交换信息，而不必开立多个账户。

为了实现互联互通，政策制定者打算在两种方法中进行选择：鼓励业内机构依靠自身力量实现互联互通，如果该行业不能实现预期进展，在某些情况下可以采取承诺授权的方式；或者主动提出由政府主导的解决方案。坦桑尼亚近来采取的是行业主导移动货币互联互通方式。在国际金融公司（IFC）支持下，4家主要移动网

① 中国人民银行数据。
② 一些地区，如南部非洲发展共同体（SADC），也正探索地区互联互通；跨境互通性不是本报告探讨的问题。

络运营商在一年之内共同商定支付方案规则，规则包括交换费、争议解决和结算安排。坦桑尼亚银行支持此项讨论，并随时了解讨论的进展情况，以便在协议最终确定之时，所有相关方，包括监管机构都充分了解并支持此项协议。

自从推动该方案后，这种方法的影响力已经在不断增长的跨运营商交易（确切来说，使用不同服务提供商的移动货币客户之间的交易）中得以体现：2014年10月，当新方案开始实施时，坦桑尼亚个人客户之间跨运营商的交易每月只有大约不到10万次，目前每月已高达400万次，月增长近15%。[①]这些跨运营商交易现在约占所有交易量的1/4，且这种增长先于运营商开展公开新互联互通规则的营销活动出现。坦桑尼亚的方案以现有基础设施为出发点，通过业界制定规则实现互通，通常被证实为解决互联互通问题最成功和持久的方案。

在其他情况下，政策制定者会支持集中统一的解决方案：无论是政策制定机构建立全国交换平台，抑或是鼓励行业制订统一解决方案。后一种方式最近的代表性例子就是秘鲁模式，秘鲁的多个利益相关者努力在所有金融参与者之间推动互联互通，并致力于推广金融服务，在无法获得银行账户服务（特别是在农村地区）的秘鲁人中，金融服务的覆盖率已达71%。在秘鲁模式（Modelo Peru）[②]中，许多不同的参与者携手创建一个无缝连接的支付生态系统，作为全国范围内互联互通的典型，秘鲁模式受到国际社会的肯定（见专栏8）。

专栏8：秘鲁模式

2016年2月，秘鲁模式启动，该模式由秘鲁银行家协会（ASBANC）领导，旨在建立一个互联互通的全国性支付平台。最关键的是，这项努力得到了政府官员和银行业监管机构SBS以及秘鲁中央银行的大力支持，这有助于说服非银行市场参与者（如移动网络运营商）加入平台建设。监管机构和政府的扶持措施包括《2013年国家电子货币法》，这一举措有助于为这个新的生态系统制定基本规则。

此平台被称为Bim（Billetera Móvil），它将30多家金融机构、政府、电信公司、大型付款人和收款人连接到一起，共享支付基础设施。其目标是提升秘鲁人（包括有银行服务的人和无法获得银行服务的人）的银行服务可得性，重要的是该

① 据坦桑尼亚银行数据。

② http://www.centerforfinancialinclusion.org/publications-a-resources/browse-publications/794-modelo-peru-cfi-brief

平台设法降低金融服务提供商和其他企业与现金相关的交易成本。

该平台提供的主要产品是互联互通的电子钱包，联合品牌为Bim，该电子钱包支持具有非结构化补充业务数据（USSD）或短消息服务（SMS）功能的移动电话，这样所有移动电话都可以在该平台上使用。新用户无需预先开立银行账户，无需用移动电话访问互联网，甚至不需要给手机账户预付话费。他们可以在他们的手机上直接注册并开立一个电子钱包，目前全国已有超过8 500个与Bim合作的实体销售点，新用户也可以在这些实体销售点中任选一个进行注册和开立电子钱包。开立账户时，只需要新用户提供个人的全国性身份证号码和编码，设置个人密码，选择提供个人账户的金融机构。电子钱包最初由9家机构（包括3家MNO）发行，可用于任何冠以Bim品牌名称的商店或代理商进行支付或存取现金，也可用于接收个人之间的付款及政府转移支付款项。

Pagos Digitales Peruanos（PDP）是一家为运营Bim平台而成立的公司，其股权结构独特，51%的股权由秘鲁银行家协会设立的非营利性实体控制，剩余的股权由33个小股东所有，在公司创立时每个股东认购了2.45%的份额。该公司为Bim平台制定项目规则，并为该国所有的电子货币发行者提供服务。

该项目经理估计该平台至少需要100万活跃用户或每月300万次交易，系统才能达到盈亏平衡。到2016年年底，活跃用户已经达到24万个，略低于他们当年的30万个初始目标。此时，平台的运营面临一些挑战，特别是交易数量、农村覆盖率，以及将Bim融入现有银行和商户的POS系统等挑战，但为进一步提升交易量和规模，并使Bim平台成为真正统一的全国性支付系统，PDP决心迎接这些挑战。

墨西哥交易数据库

墨西哥央行（Banco de Mexico）开发了一个数据库，为银行提供其客户跨境交易的整体情况。墨西哥央行建设数据库的目的是，这一开放、高效的数字基础设施将有助于加强反洗钱/反恐融资力度，并降低去风险影响。该数据库囊括了客户和其他用户向境外转账的交易信息。

自2016年3月起，银行开始按日报送客户基本信息、收款行和受益人姓名，以及向境外转账信息（包括数量、币种、交易原因）。作为回馈，银行将收到关于其客户在金融体系中状况的汇总数据。墨西哥央行考虑，未来也把向境内转账信息纳入数据库中。

国家数据库的预期效益包括：数据验证、客户通过金融系统交易的合计数据，以及国家机构能够掌握这些数据。基于这些数据，银行将建立交易指数，交易指数能反映客户行为的基本特征，从而有助于诊断客户异常交易。此外，银行还可获取必要的信息，以便在基于其客户整体行为（而非客户在一家银行的行为）的基础上了解客户。墨西哥财政和公共信贷秘书处（SHCP）已颁布法规，授权将这些数据纳入银行的风险分析中。

目前，基于上年报送的数据，计划与参与行分享145个数据点，诸如资金流向国、发起和/接收转账的银行数量，转账的总笔数，完成转账所需天数等。

数据共享平台一旦在2017年推出，银行可按需求获得客户近360天内的报告数据，该平台支持银行按客户分类分析单个的和加总的数据。预期功能包括客户申请新的国际转账时可按需查询。由于该平台信息每天持续更新，因此应有利于进行更全面及时的风险评估。

墨西哥央行数据库等是支持金融市场顺利运作以及改进反洗钱/反恐融资监管的数据共享案例。对于政策制定者而言，接下来非常重要的一步是，除与非银行金融机构（包括金融科技公司）建立更多的联系外，还考虑开放除征信机构以外的其他有用数据来源（如政府数据库），以扩大金融服务的普及率，使更多无法获得银行服务者能够融入金融系统。虽然提高数据的可得性的潜在收益可能很广泛，但是数据隐私和保护措施将是最为关键的尝试。

扩大商户对数字支付方式的接受度：肯尼亚、墨西哥和阿根廷

扩大数字支付生态系统的一个重要环节是赢得大量商户支持，使他们能够接受数字支付。要想实现有针对性地服务金融服务不足群体的目标，将处于低收入社区服务低收入群体的小商户囊括进来尤为重要。此类商户通常不会采用接受银行信用卡的标准POS系统，因此有必要为这些商户提供可负担的解决方案，使其接受简单的数字卡和移动支付方式。同时，如果顾客能够有多种支付选择，小商户通常必须决定接受哪种类型支付，进而确定要购买哪种POS系统。面对这些决定，许多商户自然选择继续接受现金。

肯尼亚的一家创新型企业为小商户提供了一种低成本的支付系统，小商户在支

付方式上将拥有多种选择而无需购买新的POS终端。Kopo Kopo早在2012年初就开始为商户服务，并为他们提供一个基于网络的平台，可通过安卓系统、桌面、短消息服务（SMS）和非结构化补充业务数据（USSD）进行访问，使得新兴市场上的中小型企业能够接受、处理和管理多种移动货币支付。Kopo Kopo目前已经成为Safaricom公司最大的商户聚合平台，也是撒哈拉以南非洲最大的商户聚合平台之一。这个例子中的监管者——肯尼亚中央银行（CBK），关注了Kopo Kopo的经营活动，但并没有将其作为受监管的机构看待，而是决定让该平台正常为市场提供增值服务。肯尼亚中央银行的观点是，移动货币运营商对其与合作商户间的关系负责。类似Kopo Kopo这样的公司把中小企业和贫困客户视为其主要客户，允许Kopo Kopo这类新的和不同类型的公司进入，是促进数字支付生态系统在所有收入水平上发展的一个重要因素。

拉丁美洲的Tienda Pago是另一个初创企业，该企业专注于促进零售商和供应商之间的交易。由于供应商频繁地从零售商处收取大量现金（对他们而言甚为不便），因此他们对能减少这些痛点并降低交易成本的商业方案很感兴趣。这些供应商运用他们与商户较好的关系和现有分销模式，与传统支付服务商（PSP）合作，协调行动为商户提供支付解决方案。Grupo Bimbo公司（总部位于墨西哥的面包公司）旗下的一家合资企业，成为非传统支付商通过与一家大型银行及一家支付处理公司（Blue Label Technologies）合作，尝试非传统支付服务的一个案例。Grupo Bimbo公司在全国数万家小型便利店安装了银行卡收单机器。①

2016年8月，阿根廷央银确认，银行应通过“移动支付平台”提供即时资金转账（网上贷记转账和直接借记）。通过定期向“Pago Electronico Inmediato（PEI）”支付费用，商户可以收到通过手机、平板电脑或笔记本电脑发起的支付，并实时贷记他们的账户。客户（买方）每天转账累计上限为最低工资水平（约520美元），更高金额的转账则要受银行实行的补充安全措施约束。在每月约18 800美元的限额下，资金贷记时不向商户收取费用，从而使PEI成为一个成本节约的支付

① http://documents.worldbank.org/curated/en/765851467037506667/pdf/106633-WP-PUBLIC-Innovative-SolutionsAccelerate-Adoption-Electronic-Payments-Merchants-report-2016.pdf

解决方案。

2016年世界银行集团的一份报告[①]专门研究了数字化商户支付问题，确定了严重影响这些类型支付深化的6个主要障碍（尤其是发展中国家）：①商户的价值认同不足，包括产品设计不足以激励他们从现金支付转为电子支付；②传统银行卡模式中产品不适用，利益相关者也难以从中获益；③客户总需求不足，尚未达到驱动需求和供给向能够支撑数字支付生态系统发展的“临界点”；④在处于发展的市场中，技术基础设施和监管环境多变，难以支持数字支付发展；⑤无效的分销模式，难以为经济落后地区（即中小微企业和客户群体密度低的地区）那些不可触及的商户提供服务；⑥企业正规化面临困境，商户不愿全额交纳销售税。

尽管行业将会在消除其中某些障碍方面发挥重要作用，但政策制定者在促进形成有利的电子支付环境方面也可发挥关键作用，从以上某些约束中可清楚看到这一点。政策制定者已采取的行动包括：

• 简化对那些正积极接受电子支付的商户客户尽职调查（CDD）要求；促进商户正规化，包括给与一定程度的税收减免（尤其在早期阶段），以便不对规模较小的（也许规模较大的）商户选择造成逆向激励（卢旺达有以税收减免促进小商户正规化的案例）；[②]

• 采取措施，激励消费者和商户以电子方式进行交易（例如，韩国的数字交易退税，在斯洛伐克每次以电子方式交易后可以用收据参与数字博彩）；

• 政府服务接受电子支付方式（例如，秘鲁模式即在小型零售商店进行小商户税收支付数字化试点）。

公共物品基础设施投资：赞比亚和秘鲁

在某些情况下，政策制定者会自行投资建设宽带基础设施，通常会将服务延伸到农村地区，而这对私营企业而言在经济上是不可行的。近来的一个例子出现在秘鲁。秘鲁于2016年6月宣布，[③]该国的国家光纤骨干网络（Red Dorsal Nacional

---

① http://documents.worldbank.org/curated/en/765851467037506667/Innovation-in-electronic-payment-adoption-the-caseof-small-retailers

② https://www.itu.int/en/ITUT/focusgroups/dfs/Documents/09_2016/FINAL%20ENDORSED%20Enabling%20Merchant%20Payments%20Acceptance%2030%20May%202016_formatted%20AM.pdf

③ http://www.fomsn.com/fiber-optic-news/fiber/rdnfo-is-getting-ready-for-completion-in-peru/

de Fibra óptica，RDFNO）已接近完工，并计划将RDFNO的受益地区扩大到195个地区首府城市，覆盖约62.5万人。建设RDFNO的目的是连通农村地区（特别是秘鲁的高地和雨林地区），并向发达地区提供高速有线网络。秘鲁运输与通信部希望通过使用RDFNO作为回程线路（backhaul），藉此鼓励各移动网络运营商将其移动网络扩展到偏远的农村地区。

该项目既包括了对在PPP模式下建设和运营的宽带网络进行拓展，也包括提供数字内容和技能培训，包括以下几项：①创建一个农村开放数据平台，向公众发布农村地区的信息；②创建支持农村地区公共服务交付的应用程序、内容和数字业务；③在对农村社区重要的领域（如预警系统和灾害风险管理），开发新技术应用模板；④与农村社区相关的数字技术培训课程。

早在2014年，赞比亚就更进一步，[①]赞比亚信息和通信技术管理局（ZICTA）在该国农村地区首批建造了169个移动通信塔。这些塔由ZICTA拥有，供该国的3个移动电话服务提供商使用。

---

① https://www.telegeography.com/products/commsupdate/articles/2014/11/13/zicta-confirms-147-of-169-planned-ruralcommunications-towers-are-up-and-running/

3.对数字普惠金融新兴政策与方法的总结

从本报告中所介绍的众多案例可知，金融业数字技术的创新及应用步伐在不断加快，复杂度也日益提升，这意味着政策制定者和监管者所采用的方法也必须与时俱进，并符合本国国情。需努力提升金融服务的普惠性并服务目前无法获得金融服务的群体。将对此努力予以支持考虑在内，对我们提出了更大挑战。尽管没有任何两个国家的方法甚至特定的市场情况是相同的，但我们仍可以从报告介绍的案例中提炼出如下结论：

• 积极主动的领导和政治意愿是全局性成功的关键因素。政府各部门的整合和协调很重要，这些部门包括财政部、中央银行和其他监管部门，也包括传统上与得不到银行服务的转移支付接收人打交道的社会福利部门等。广义上讲，涉及政府和业界的跨领域项目通常难以协调，需要耗费大量的尝试、时间及成本，但在解决利用数字技术方面的众多问题上，跨领域项目可能比较有效。印度案例说明了，得益于各政府部门和非政府实体之间的强有力的领导和协调，在数字交易账户使用快速增长的同时，强大的数字基础设施也得到发展（现在被称为“印度数字平台”）。中国政府发布了《指导意见》和规则，支持互联网金融的健康发展，为行业参与者提供了行为准则，推动了非银行互联网金融公司的增长。

• 开发更多数字工具，协助监管者做好监管工作。由于数字创新正在迅速改变人们对金融服务提供者的认识，金融监管者须采用更积极主动、数据驱动的方法，以加深对行业（包括服务金融排斥群体的大量非正规小微企业）的理解。许多监管者采用“以风险为导向”的监管方法，并寻找安全促进创新的新路径，这包括边试边学项目，也包括和业界开展更深入的合作和信息共享。在英国的案例中，FCA的“项目创新”计划使英国监管者得以指导创新金融服务发展并确保消费者得到充分保护，同时跟上金融科技的最新发展。同样，在加纳，中央银行、保险监管机构和电信监管机构之间的合作，促成了以风险为导向规则的发布，以支持通过手机提供小额保险服务。

• 处于交易量巨大（及更多使用快速或实时支付交易）的时代，监管数字金融服务提供商要求可以提供实时监测和分析的、更复杂和自动化程度更高的系统。一些国家在开发这样的系统，但需要更多的努力来设计强大、灵活的系统，并提供全面实施它们所需的能力建设支持。例如，在卢旺达的例子中，中央银行实施数据仓库项目预计将提供更有效和及时的机制来获取粒度数据，以跟踪按性别、不同目标市场和地理位置维度定义的普惠金融进展情况。

• 虽然监管者正在积极努力拥抱新技术并加强与业界的沟通，在可能的情况下，尽早（必要时持续地）厘清监管框架和预期也会行之有效。其目的是为了引导和塑造创新，使其与金融监管的重点事项相一致，并避免被未预见到的发展变化弄得措手不及。

• 推动互联互通的、开放的数字金融服务技术平台有助于建立一个广泛的生态系统，让私人实体和政府机构更好地服务消费者，最终改善其金融生活质量。实现互联互通的方法和时机不一，但政策制定者需弄清楚互联互通是一个发展方向。开放技术平台的一个重要相关要素是其应该让消费者（在技术上）能够非常容易地掌握和控制个人信息，并在不同的服务提供商之间转移信息。在坦桑尼亚，业界主导开发的移动货币互通性项目规则和安排，促进了跨运营商交易的迅速增长。基于现有基础设施上的诸如此类方案，通常表明是实现互通性的成功和持久的解决方案。

• 数字本身是公共数字基础设施的重要基石，为在整个经济体中普及金融服务乃至其他服务创造了机会。各国政府需要将获得强大及易于验证的数字 ID 置于优先地位，无论是生物统计学的或其他（基于数据的）类型的，只要其可用于促进数字金融服务可得性的提高。人们对隐私权和公民自由权问题的担忧是有根据的，这些担忧有待解决。建立惠及所有人的身份证明项目的必要性，凸显了尽快解决这些担忧的重要意义。正如在印度和巴基斯坦所看到的，广覆盖的数字身份证明项目具备激发迅速提高数字金融服务可得性的潜能。在广覆盖的数字身份证明项目尚未建成的国家，为确保效率和持续性，临时性的部门性方法可被吸收整合入更宽泛的全国性身份证明方案中。

• 各种数字服务的迅速增长，引起了一些担忧，即金融政策制定者和监管者传统上还勿需对一些日益重要的问题加以关注，这些问题包括数据保护[①]、第三方获得数据，以及服务和网络的可靠性。这些担忧要求与电信监管机构、数据保护监管机构、消费者保护监管机构进行更深入合作。尽管监管机构有正当的理由关心各自的职权和授权，但这种情况清晰表明，各方应以信息共享和对双方感兴趣和关注领域达成一致意见的方式更紧密地进行合作。

① 普惠金融全球合作伙伴（GPFI）在负责任金融论坛（RFF）内的独立工作主要集中于数据隐私和保护问题。

报告三

G20政策指引：数字化与非正规经济

利用数字普惠金融服务非正规经济中的个人和中小微企业

BUILDING CONSENSUS FOR FAIR AND SUSTAINABLE DEVELOPMENT

致谢

这份G20政策指引（G20 Policy Guide）系代表G20普惠金融全球合作伙伴（GPFI）而作。该成果基于GPFI执行伙伴所起草的基础论文，这些执行伙伴包括优于现金联盟（BTCA）、扶贫协商小组（CGAP）、经济合作与发展组织（OECD）和世界银行集团（WBG），以及国际征信委员会（ICCR）。所参考的基础论文是为GPFI各工作小组而起草的，包括监管及标准制定主体、市场和支付体系、中小企业融资和金融消费者保护与金融教育等四个小组。按照GPFI章程所规定的咨询程序，本指引也受益于GPFI成员代表的同行评议。最后，一些非G20国家（在普惠金融联盟（AFI）的推动下）、比尔及梅琳达·盖茨基金会、中小企业融资论坛以及联合国秘书长普惠金融特别代表等，均为本指引提供了宝贵支持。

缩略词

AFI: 普惠金融联盟（Alliance for Financial Inclusion）

AML: 反洗钱（Anti-Money Laundering）

ARCO: 访问、修正、删除及反对权（Access，Rectification，Cancellation，Opposition rights）

BTCA: 优于现金联盟（Better than Cash Alliance）

CDD: 客户尽职调查（Customer Due Diligence）

CFT: 反恐怖融资（Countering Financing Terrorism ）

CGAP: 扶贫协商小组（Consultative Group to Assist the Poor）

CRSP: 征信服务提供者（Credit Reporting Service Provider）

DFI: 数字普惠金融（Digital Financial Inclusion）

DFS: 数字金融服务（Digital Financial Services）

DFSP: 数字服务提供者（Digital Financial Service Provider）

EU: 欧盟（European Union）

FATF: 反洗钱金融行动特别工作组（Financial Action Task Force）

G2P: 政府对个人（Government to Person）

GDPR: 通用数据保护条例（General Data Protection Regulation）

GPCR: 征信原则（General Principles of Credit Reporting）

GPFI: 普惠金融全球合作伙伴（Global Partnership for Financial Inclusion）

HLP: 高级原则（High-Level Principles）

ICCR: 国际征信委员会（International Committee on Credit Reporting）

ID4D: 促进发展身份证明（Identification for Development）

IP： 执行伙伴（Implementing Partner）

LEI： 法人身份证明（Legal Entity Identification）

MSME： 中小微企业（Micro Small and Medium Enterprise）

OECD： 经济合作与发展组织（Organisation for Economic Co-operation and Development（OECD））

P2G： 个人对政府（Person to Government）

P2P： 个人对个人（Person to Person）

PSD2： 支付服务指令（Payment Services Directive）

PSP： 支付服务提供者（Payment Service Provider）

QR-Code： 二维码（Quick Response Code）

目录

摘要

金融服务的获取和使用在支持包容性和可持续发展方面起着重要作用。尽管普惠金融领域已经取得了引人注目的进步，但仍有大批人口被排除在正规金融体系之外。许多受到金融排斥的个人和企业处于非正规经济领域。

非正规个体和企业获得正规普惠金融服务面临着资格和可负担性障碍，数字化为解决这些障碍提供了前所未有的机会。特别是数字化可以促进身份验证，推动数字支付和改善信息环境。然而，要充分发挥数字化的潜力，还需要关注金融消费者保护和金融素养。

本政策指引提出了一套关键政策，有助于推出一些举措，促进非正规经济领域中的个人和企业获得金融服务。它聚焦于四个关键领域来缓解资格和可负担性障碍。

下表概述了每个政策领域的主要建议。

一、发挥数字身份作用	**二、数字支付基础设施建设**
提升新客户身份证明和验证能力 1）确保统一的身份体系 *合法的数字身份系统有助于身份识别和验证*	*建立开放和包容的支付生态系统* 1）优先发展互联互通的、能实现快速支付的支付系统 *政策制定者需要建立市场化、安全、高效和互联互通的支付系统*
2）调整和升级监管体制 *合适的监管体制应认识到数字身份的潜力*	2）实施鼓励商户接受数字支付的激励措施 推动商户使用数字支付时，业务模式应当可持续
3）在金融领域建立强大和安全的数字身份基础设施	3）实施鼓励消费者使用数字金融服务的激励措施

可在金融服务业建设和使用数字身份系统 4）利用合法身份基础设施促进私人部门主导的服务的发展 *私营部门可以提供创新解决方案* 5）监测身份领域的新发展及新方法 *监管应跟上技术发展的步伐*	*最终消费者对数字支付的使用应当可负担* 4）支持跨境支付系统 *探索新的跨境支付方法*
三、征信中替代性数据的使用	**四、金融消费者保护、金融教育和数据保护**
利用替代性数据提高征信质量 1）提高信息的可得性和准确性 *划分替代性可靠数据的主要类别* 2）扩大信用信息共享 *信用信息共享可扩展到替代性数据* 3）实现负责任的跨境数据交换 *区域合作有助于提高数据的一致性和可比性* 4）平衡市场诚信、创新与竞争 *实施功能要求确保市场监管质量*	*缓解风险，并增加机会* 金融消费者保护： 1）改进金融消费者保护监管措施并提高监管能力 *监管者应在保持高消费者保护标准的同时拥抱技术* 2）加强信息披露并提高透明度 *技术可被用于改进并提高信息披露和透明度标准* 金融教育： 3）加强有关数字金融素养的数据收集、协调和新核心能力的识别 *新数据应以协调一致的方式用于确定能力范围* 4）加强数字金融服务的金融教育，支持对其进行评估 *数字技术可用于提供金融教育项目及对其开展评估* 数据保护： 5）构建安全有效的同意模式 *采用能确保数据得以保护的同意模式* 6）强化访问、更正、删除和反对的权利 *消费者应有访问和修改其数据的选择权* 7）解决数据安全问题 *采用安全措施有助于防范操作风险*

一、数字化和非正规性：

为什么重要

金融服务的获取和使用在支持包容性和可持续发展方面起着重要作用。虽然在普惠金融领域已经取得了引入注目的进步，但是全球大约仍有17亿成年人没有金融机构或移动支付机构的基本账户。[①]无银行服务的成年人中超过一半是女性，全球的性别差距估计为7个百分点：2017年有72%的男性拥有账户，而只有65%的女性拥有账户。[②]虽然账户拥有率近年来已上升至69%，但是声称在过去12个月内有过正规储蓄的成年人仍然只有27%，而同期全球范围内有过正规借贷的成年人比例仅为11%。[③]此外，新兴市场中的4亿中小微企业（MSMEs）有一半因缺乏足够的融资，其繁荣和成长受到影响，信贷缺口总额据估算在2.1万亿至2.6万亿美元之间。[④]可见，所有许多个人和企业缺乏安全、可靠的方式进行储蓄、投资、支付和购买保险，从而对于生活、劳动生产率、增长和均等产生了负面影响。

经济的非正规性对普惠金融来说是一大障碍。为此，本政策指引将非正规性宽泛地定义为“一切工作人群和经济单位所从事的、未被法律或实践中的正规约定所覆盖或覆盖不充分的经济活动”。[⑤]导致金融排斥的因素有很多，然而非正规经济中的个人和中小微企业尤其难以获得和使用正规金融服务。[⑥]大约80%的中小微企

---

① Demirgüç-Kunt, A., Klapper, L., Singer, D., Ansar, S. and Hess, J. (2018). The Global Findex Database 2017: Measuring Financial Inclusion and The Fintech Revolution. Washington DC: The World Bank Group.

② World Bank Group (2018). The Little Data Book on Financial Inclusion. Washington DC: The World Bank Group.

③ 同上。

④ International Finance Corporation (2017). Alternative Data Transforming SME Finance. Washington DC: IFC.

⑤ 参见 International Labor Organisation (2013). Decent Work and the Informal Economy. Geneve: United Nations. 另参见 ILO's 2002 International Labour Conference Resolution and Conclusions concerning decent work and the informal economy.

⑥ International Labor Organisation (2014). Transitioning from the Informal to the Formal Economy. Geneve: United Nations.

业是非正规的，[①]这些企业一贯认为融资问题是它们面临的最大约束。[②]在非正规经济规模越庞大的国家，个人和中小微企业的金融排斥越普遍。图 1 表明，当非正规经济在整个经济中所占比例越高时，账户拥有率以及从正规金融机构获得贷款的小企业比例就越低，同时使用现金和非正规借贷的情形也越普遍。

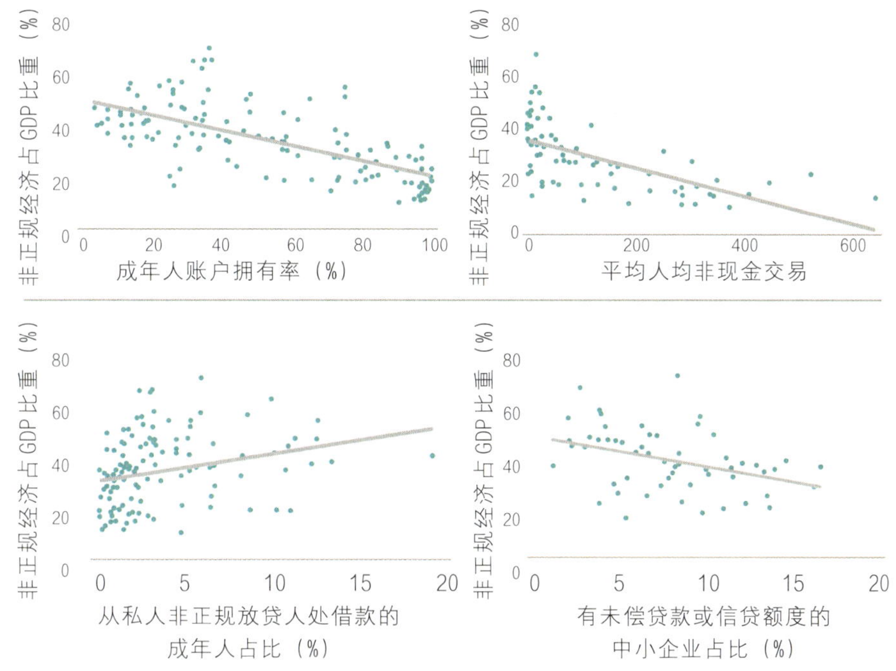

图 1：金融排斥与非正规性

妇女是构成非正规经济的最大群体。无论是街头商贩、家政人员、自己自足的农民，还是季节性农业工人，妇女都构成了非正规经济中劳动力的主体。[③]这些妇女有自己的收入，也做生意，但通常无法从传统的金融体系中获益。她们缺乏抵押物、信用记录，有些移民还缺乏证明文件。在非正规经济中工作的妇女需要获得全

① MSME Finance Gap Database. Washington DC: The World Bank Group.
② World Bank Enterprise Surveys (various years).
③ International Labor Organisation (2014). Women and Men in the Informal Economy: A Statistical Picture. Geneve: United Nations.

方位的金融服务来创造收入、积累资产、平滑消费并管理风险，但她们通常难以获得这些服务。这凸显了性别维度在观察普惠金融与非正规性联系中的重要意义。①

数字化或采用数字技术与方法，为非正规性导致的金融排斥问题提供了改善途径。飞速的技术创新深刻重塑了产品和服务的生产与消费。新技术（尤其是数字技术）在普惠金融这一重要领域产生的颠覆性冲击已经显现。近年来移动货币和数字支付的使用大幅增长，把越来越多的人纳入了正规金融体系。②对于非正规经济的参与者，以及有新工作规划但缺乏稳定和正规收入来源的人群，利用数字化使其享受金融服务是一个重要机会。

数字化有助于解决资格和可负担性障碍，这些都是非正规经济中个人和中小微企业获得金融服务时最主要的障碍。③非正规经济中的个人有时无法提供可靠的身份证明文件，从而无法满足开立银行账户时的客户尽职调查（CDD）要求。他们通常也无法负担使用支付服务的费用。非正规经济中的中小微企业抵押品有限，且由于信息不对称而无法令人信服地证明自己的还款能力，往往在申请贷款时会遇到更大的障碍。

为了发挥数字化在非正规经济中的潜在价值，需要广泛的移动联结及手机的普遍使用。这是抓住数字化所带来机遇的重要前提条件。为了提高数字金融服务的可得性，非正规经济中的个人和企业应拥有一部能在任何地方使用的手机。从各国情况来看，网络覆盖率总体较高，手机话费和智能手机的拥有率都增长很快。然而，某些群体仍然无法使用或不能充分使用手机。这一挑战对妇女而言尤其严重，在大多数国家，她们拥有手机的可能性相对较低。在低收入和中等收入国家，女性拥有手机的比例平均比男性低14%，不同地区间的差别也很大。④因此，必须继续努力

---

① 促进非正规经济中有关妇女的普惠金融发展要求改进分类数据质量。参见2018年6月1日在加拿大举行的G7发展及财政部长联席会议共同主席关于会议的总结。另见 Women Financial Inclusion Data Partnership (2018). The Way Forward: How Data Can Proper Full Financial Inclusion For Women。

② 同上。

③ 虽然物理网点及物理联结对普惠金融发展非常重要，但近来的有关证据表明，非正规部门的资格和可负担性也起着重要作用。参见Honohan, P. and M. King (2012). Cause and Effect of Financial Access: Cross-country Evidence from the Finscope Surveys, in R. Cull, A. Demirguc-Kunt, and J. Morduch (eds.), Banking the World: Empirical Foundations of Financial Inclusion. MIT Press, Cambridge; King, M. (2012). The Unbanked Four-fifths: Informality and Barriers to Financial Services in Nigeria. IIIS Working Paper 411。

④ GSMA (2018). The Mobile Gender Gap Report. February 2018.

保证移动技术的普及和平等获取。

本政策指引重点关注数字化如何帮助非正规经济中的个人和中小微企业获取金融服务，以改善他们的生活和经营。数字化并不是实现正规化的方法，但是从长期来看，获取正规金融服务有助于降低非正规性。获取正规金融服务能够提升受金融抑制的个人和企业的可信度，帮助他们克服进入正规部门的障碍；[①]同时也能提高生产率，减少机会主义导致的非正规性以及选择在非正规部门生产和交易的个人和中小微企业的数量。[②]然而，非正规性仍然是一个复杂的问题，需要多方位的政策举措，特别是机制建设、就业监管和税收，不过这些超出了本政策指引的范畴。

为了将非正规经济中的个人和企业纳入金融体系，本政策指引列举了一系列关键的非强制性政策。它汇集了有证据支持且各方认同的政策建议和指引，涵盖四个政策领域。为了将非正规经济中的个人和中小微企业纳入正规金融部门，向其提供公平、可负担的金融服务，以下领域的政策措施十分重要：

（1）发挥数字身份的作用；

（2）数字支付基础设施建设；

（3）征信中替代性数据的使用；

（4）金融消费者保护、金融教育和数据保护。

本政策指引与《G20普惠金融行动计划》一脉相承，是建立在此前G20历任主席国工作，包括最近两年中国和德国担任G20主席国期间所做工作的基础上的，并支持《G20数字普惠金融高级原则》的实施。政策领域的选取也体现出了借助数字化解决非正规经济中金融排斥问题的技术关联性。从这个角度看，本政策指引将重点关注非正规性、普惠金融和数字化交叉领域中的重要问题，从而进一步推动GPFI议程。然而，由于会出现有关有效干预的新证据，所以政策建议也需与时俱进。基于这个原因，本政策指引应当被视为一份有活力的文件。

本政策指引的目标群体包括G20和非G20国家负责制定、执行和评估普惠金融战略、规划和项目的政策制定者，以及那些来自能够影响普惠金融效果的部门（特

---

① Capasso, S. and T. Jappelli (2013). Financial Development and the Underground Economy. Journal of Development Economics, 101(C): 167–178.

② Beck, T. and M. Hoseini (2014). Informality and Access to Finance: Evidence from India. Centre Discussion Paper Series No. 2014–052.

别是处于非正规经济中的部门）的个人或企业。此外，在向非正规部门提供数字金融服务的过程中，许多政府以外的利益相关者都可以扮演重要角色，包括民间社会团体、专业协会以及广泛的私人部门。因此，要想抓住数字化带来的机遇，公共和私人部门的共同努力尤为重要。

本政策指引旨在支持政策对话、战略规划、优先事项安排以及实施计划。然而，本政策指引既不是为了影响也不是为了阐述全球金融标准制定机构的工作。在充分考虑本国国情的基础上，本政策指引提供的关键政策措施，可以被应用于可行的普惠金融国家战略中，以及应用于致力于推动普惠金融发展的国家行动中。本政策指引的很多重要部分具有一定的弹性，可以根据需求作为政策备选清单，并不一定要按顺序实施。由于结构性失衡，政策举措对于女性和男性而言具有不同的影响。我们鼓励G20和非G20国家的政策制定者和利益相关者对其政策和项目进行系统性分析，以帮助消除金融可得性方面存在的性别差异。

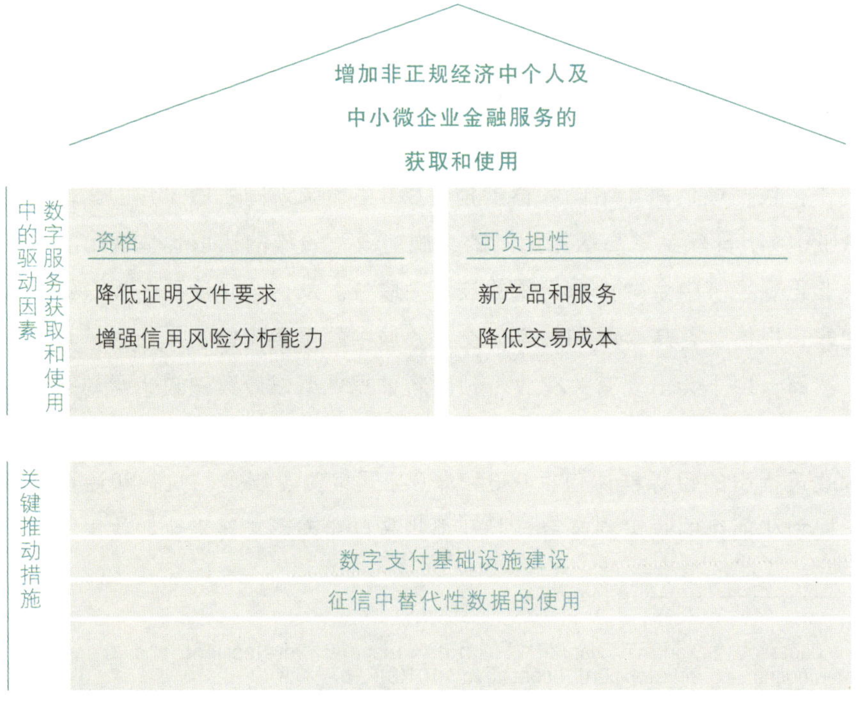

图2：数字化与非正规性

“

数以百万计的个人和小企业以非正规经济形式存在，为生存而不断努力，但却无法获得能使自己免受冲击并为自己带来机会的正规金融服务。因此，解决非正规问题是提高金融包容性的当务之急。

G20关于数字化和非正规性的政策指引是一个好的开端，它有助于我们理解数字化在降低非正规性方面的潜能。但我们还必须解决其他问题，如加强金融信息基础设施和数据建设，以及建立能促进正规化的法律和监管体系。

我希望G20政策指引能够激发更多目标明确的研究，藉此弄清普惠金融在降低非正规性方面所能做出的确切贡献（也包括实例），以及非正规性如何影响普惠金融发展。”

—荷兰马克西玛王后陛下，联合国秘书长普惠金融特别代表（UNSGSA）

二、数字化和非正规性：如何利用机会

（一）发挥数字身份的作用[①]

身份证明系统在促进普惠金融发展方面发挥了重要作用。个人只有拥有唯一、合法的身份，才能充分参与社会和经济活动。身份验证对中小微企业也很重要，因为它可以帮助它们确定经授权启动、运营和指导业务变更的员工和经理的身份。身份验证能方便服务提供者注册，最大限度地减少欺诈风险，并满足客户尽职调查（CDD）规定的要求。[②]据估计，全世界约有10亿人缺乏官方认可的身份证明。[③]妇女和诸如流离失所者等弱势群体尤其如此。[④]已有数据表明，未登记人口中女性所占的比例往往超过50%。[⑤]因此，开发身份证明系统的进展可对金融包容程度产生积极影响——特别是对那些处于非正规经济中的个人和中小微企业而言，因为这些社会群体普遍存在资格障碍。

技术可以提供解决方案，改善对新客户的身份证明和验证。数字身份证明系统的引入，可能会导致更多的金融服务数字化：（1）在简化文件要求的同时，使无银行账户者更容易开立交易账户[⑥]；（2）使能够远程实施的、具有成本节约效应的客户引导得以进行；（3）有助于为个人提供额外服务。数字身份证明系统还可以增强安全凭证的可信度，在满足反洗钱/反恐怖融资（AML/CFT）监管要求的同时，使普惠金融推进进程更加安全。

---

① 本节建立于世界银行的相关研究论文基础上：“G20 Digital Identity Onboarding Paper”. Washington DC，2018。

② 客户尽职调查标准系根据反洗钱金融行动特别工作组（FATF），反洗钱和反恐怖融资领域主要标准制定机构）的《建议》而阐述。本政策指引无意解释FATF 的建议或对其相关指引进行总结。

③ World Bank Identification for Development（ID4D）dataset.

④ Global Partnership for Financial Inclusion（2017）: GPFI Policy Paper Financial Inclusion of Forcibly Displaced Persons.

⑤ 同上。

⑥ 交易账户广义上指在银行或其他授权及（或）受监管的服务提供者（含非银行机构）开立的可用于收付款的账户。交易账户可进一步分为存款交易账户和电子货币账户。参见Committee on Payments and Market Infrastructures and World Bank Group（2016）. Payment aspects of financial inclusion. Bank for International Settlements and World Bank Group，2016。

世界银行集团《可持续发展身份证明原则》为推进强大和包容的身份证明系统，特别是数字身份证明系统提供了指导。[①]正如原则二所强调的那样，新的数字方法（如生物特征识别法）的出现，使个人和小型企业能以更有效的方式获得身份证明服务。国家和地方政府在注册和认可合法身份方面起着主要作用。正如《G20数字普惠金融高级原则》原则七所指出的，在金融领域，重点是政府出于官方目的所提供和（或）承认的合法身份证明。

法律体系是身份证明系统最重要的方面之一，尤其是当系统扩展到多种功能应用时。在法律体系内解决个人和企业缺乏身份的问题，是普惠金融取得进展的关键。需评估新技术大规模应用的方式，包括探索私人部门在构建数字身份证明层方面发挥的作用。还应密切监测不断涌现出的身份证明新技术和新方法，并使政策体系适应这些新变化，以推动生态系统向前发展。

根据迄今为止从政府身份证明方案和私营部门举措中获得的经验教训，本指引提出以下政策建议：

（1）确保统一的身份体系；

（2）调整和升级监管体制；

（3）在金融领域建立强大、安全的数字身份基础设施；

（4）利用合法身份基础设施促进私人部门主导服务的发展；

（5）监测身份领域的新发展及新方法。

1.确保统一的身份体系

一个合法的或基础性的身份系统对于可靠地确定为政府和私人部门认可的身份至关重要。在开户过程中，客户必须提供凭据以证明身份，以便金融服务提供者能够执行客户尽职调查程序。然后，需对这些凭据进行验证，并允许金融服务提供者访问其他信息来源（如征信机构），以验证所提供的信息及评估产品对客户的适用性。一旦完成以上步骤，金融服务提供者会下发交易识别码，用于在交易中进行身份验证。一个合法的或基础性的身份系统构成了获取关键性服务（包括建立超出特定风险阈值的账户关系）时身份验证的法律基础。在金融领域，一旦身份验证完

① World Bank Group (2017). Principles on Identification for Sustainable Development: Toward the Digital Age. Washington DC: The World Bank Group.

成，客户与金融服务提供者后续发生业务时，就可以在服务交付过程中使用其他方法进行身份验证和授权。

政策制定者可以设计出符合实际的数字基础设施，包括针对偏远地区的战略和确保“打通最后一公里”的战略。线下解决方案可以弥补在线连接的缺失或漏损。制定健全的采购准则和开放的设计标准可以促进创新，同时无论在国内还是在跨境领域，都应当考虑赋予系统更大的灵活性、更高的效率和更多的功能。此外，应确保政府机构、私人部门和数字身份生态系统（包括终端用户）中的其他利益相关方有操作和维护新系统、新设备的技术能力。

在遵守反洗钱/反恐融资法规的同时，基于生物统计的合法身份系统还可能支持认证服务，在此基础上，服务提供者还可进一步开发授权流程。然而，在提供金融服务的多个阶段广泛运用合法身份基础设施，会在几个层面产生影响，包括更换现有的为这些流程而建立的基础设施所付出的成本；这些服务的定价；有关生物统计凭证的误报与漏报的责任安排；如果生物统计信息受到损害，就不可能在集中化的合法身份数据库中替换身份验证凭证。因此，需要认真考虑如何使用国家基本身份基础设施进行持续的交易认证和授权，并考虑是否要将这些功能拆分，并将基本身份基础设施与其他基础设施相隔离，如果其他功能具有存在已久、可靠、高效和安全的流程的话。

2. 调整和升级监管体制

每个国家的金融服务监管体制应能认识到数字身份服务的潜力，并确保对账户如何开设、何处开设、为谁开设所进行的限制与这些技术的潜在益处相一致。认识到这一点非常重要。同时，任何这类监管改革都必须与反洗钱金融行动特别工作组的建议保持一致。

一些特定问题可能需在有利于数字身份服务发展的监管体系内加以解决，这些包括（但不限于）以下内容：数字身份验证是否符合现行的反洗钱/反恐怖融资要求；是否能够保证数字签名与物理签名之间法律效力的确定性和对等性；是否承认由私人部门管理的第三方认证服务在法律上等同于银行自身进行身份验证；是否要求所有银行客户提供特定类型的身份凭证，如某一种被认为是唯一且具有数字功能的身份凭证；当新的数字识别服务成为主流时，消费者的利益是否受到保护，特别是确保没有任何客户群体处于劣势地位。

3.在金融领域建立强大、安全的数字身份基础设施

数字身份系统可能带来新的挑战和风险，需要一套适用于传统上受监管金融机构（及第三方）的、适当的监督管理体系加以解决。值得注意的风险包括数据安全性（确保数字身份的底层技术、系统和流程稳健可以缓解这一风险），隐私保护，以及金融领域数字身份基础设施使用的有效治理安排（尤其是将数字身份基础设施服务应用于不受监管的实体时）。

数字身份系统应有配套的安全措施来保护数据。考虑到存储在系统中的数据的性质，安全性应该遵循一种三维方法（逻辑、物理和组织），包括存储数据系统、支持系统访问的网络、备份系统和任何与个人数据（以及执行身份系统中个人数据相关任务的第三方）连接的其他系统。

4.利用合法身份基础设施促进私人部门主导服务的发展

合法的身份基础设施可以为私人部门构建解决方案提供基础，以满足金融部门和其他部门的需要。这对身份平台提出了要求，特别在开放式接口和可持续收费模式领域，这通常也使得数字身份可以更快推出（比政府推出的速度要快）。正是因为如此，《可持续发展身份证明原则》有两项原则明确要求利用开放标准创建互联互通的平台。[①]

5.监测身份领域的新发展及新方法

有一些新兴技术和现有技术的新组合，有可能超越某个特定的国家身份平台不论数字化平台或传统平台。这些方法包括使用分布式分类账簿技术和社会数据。然而，这些方法目前处于非常早期的发展阶段，并不能作为一种可行的替代性方案来全面构建基本的合法身份基础设施。与任何创新一样，这方面的能力可以大幅提高，因此当局需要密切关注发展动态，使用通行的最佳实践，并考虑运用开放接口和模块化方法来构建合法身份平台。

专栏1：客户尽职调查要求和生物识别技术

印度储备银行允许受其监管的主体接受印度政府签发的Aadhaar身份识别码作为身份证明和地址，以满足对开放账户的客户尽职调查监管要求。

---

① World Bank Group (2017). Principles on Identification for Sustainable Development: Toward the Digital Age. Washington DC: The World Bank Group.

Aadhaar数字ID系统已经与电子客户尽职调查（电子化方式了解你的客户（e-KYC））服务相结合，加快客户身份验证速度。e-KYC使得拥有Aadhaar号码的个人可以授权印度唯一身份证明管理局（UIDAI）向希望立即激活移动联接和银行账户等服务的服务提供商披露其个人信息。

e-KYC是无纸化的、基于同意的、私密的、即时的。因此，可以与报告主体实时共享准确可靠的客户尽职调查数据。此外，由于KYC数据只有在客户同意的情况下才会直接发送给服务提供商，因此用户的隐私仍然受到保护。到目前为止，通过Aadhaar完成的e-KYC交易共计59亿笔。

银行和支付网络运营商已经将Aadhaar认证嵌入到微型自动取款机中，以实时、规模化和互联互通的方式在全国各地提供无网点银行服务。从金融服务提供者的角度来看，它几乎消除了文书工作和随之而来的记录负担，并通过电子化储存信息便利了审计和鉴定，因而为金融服务提供者带来了巨大的好处。

在巴基斯坦，国家身份证明使所有SIM卡得以注册，而这些SIM卡依赖于无网点银行服务提供者所建立的广泛的代理网络。这些身份证使开立交易账户成为可能，从而扩大了无网点银行网络。

生物识别技术，如其名称所示，是与人的特征相关的度量标准，这些特征是独一无二的，因此被用作证明个人身份的一种手段。作为对反洗钱和反恐融资及其他问题的回应，世界各国对探索生物识别技术用于身份证明的兴趣日益浓厚。印度和巴基斯坦的身份识别服务建立在生物识别技术的基础上，预计孟加拉国也会效仿。

生物识别技术大致可分为初级虹膜扫描、指纹和面部识别以及软生物统计——这些技术与行为特征和习惯更相关。虽然它们都被认为是身份验证，但前者更为普遍，而后者通常被用于理解模式和趋势，从而识别异常或未经授权的交易。

南非支付协会正在与万事达（Mastercard）和维萨（VISA）合作，设计一种在南非互联互通的解决方案。该规范提供了一系列生物统计解决方案，从指纹验证到手掌、声音、虹膜或面部生物识别技术。然而，也有人担心，由于更换销售终端（POS）设备的成本很高，零售商对此的接受程度会比较低。

2015年，尼日利亚开始对所有公务员进行生物统计验证方法的测试，以期获得全部人员的准确记录，并确保“虚构人员”吃空饷的现象不再发生。尼日利亚央行要求所有客户在其银行登记，以获得由尼日利亚银行间结算系统（NIBSS）发放的唯一的银行验证号（BVN）。2016年年初，他们宣布解雇2.4万名工作人员，此后这一数字翻了一番，为纳税人节省了相当于7 400万美元的税款。

（二）数字支付基础设施建设[①]

实现数字支付的更广泛获取和使用对普惠金融发展至关重要，对于那些处于非正规经济中的个人和中小微企业而言尤其如此。最新数据显示，全球范围内数字支付的使用正在增加。[②]然而，性别之间的差异仍然存在：男性使用数字支付的可能性比女性要高出约5%。[③]改进支付基础设施，可通过增加正规支付服务的使用来推动普惠金融快速发展和抓住经济发展机遇。[④]正如《G20数字普惠金融高级原则》原则四（扩展数字金融服务基础设施生态系统）所指出的，支付基础设施的发展是建设一个更具包容性、开放性的数字支付生态系统的核心驱动因素之一。[⑤]

许多政府认识到，一个高效、广泛可得、开放、安全、包容的数字支付基础设施是实现经济包容并不断增长的重要推动因素。根据通用定义，一个开放的支付基础设施是指任何受监管的支付服务提供者[⑥]都可以接入的支付基础设施。包容性的支付基础设施使支付服务（在理想状态下）可以惠及本国任何个人和中小微企业。既开放又包容的支付基础设施可以增加数字支付的交易量。反过来，交易量的增长可以降低单位成本，并最终降低终端用户的费用。它还促进支付服务提供者之间的

---

① 本部分基于优于现金联盟（BTCA）起草的基础论文：Better than Cash Alliance (2018): “Achieving Development and Acceptance of an Open and Inclusive Digital Payments Infrastructure. A Guidance Note for the G20/GPFI Markets and Payment Systems Subgroup”. New York，2018。

② World Bank Group (2018): The Little Data Book on Financial Inclusion. Washington DC: The World Bank Group.

③ Demirgüç-Kunt et al. (2018)，op. cit.

④ 当墨西哥政府数字化并集中化其支付时，发放工资、养老金和社会福利的成本下降了3.3%，或节省了近12.7亿美元。参见Better than Cash Alliance (2013). Sustained Effort, Saving Billions: Lessons from the Mexican Government’s Shift to Electronic Payments. New York。

⑤ Global Partnership for Financial Inclusion (2016). Guidance Note on Building Inclusive Digital Payments Ecosystems.

⑥ 支付服务提供者是提供支付服务（包括汇款）的实体。支付服务提供者包括银行和其他存款机构，还包括诸如货币转账支付运营商和电子货币发行商等专业化实体。参见Committee on Payments and Market Infrastructures and World Bank Group (2016)，op. cit。

竞争，进而推动改进产品和服务以及扩大产品和服务的使用。此外，通过正确的激励措施鼓励个人和中小微企业接受数字支付是非常必要的。①

对一些国家而言，完全开放的支付基础设施并不总是立即可行的或者理想的方案。由于监管和财务等要求（如为降低金融稳定风险），或由于现存的运营问题，接入这样的基础设施对某些支付服务提供者来说可能是不可行的或无法实现的。此外，一些支付服务提供者可能因为担心开放其闭环支付系统后会丧失创新优势而放弃接入公共基础设施。这些问题，以及诸如一国的基础设施发展等其他特定情况，须在向更开放、更包容的支付基础设施转变的背景下予以看待。②

从支付服务提供者的角度看，支付生态系统向更开放、更包容方向发展的进程，在某些情况下会受到与参与现有支付基础设施有关的复杂性的阻碍。正如上文所提及的，新的支付服务提供者通常不会寻求或被准许接入已有的支付基础设施。例如，新兴经济体将移动货币作为鼓励新型交易账户提供者为无银行账户群体提供服务的手段。这些通常作为一个闭环系统被引入，其成功范围仅限于国内个人对个人间的转账。原因是多方面的，包括服务提供者的商业做法、满足监管要求的成本和困难、管理代理网络和流动性的成本。

从终端用户角度看，构建一个更加开放和包容的支付生态系统的主要挑战在于缺乏互通性。缺乏互通性意味着不同支付服务提供者的客户之间很难进行交易或兑付资金，而且移动货币客户不方便与有银行账户的个人或实体发生资金往来。另一个问题与小商户尤其相关，由于接受成本高，以及延迟清算及结算流程导致资金到账不及时，因此现金相对于电子支付的价值较高。因此，如果各国大力开发更为开放和包容的支付基础设施，不仅对于提升电子支付服务间的互通性很重要，而且对于考虑推出激励措施也很重要，因为激励措施可以提高此类服务相较于现金的使用率，使正规金融服务对于非正规经济中的零售商和消费者更具吸引力。就此而言，

---

① Better than Cash Alliance (2018), op. cit.

② Committee on Payments and Market Infrastructures and World Bank Group (2016), op. cit.; CPMI (2014). Non-Banks in Retail Payments. Bank for International Settlements; and International Telecommu-nication Union (2016). ITU-T Focus Group Digital Financial Services. Access to Payment Infrastructures. Geneve.

实用性、成本和信任对终端用户使用金融服务来说至关重要。[①]

以下政策建议旨在推动向更加开放和包容的支付生态系统迈进，以及有效解决上述服务提供者和终端用户面临的挑战。而且，政策建议旨在提高个人和中小微企业（特别是那些非正规经济中的个人和中小微企业）对系统的使用和接受度。不言而喻，为确保数字支付基础设施得以健康发展，重要前提之一就是构建广泛的互联互通体系。同时也要确保获取广泛及可负担的电信网络服务。主要政策建议可归纳如下[②]：

（1）优先发展互联互通的支付系统，实现快速支付；

（2）激励商户使用支付系统；

（3）鼓励消费者使用数字支付；

（4）支持跨境支付系统。

1.优先发展互联互通的支付系统，实现快速支付

数字支付系统应当可互联互通，允许所有支付服务提供者接入同一系统。很多国家已经将其付诸实施，旨在提高传统支付系统效率并达成普惠金融目标。可互联互通的数字支付系统需要所有利益相关者的合作，它能提供低成本、低风险交易，从而便利支付系统有更多方参与及提高支付效率，藉此促进更加开放和包容的支付基础设施发展。此外，使快速支付（Fast Payments）得以实现的系统未来能够采用数字支付方式进行日常支付，并将日常支付能力提高到新的水平。

快速支付系统的一个典型特征就是支付信息和资金的快速传递能力，即支付信息的传递和收款人的资金尽可实现7天24小时（24/7）实时或者接近实时“最终”到账，且不可撤销。为达到这一目标，某些与清算相关的活动必须实时或接近实时并按每个支付命令持续发生，传统支付中的延迟现象不会再出现。然而，支付服务提供者并不必按每个支付命令进行即时资金结算。收款方资金到账和支付服务提供者之间的结算可能是耦合的(即实时结算)，也可能是解耦的(即延迟结算)。[③]

---

① World Bank Group and World Economic Forum (2016). Innovation in Electronic Payment Adoption: The Case of Small Retailers. Washington DC.; and BTCA (2018), op. cit.

② Better than Cash Alliance (2018), op. cit.

③ Committee on Payments and Market Infrastructures (2016). Fast Payments Enhancing the Speed and Availability of Retail Payments. Bank for International Settlements.

在许多情况下，在现有基础上一步建成一个覆盖范围广、易于使用、可互联互通，以及运行稳健高效的支付系统，或许是不实际或不可行的。因此，分阶段进行支付系统建设尤为重要。尽管不存在某种最佳操作方案，但应当考虑以下设计要素：

- 采用国际标准，尤其在系统间信息交换方面，包括交易处理信息。
- 终端用户的成本问题至关重要。很难在早期阶段确定成本，但是，成本估算应基于预期交易量而不是短期的成本回收。这是一个服务定位问题，服务应为所有参与者的长期利益考虑。
- 确定所需的系统组成部分，并尽可能实现原有系统中已使用组成部分的再利用。例如，如果结算系统被设计为可处理多个支付流，那么该系统也可用于处理新的支付流。
- 扩大市场认可度，构建信任，推动并确保能够开展大容量业务。在这方面，来自政府实体的支付流及应支付给政府实体的支付流（即政府对个人（G2P）、政府对企业（G2B）、个人对政府（P2G），以及企业对政府（B2G）支付）起着关键作用。
- 在可行的情况下，如果支付服务提供者尚未使用国家身份证明系统，为确定支付款项的个人或法人的真实身份，感兴趣的利益相关者将因使用国家身份证明系统而受益。这样做将增加实用性，并使得采取有信息依据的风险缓释措施成为可能。
- 确保所有接受监管的支付服务提供者能够直接或通过某种形式的聚合器访问支付系统。这并不意味着每个支付服务提供者都应被授予访问权限，而是意味着使用标准要根据支付服务提供者引发的风险以及参与系统的技术/操作能力来具体判断，且不能将某些特定类别的支付服务提供者排除在外。

快捷支付系统应该是市场化、安全、高效、低成本的。参与者应该能够在基础设施层面上进行协作（如创建共享平台并使它们的系统互联互通），在服务层面上通过创新进行竞争。这可以为竞争和创新提供空间，同时可对支付服务提供者保持开放性，且使其能够访问。此外，这有助于为支付服务提供者提供公平的竞争环境，并给予创新者和用户同等的访问机会。共享基础设施的方法可以确保数量集中，使得“触及”（任何付款人触及任何收款人的能力）变得非常简单，同时保持交易成本低廉、可负担，从而促进普惠金融发展。不过，支付服务提供者应该能够负担持续运营的成本并实现盈利。

为了使快捷支付系统充分发挥潜力，应建设现代化结算系统，从而促进交易的日内结算、实时结算和7×24小时交易结算服务。随着支付生态系统内参与者数量增多，风险监控的复杂性也随之增大，监管机构可以提高监管效能，使用改良工具，特别是数据管理和分析工具，以便能够执行监管响应。

政策制定者最终可以考虑优先推出大规模的应用场景，以此来验证快速支付系统的效率、安全性和可靠性。关注优先使用场景，如交通运输系统、公用事业缴费以及集市/街头流动商贩，这些应用场合可以增加支付交易量和提高市场认可度。政府可以考虑在支付生态系统中发挥积极作用。例如，政府通过支付系统向个人发放社会福利或工资，能增强社会公众对支付系统的信任，并能迅速扩大使用支付系统的家庭覆盖面和占比。

2.激励商户使用支付系统

在注重创新、推广和业务发展的同时，快速支付系统也应可持续。这需要一个强大的商业模式，也意味着定价应有商业可行性。然而，不应向商户或诸如开账单者等其他支付接受者收取收款费用，以免对其造成负向激励，同时要确保快速支付系统的商业可持续性，尤其是对小型企业和非正规零售商，更要考虑到这一点。应当认识到每个国家的情况都有不同，因此政策制定者应结合本国具体国情，考虑各种激励措施。其中包括：

- 确保对数字金融服务提供者不征收“额外交易费用”，这些费用通常会转嫁给商户，并且会给他们使用数字支付带来很大的障碍。
- 在支付体系发展初期，对数字支付的接受成本给予补贴，进而引导私人部门降低商户接受、使用数字支付的初始成本，并实现更大范围的推广。
- 考虑使用与清算所连接，且能将非正规和正规商户分组的正规聚合器。从这个意义上讲，商户可以接受支付而无需考虑支付机构的规范化程度，从而能显著增强支付基础设施的服务能力。
- 确保为商户服务的机构在满足监管要求的同时，还具有足够的能力影响业务链条上有关联的金融机构和非金融机构。
- 披露交易费用、折扣率和其他费用，提高市场透明度。

• 引入财务激励措施，如商户豁免、服务费减免、降低商户赊购比率、费用政府返还。

• 为单笔交易设置现金支付门槛，超过这一门槛的，拒绝消费者使用现金支付。[①]

• 在符合国家税收体制和监管要求的情况下，有关当局应考虑通过向使用电子渠道购买商品和服务的商户提供税收优惠，鼓励商户与供应商之间（B2B）使用系统进行交易。但是，由于没有对相关政策措施和方案的影响进行评估，因而这方面的文献比较缺乏。[②]

• 可以考虑非财务的激励措施，如自动报告（财税的、合规方面的）、培训和实时支持等措施。

为从消费者处接受付款，应鼓励商户不要依赖其与不同支付服务提供者之间达成的不同商业协议或技术协议。公私合作企业可以与数字支付服务商（DFSP）之间就标准化技术的开发进行合作，如商户付款二维码（QR码）。标准化可以支持不同服务商系统之间的互联互通，提高支付系统对商户和客户的可用性和满意度。

3.鼓励消费者使用数字支付

对金融服务不足人群在目标使用场景下的消费所收取的费用应该是可负担的。消费者抽奖活动（“您的下一张公共汽车票是免费的吗?”）也许对可感知成本和消费者意识都能产生影响。通过使用折扣或其他鼓励使用电子支付的激励措施，可以增加消费者与政府之间的互动。对于消费者来说，财务激励可包括现金返还、消费者奖励、客户忠诚度方案或政府发起的彩票抽奖。

正如《G20数字普惠金融高级原则》关于消费者保护建议所指出的围绕保护消费者账户资金安全、建立赔偿机制和使用消费者保护信息等，制定明确而统一的监管规定十分重要。再如《G20数字普惠金融高级原则》原则六关于金融素养的建议所指出的，政策制定者考虑市场教育倡议（尤其是有关新引入的快速支付系统）也

---

① Ernst & Young and Master Card (2017). Reducing the Shadow Economy through Electronic Payments.

② World Bank Group (2016). Supporting Payment Sector Development: B2B Corporate Payments Requirements in the Traditional Retail Sector". Washington DC: The World Bank Group.

很重要。如果所涉及的支付服务提供者已经就共同的消费者品牌达成一致，这会变得更容易些。

4.支持跨境支付系统

目前有一些正在开展或计划开展的支付系统建设方案。其中一些仅仅侧重于跨境交易，而另一些视野更广阔，同时着眼于支持国内和跨境交易。区域内各国政府正积极探索运用一些方法处理国内支付交易的可能性，这些方法与G20政策指引所推荐原则及可行的监管框架相一致。跨境基础设施对于建设服务于普惠金融目标的基础设施，或许是有益的。更大量交易通过区域化处理可大幅降低成本，而成本可负担及使用的便捷性又可激励各方参与。

专栏2：抽奖、忠诚度方案和POS机补贴

FIMPE是根据2004年墨西哥的一项总统令而设立的，它是一个私人信托基金，旨在扩大电子支付渠道的使用范围。收单机构可自由加入，向基金投资。基金将支持联合项目，推动POS机的安装及数字支付的使用。FIMPE由收单机构捐款筹集资金，这些捐款尔后又通过财政豁免予以返还。该项目主要分为两个阶段：

一是需求阶段：组织彩票抽奖，向支付卡使用者奖励汽车（奖出的汽车有3 100多辆）。通过实施该项目，墨西哥通过POS机的交易量从2003年到2006年增长了167%，有1/5的受访者表示，他们在这一时期增加了银行卡的使用。

二是供给阶段：通过该基金，给没有POS机的商户免费安装POS机，并且这些商户还可以按月获得固定的补贴，直到达到一定的交易量为止。该方案还包括针对商家的全国性宣传活动，让更多的人了解使用支付卡的好处。据FIMPE称，POS网络从2003年到2006年增长了96.3%。

泛美开发银行（IDB）的一份报告显示，通过FIMPE项目，总共给商户免费安装了205 000台POS机，而通常这些商户安装一台POS机需要支付6 000~7 000墨西哥比索（约合322~376美元）。墨西哥银行的数据显示，2005至2008年间，墨西哥使用POS机的交易量平均每年增长24%；而在FIMPE项目结束后，使用POS机的交易量出现了停滞，2009年仅增长了0.2%。

最近，墨西哥财政部门通过一项活动（Tablet para el Regimen de Incorporación Fiscal），向注册纳税的微型企业提供一台得到补贴的平板电脑，其中配备了移动POS机和会计软件。

就现金支付上限而言，从2014年开始，根据《所得税法》第55条，当累计每月现金存款超过15 000比索（约合806美元）时，金融机构必须报告纳税人账户现金存款的变动情况。此外，墨西哥银行还设定了5 000比索（约合268美元）的支票支付金额上限。

基于积分的忠诚度激励项目是尼日利亚中央银行（CBN）和“尼日利亚银行间结算系统（NISS）效率奖”所认可的创新项目，旨在“认可、鼓励、奖励和支持”支付机构的普惠金融创新活动。该项目对消费者通过POS机进行的每笔卡片交易给予忠诚度积分奖励，积分可以累积，并可以用于在CBN忠诚度门户网站线上购买礼品和商品。

（三）征信中替代性数据的使用[1]

现今，约80%的中小微企业以非正规形式存在。有限的公共基础设施和不完善的制度等诸多挑战，给这些企业的经营和成长带来了不利影响。[2]然而，根据世界银行集团企业调查，融资渠道的匮乏一直被视为这些企业面临的最大障碍。[3]对于个体经营者尤其是妇女来说，融资可能是他们创业的一个重要前提条件。例如，只有37%的妇女能够使用自有资金去创业，对于男性来说这个比例高达68%。[4]非正规企业贷款和银行账户的使用率通常较低，绝大部分企业通过其他渠道而非金融机构为运营融资，这些渠道包括内部基金、放贷人、家人和朋友等。[5]许多这样的企业希望能够正规化（即注册），认为这样做最大的好处是更容易获得融资支持。[6]

最新证据表明，对非正规的中小微企业来说，降低初始注册成本、公开登记流程对企业正规化的影响很小，而缴税等与企业正规化有关的可变成本相对而言影响

---

① 本部分基于国际征信委员会和普惠金融全球合作伙伴起草的基础论文：“Policy Guidance Note on the Use of Alternative Data to Enhance Credit Report ing”. Washington DC，2018。

② MSME Finance Gap Database. Washington DC: The World Bank Group.

③ World Bank Enterprise Surveys.

④ UN Women (2015). Progress of the World's Women 2015 2016: Transforming Economies, Realizing Rights. New York: United Nations.

⑤ Farazi, S. (2014). Informal firms and financial inclusion: Status and determinants. Policy Research Working Paper No. 6778. Washington, DC: The World Bank Group.

⑥ 同上。

更大。[1]除非这些企业发展壮大，能够获得足够的利润来覆盖这些成本，否则它们很难进入正规队伍。提高对非正规中小微企业的金融包容性，可能有助于它们的发展，并为其正规化铺平道路。[2]考虑到发展中经济体中约2/3的全职岗位是由非正规中小微企业所提供的，因此进一步拓展融资渠道，尤其是银行信贷等正规融资方式，对这些企业来说至关重要。

信贷数据的匮乏是导致非正规中小微企业受到金融排斥的一个常见原因。大多数非正规企业未建立会计系统来记录其交易情况，生成可信的财务报表和进行预测。通常，评估它们信誉的唯一可得的标准信息是个人信用档案或公司所有者的历史。然而，后者往往没有正式的工作，以非正规形式进行的经营是她和家人的唯一收入来源。在这方面，技术可以有所帮助。

在一个日益数字化的世界里，每天都产生大量的“替代性数据”，这些数据可以补充或替代传统的金融数据。据估计，到2020年，世界数字数据存量每两年将翻一番，这得益于移动电话、云计算、大数据和电子支付等方面惊人的业务交叉及增长。[3]金融系统生成了许多具有替代性作用的数字化数据。这些信息包括网上银行交易、数字支付和自动公用事业支付。在某些情况下，金融系统之外也产生了替代性数据。每次中小微企业及其客户使用云计算服务、浏览互联网、使用移动电话、使用社交媒体、使用电子商务平台、运送包裹或在线管理应收账款、应付账款、记账时，均产生了数据足迹。通过移动电话和电信收集的数据，例如呼叫数据记录，话费充值，以及个人对个人、政府对个人和个人对政府的支付交易等，正以指数化速度增加数据足迹，包括发展中国家和新兴市场的低收入消费者的数据足迹。

---

① Bruhn, M. (2013). A Tale of Two Species: Revisiting the Effect of Registration Reform on Informal Business Owners in Mexico. Journal of Development Economics (103): 275 83.; de Andrade, G., M. Bruhn and D. McKenzie (2013). A Helping Hand or the Long Arm of the Law? Experimental Evidence on What Governments Can Do to Formalize Firms. Policy Research Working Paper 6435. Washington, DC: The World Bank Group; De Giorgi, G. and A. Rahman (2013). SME' s Registration: Evidence from an RCT in Bangladesh. Economics Letters 120 (3): 573 78; Campos, F., M. Goldstein and D. McKenzie (2013). Business Registration Impact Evaluation in Malawi. Unpublished paper. Washington, DC: The World Bank Group.

② 同上。

③ Global Partnership for Financial Inclusion and International Finance Corporation (2017). Alternative data transforming SME finance. Washington, DC.

传统及非传统的贷款人可以选择挖掘这些实时、容易获取的数据，并将其用于授信决策。贷款人可以使用替代性数据判断偿还贷款的能力和意愿。因此，利用替代性数据完善征信功能，是扩大中小微企业、特别是非正规中小微企业融资渠道的良机。贷款人可以利用公用事业或零售贷款、行为数据、在线平台和移动应用程序的信息等替代性数据，为包括中小微企业在内的新客户群体服务。除了用于提供信贷外，替代性数据还可以用于提供关于客户偏好和行为的有价值的数据粒度，从而有助于设计新的金融产品和服务，鼓励积极的金融行为，并通过将融资与能源、商业、卫生或其他部门联系起来为实体经济提供支持。

尽管有上述好处，但使用新的替代性数据来制定金融和其他敏感性决策会带来额外风险。政策制定者面临的挑战，是如何在利用进一步使用替代性数据所带来的好处（同时确保对数据的充分保护），与注重消费者保护（将在下一节中讨论）之间寻求恰当的平衡。在这方面，可以考虑以下政策建议：

（1）提高信息的可得性和准确性；

（2）扩大信用信息共享；

（3）实现负责任的跨境数据交换；

（4）平衡市场诚信、创新和竞争。

1.提高信息的可得性和准确性

第一步是确定替代性数据的主要类别。从征信角度看，替代性数据是通过技术平台收集的、便捷易得的数字化信息。替代性数据被分为两类：结构化和非结构化数据。前者是“高度系统化的信息，可被无缝纳入关系数据库中，可以通过简单、直观的搜索引擎运算法则或其他搜索操作进行搜索”。后者可能更适用于借款人首次借贷的情形，它是“没有预先定义的数据模型而且（或者）没有以预先定义的方式处理的信息”。在这两种情况下，都需要一个唯一标识符（身份证、护照、金融身份证明号码等）来唯一地连接来自所有数据提供者的数据，只要这些数据提供者与同一个人或中小微企业有关。因此，为了提高信息的可得性和准确性，政策制定者和监管者可以评估唯一标识符的使用情况，如私人护照或身份证；对于非注册中小微企业，是监管机构或金融机构生成的金融数字，或发起人的护照或身份证；对于注册中小微企业而言，则是公司（法人）登记号码。

就中小微企业和个人而言，如果存在这种系统的话，政策制定者应意识到确保国家身份证明系统的效率和一致性的重要性。在没有这类系统的国家，可将重点放在其他替代性方案上，如公共机构签发的其他身份证明文件，或考虑与金融监管机构合作建立国家金融身份证明号码。对于规模较大且地位较为稳固的中小微企业，政策制定者和监管者可以认真考虑建立一个法人机构身份识别（LEI）体系的可能性，允许多渠道连接数据以提高相连数据的准确性。此外，提供了其他数据的相关公共机构，在一定程度上也提供了特定身份证明服务，因此可以考虑这种可能性，即同意征信服务机构(CRSP)出于验证目的以某种方式访问国家身份数据库。

政策制定者还可以考虑通过以下几个方面来解决数据不可得和数据质量差的问题：一是促进数据收集、处理和及时更新的自动化，确保数据及时更新；二是探索开发并向公众提供中小微企业公开数据系统与数据标准，该系统采集公司和金融机构的公共数据；三是对收集和使用替代性数据提供指引，包括对使用结构化和非结构化数据的环境提供指引。此外，监管者和政策制定者还可以通过修订法律法规，明确规定在考虑数据隐私和保护最佳实践的前提下如何处理替代性数据。

数据不可得或数据质量差是普惠金融的另一个障碍。政府也可以考虑将纳税申报、公司注册等政府服务数字化，使得中小微企业和个人可以产生更多数字足迹。一旦数字化，应考虑鼓励政府部门主动为征信服务机构提供高效、经济的官方数据获取渠道，包括但不限于身份证明数据集、公司注册信息、法院系统数据、财产及抵押登记数据等。因而，促进公共信息的数字化是基础。

最后，应考虑促进数字平台的使用，通过宣传教育活动，通过向信贷提供者、中小微企业和消费者提供激励的方式，来解决中小微企业交易痕迹不足的难题。政策制定者应鼓励中小微企业尽可能多地使用数字服务来经营其业务，因为数字服务能够留下可被访问的数字记录。通过激励信贷提供者、中小微企业和消费者，培养消费者意识以及提高数字金融素养等措施，将中小微企业留下的数字记录与其他信息相结合，对其信用状况进行分析。

2.扩大信用信息共享

为扩大信用信息共享，监管机构和政策制定机构可以推广开放式数据平台，使征信服务机构与法院记录、公司注册、抵押登记数据等其他数字化数据对接，分析并解决数据覆盖面有限和不完整的问题。这些机构之间可以达成强制性完全信息共享协议；将强制信息共享者的范围扩大到非银行金融机构、电子商务机构和公用事业公司；降低或消除最低报告门槛；促进征信服务机构间的信息共享；消除监管及金融障碍，开放信用信息共享市场。政策制定者可以在信息共享不充分时评估建立公共征信系统或数据库的可行性。

监管机构也可以考虑修订监管规则，要求所有支付服务提供者，包括不受监管的非银行金融机构，向监管机构辖区内的征信服务机构报告信用数据和其他相关信息。同样，也可以考虑进一步完善中央银行等监管机构对其辖区内征信系统和征信机构的监管角色，以考虑到使用替代性数据评估中小微企业获贷能力的需要。

监管机构还应确保信用信息共享相关法律允许征信服务机构为其客户提供服务，包括零售商、公司和中小微企业。适用法律也应允许征信服务机构间相互合作、共享信息、联合推出产品，以避免其将中小微企业排除在外。因为在通常情况下，征信服务机构更侧重服务于消费者或公司贷款人，这容易导致金融排斥。因此，有必要降低或消除向征信服务机构报告有关贷款或债务人情况的最低门槛。此外，应鼓励企业征信机构和个人征信机构进行合作，在法律允许的范围内，共享可能对彼此及各自客户有用的数据。最终，这些机构得以共同开发某些征信产品。

3.实现负责任的跨境数据交换

目前大部分替代性数据都能在互联网平台上获得，可以从任何地方访问，没有物理边界。但是，跨境数据共享可能因一些差异的存在而受到影响。例如，不同的数据采集方式、格式、国家监管规则、保存期限、唯一身份证明、争议处理程序等，在确认导致不精确的根源方面也存在困难。为了实现长期内跨境数据的负责任交换，监管机构和政策制定机构应与相关机构协作，制定跨境数据共享标准，确定跨境信息监管机构；协调适用于替代性数据的数据隐私法律；并指导跨境信息共享流程，包括可共享的信息范围及评估征信服务机构的可行性。有必要进一步加强国际合作，提高共享并最终跨境使用的中小微企业信贷数据的可比性和一致性。

有关部门最终应协调一致，提高收集及共享数据的一致性和可比性，评估实施“全球法人识别符”（GLEI）或其他类似文件（如世界银行集团“促进发展身份证明”（ID4D）倡议的可行性。应当在国际层面就一系列核心数据达成协议，以促进中小微企业在金融数据和信用状况方面的跨境信息共享。

4.平衡市场诚信、创新和竞争

既维护市场诚信，又不致不必要地限制个人和企业获得创新性金融服务，保持这两方面之间的平衡很重要。为此，必须一致应用功能性要求以确保各方得到平等对待。为实现这一目的，政策制定者和监管机构应当要求征信服务机构加强风险管理；运用风险为本原则对征信服务机构运营进行评估，并提高评估的严格性和强度；合作制定负责任创新原则。为解决替代性数据使用不透明的问题，监管部门应鼓励征信服务机构提高透明度，披露使用替代性数据进行评分的方法。监管部门还应积极争取或参与定期进行的全球调查或类似项目，以便获取其辖区内及全球层面有关征信活动的详细、全面、系统的信息。同样，政策制定者和监管者可以考虑实施或利用监管工具的可行性，以便在各自的特定市场中能够促进以替代性数据为中心的创新，包括替代性评分技术。

专栏3：全球法人实体标识符、开放式数据系统及亚太经合组织跨境信用信息共享

法人实体标识符（LEI）是基于ISO 17442标准、由20位字母及数字组成的代码，以唯一标识在最广义上从事金融交易的不同实体。它与关键的参考信息相连接，这些信息能够清晰且唯一地识别参与金融交易的法人实体。简而言之，公开可用的LEI数据池可以被看作是一个全球名录，它极大地提高了全球市场的透明度。公开可用的LEI数据池是获取全球法人实体标准化信息的关键。根据LEI监管委员会制定的协议和程序，对这些数据进行注册和定期验证。全球法人实体标识基金会（GLEIF）与全球LEI系统的合作伙伴合作，继续专注于进一步优化LEI数据的质量、可靠性和可用性，便利市场参与者从大量的LEI信息中获益。

开放式数据系统是一些平台，在这些平台上，每个人都可以免费获得一些数据，可以随意使用和重新发布，而不受版权、专利或其他限制。开放式数据系统可以是私有的，也可以是政府发起的。一些公开数据方案的实例包括Data.gov、Data.gov.uk、Data.gov.in等网站以及开放式银行业务（open banking，当银行数据由两个或多个非关联方共享时，通过应用程序编程接口向市场主体提供更强大的功能）。

开放式银行业务是欧盟修订的《支付服务指令》（PSD2）背后的驱动力之一，它要求欧盟的金融机构使用开放式和标准化的应用程序编程接口（APIs）向授权的第三方发布客户数据。开放式APIs的潜在含意可能在于，运用数据和流动性信息，在客户明确同意情况下对其信用状况进行动态评估。一些服务提供机构，如德国的bonify.de，正在使用交易数据（账户上的借贷往来、流动性水平以及历史变化）来创建一个与过去静态方法完全不同的信用评分。它们不着眼于长期的统计方法，而是基于历史和当前交易数据始终保持最新的评分。

国际金融公司和工商信息业协会应亚太经合组织（APEC）商业咨询委员会邀请，开展了一项关于中小微企业信用信息跨境访问的试点，作为实施APEC金融基础设施开发网络（FIDN）信用信息系统要素的一部分，试点中有关小微企业的信用信息涉及泰国、柬埔寨、老挝、越南和中国五个国家的一些征信服务机构。目前，实施方正努力建立一个区域数据术语词典以便更容易地解释跨境征信报告，并且还将对可能禁止在特定管辖范围内报告但在其他司法管辖区通常应以报告的任何数据元素（如性别）进行识别。

（四）金融消费者保护、金融教育和数据保护[1]

数字化有利于提升消费者金融素养、信心和金融体验。金融服务提供者通过分析消费者和创业者的数据（可能也包括大数据），深入了解相关主体的消费习惯，有助于开发定制产品以及识别欺诈行为。在适当的数据保护制度框架下，上述数据分析对全世界消费者和创业者都大有裨益。金融服务提供者还可以通过创设替代性行为指标来评估客户风险，从而为低收入或金融排斥群体创造进入正规金融体系的机会。例如，全世界民众的金融素养存在明显的性别差异，女性的金融知识获取率比男性低5%，而借助数字科技可以缩小这一差距。[2]

数字技术可以通过数字界面为金融服务提供者与消费者之间建立有效互动提供更多的机会。这些互动可利用对行为的洞察，从而加深消费者和创业者对相关金融

① 本部分基于经济合作与发展组织（OECD）的二十国集团—经合组织消费者保护特别工作组（G20 OECD Task Force on Financial Consumer Protection）起草的基础论文："Policy Guidance Note Financial Consumer Protection Approaches in the Digital Age". Paris, 2018, for the Consumer Protection sub-section; the Organisation for Economic Co-operation and Development through OECD International Network on Financial Education: "Policy Guidance Note on Digitalization and Financial Literacy". Paris, 2018, for the Financial Literacy sub-section; and The World Bank and Consultative Group to Assist the Poor: "Data Protection and Privacy for Alternative Data". Washington DC, 2018, for the Data Protection sub-section。

② Hasler, A. and A. Lusardi (2018). The Gender Gap in Financial Literacy: A Global Perspective. Global Financial Literacy Excellence Center. The George Washington University School of Business.

产品和金融决策的理解。这也有助于扩大金融服务的供给范围。数字革命产生了新型服务提供者，它们进入市场并通过数字渠道直接向个人提供金融服务。这些金融科技公司通常只专注于提供一种产品或服务。它们能够提升金融市场的竞争程度，有助于降低金融服务成本，并为个人和创业者提供更好的用户体验。

与此同时，数字化也给金融消费者带来了新风险。这些风险可能包括：

- 市场驱动型：可能包括消费者对不了解的（或新型）产品的误用，或服务提供者将产品推销给不知情的消费者；通常利用消费者对于数字环境的不熟悉而实施的新型欺诈；数据缺乏安全性、隐私性和机密性；服务提供者不恰当或过度使用数字信息收集分析方法，以识别潜在客户而排除不想要的客户；消费者能轻易获得高成本/短期信贷，或本质上是投机性的产品（例如首次代币发行（ICO）），以及采取其他加剧行为偏差的市场行动。

- 监管驱动型：可能包括国内保护水平的不平衡（披露不充分和救助机制不完善）和国家之间保护水平的不平衡（各类服务提供者的跨境销售和监管套利）；对于数据保护问题考虑不够；政府各部门之间对新型数字金融服务等缺乏协调。

- 消费者驱动型：日常生活和金融决策日益增加的数字化程度与数字和金融素养水平的持续提升仍不匹配①，即使年轻群体也是如此。②

- 技术驱动型：使用的各种算法越来越多，这会影响信贷或保险决策，并且可能导致消费者不能使用一些服务或导致对消费者的不当收费，这可能是因缺乏人工阐释所致的不准确或谬误相关而引起的；数据滥用，既包括大数据的滥用也包括小数据的滥用；移动网络和数字金融平台的不可靠可能导致交易无法正常进行；无法得到资金或网络安全风险等。

这些风险既可能会对消费者产生负面影响，也可能导致一系列负面结果。它们可能使消费者对于数字金融服务、金融系统和技术创新难以信任（或难以始终信任）的问题持续存在。金融服务提供者必须采取安全措施，以避免交易欺诈或其他

---

① 参见OECD/INFE (2016). International Survey of Adult Financial Literacy Competencies. Paris: OECD; G20/OECD INFE (2017). Report On Adult Financial Literacy in G20 Countries. Paris: OECD。

② 参见OECD (2014). PISA 2012 Results: Students and Money: Financial Literacy Skills for the 21st Century (Volume VI). Paris: PISA, OECD Publishing; OECD (2017). PISA 2015 Results: Students' Financial Literacy (Volume IV). Paris: PISA, OECD Publishing。

安全风险。消费者在使用数字渠道时应采用安全预防措施。在信贷和保险决策中，当使用大数据和数字信息收集分析技术时，可能会导致某些群体（可能包括老年人、妇女和创业者）遭遇新型金融排斥。数字和金融素养较低，以及对金融产品和新服务商的不熟悉等，都会增加消费者自愿排斥的可能性。最后，还可能产生过度负债等意外后果。如果消费者（特别是那些弱势群体）受到即审即贷的诱惑（这利用了人们对立即满足的偏好），或是在没有适当监管情况下服务商不对贷款对象的可负担性做认真调查就发放高成本信贷（贷款对象可能包括年轻人，尤其是学生，以及难以获得较低成本信贷的低收入群体），就会出现一些不良后果。

要最大限度地利用好数字化机会，需要更好地了解消费者对待数字金融服务的行为和态度，以及伴随技术应用而产生的金融和数字素养需要和需求。健全的金融消费者和数据保护体制以及提升消费者数字和金融素养，对于金融数字化的负责任的、有益的发展至关重要。要使金融排斥群体在获取和使用数字金融服务中建立信任和树立信心，就需要既能促进创新又注重金融消费者保护的监管法规。从这个意义上讲，政策和方法需要根据环境不断改进和完善。

在此背景下，提出以下政策建议：

金融消费者保护

（1）改进金融消费者保护监管措施并提高监管能力；

（2）加强信息披露并提高透明度；

金融素养

（3）加强有关数字金融素养的数据收集、协调和新核心能力的识别；

（4）加强数字金融服务的金融教育，支持对其进行评估；

数据保护

（5）构建安全有效的同意模式；

（6）强化访问、更正、删除和反对（ARCO）的权利；

（7）解决数据安全问题。

金融消费者保护

1.改进金融消费者保护监管措施并提高监管能力

正确平衡促进技术创新与金融消费者保护非常重要，尤其是不能对技术创新设置过度的限制，同时确保适当程度的金融消费者保护力度。监管安排和能力涉及监管和实施消费者保护所需体制的有关法律和制度安排，包括其权力、架构和能力。技术的发展对国内负责金融消费权益保护的监管部门带来了一系列挑战和机遇，包括在确保适当的金融消费者保护水平的同时平衡金融科技创新发展，以及能够拥有足够的工具、资源和能力来监管数字金融服务。

监管主体自身需要拥有充足的金融市场相关知识，通过密切接触企业、行业代表和消费者，了解新型数字产品与服务，了解金融市场的趋势和存在的问题。金融监管部门还应确保拥有适当的、与数字环境发展相适应的监管资源、监管工具和监管方式，其中包括获取各类数据、探索运用科技手段辅助市场监管等。

监管主体还应能有效应对技术创新，同时确保金融消费者得到适当保护。监管方式需要根据环境变化而变化。比如，建立“监管沙箱”机制，准许在受控的环境中测试新的商业模式；提出适当的监管要求，并在运用监管框架时提供监管支持、建议或指引。

旨在确保消费者使用电子渠道时能受到保护而开展的跨境合作，能够促进跨境交易，从而提升监管的一致性，减少监管套利，并对执法活动形成支持。这可以通过不同国家（或地区）监管机构间的信息共享来实现。考虑到借助数字渠道提供金融服务能促进跨境交易，但也会产生特定风险，所以不同国家（或地区）的监管机构应加强合作以保证金融消费者得到充分保护，比如支持有效的投诉处理或执法活动。

2.加强信息披露并提高透明度

对加强信息披露和透明度做出相关要求，是大多数金融消费者保护机制的基础性组成部分。技术发展（包括数据可得性）为改进信息披露方法（基于对消费者决策更好的理解，及对披露有限性日益加深的认识）提供了机会，也为探索其他方法提供了机会。

政策制定者可以重点考虑推进以下措施：

- 在数字金融服务的背景下评估现有的信息披露规定，以确保其充分考虑了以数字方式提供的金融服务相关的信息披露问题。
- 深入了解消费者决策过程和其行为偏差可能导致的影响，以消费者为中心制定方法。
- 鼓励金融服务提供者探索不同的数字化信息披露方式，提高披露方式的有效性，充分考虑以下因素：如不同的屏幕尺寸、通信格式，不同的地区语言和方言，以及金融产品目标消费者的数字素养。

技术发展和大数据可得性的日益提高，也为探索传统方式之外的新型披露方式提供了潜在机会。例如，发布针对某项金融产品或服务特定指标（如消费者投诉）就对消费者决策非常有帮助。又如，为消费者预设特定选项的“智能默认”；亦或是允许消费者采取措施终止金融交易的“个性化摩擦”等。在建议（包括数字化建议）提供方面，有待政策制定者考虑的方法有：确保所有生成数字化建议的底层算法的客观性和一致性，以及确保构成数字建议服务基础的方法（也包括追索权）是清晰和透明的。

金融素养

3.加强有关数字金融素养的数据收集、协调和新核心能力的识别

政策制定者应优先收集和分析那些体现数字金融服务影响消费者和创业者的数据，并确定供需双方的关键指标。供给侧方面，数据收集应侧重于收集可获得的产品和服务、服务提供者使用的分销渠道，以及相关的安全开发数字金融服务所需的物理基础设施及实现这一目标的技术要求；需求侧方面，除了消费者的态度、行为、具备的数字和金融素养外，政策制定者还应调查对数字金融服务的需求和使用情况。这些数据的收集和分析有助于确定那些最需要特定金融教育干预措施的目标群体。

在制定这些举措的准备期，政策制定者还应协调好参与金融知识普及和金融创新的私人机构和非营利机构之间的关系，避免利益冲突。首先，应弄清数字金融服务提供者的总体情况及其在线平台和工具的基本情况，以理解传递的信息及不知情的消费者可能面临的风险。这个过程还应使相关方参与其中，包括那些具有专业知识并与决策者信息对称的人，使其也参与到数字金融知识普及倡议的设计和发展中。

政策制定者应利用现有数据和研究来为所确定的目标群体制定或微调核心能力框架，并制定适当的金融教育内容。政府机关应在现有的金融素养核心能力框架（包括国际层面的框架）的基础上，对安全和正确使用数字金融服务[①]所需的其他

---

① 具体请参见 OECD / INFE Policy Guidance Note on Digitalisation and Financial Literacy. Paris: OECD。

核心能力加以考虑，这些能力有助于：

- 建立信任并培养正确使用数字金融服务和相关技术创新的行为。
- 保护消费者和小微企业免受数字犯罪、滥用以及不当销售的影响。
- 当滥用数据源（包括数据分析和数字信息记录分析）的情况发生时，让消费者能够应对因此导致的新型排斥。
- 给予那些因过度依赖易获得的在线授信而面临风险的消费者以帮助。

4. 加强数字金融服务的金融教育，支持对其进行评估

基于这些核心能力，负责金融教育的机构应与利益相关方合作，支持通过数字和传统手段提供有效的金融教育，并通过有针对性的方法满足目标群体的需求。尤其应该利用数字化交付的优势推进此项工作。数字工具首先可以通过以下方式改善金融教育的可得性：

- 使金融教育对更广泛的群体而言更易负担、更易获得。
- 鉴于其能够以灵活、动态和平面化的方式描绘信息，以及能够使目标受众更加容易接受，因而可以使金融教育更适合所有人的口味。
- 通过探索在数字平台上上传个人资料或设立账户以及获取个性化信息、指导和建议，有针对性地开展金融教育。

数字化工具还有助于增强消费者关于数字金融服务的核心能力、信心和体验，因为数字工具可以实时测试金融概念和产品，通过反复试验来学习，并在受控（和人工）环境中体验失败，从而帮助塑造消费者的金融习惯和态度，以及强化总体金融决策过程。这可以提高消费者的资金管理技能和自身财务控制能力，并有助于消除消费者的个人偏见，同时通过个人目标设定、反馈机制和提醒来激励消费者形成积极的金融行为。政策制定者还应该考虑到，特定的弱势目标群体或创业者仍然可以从学习班等更加传统的交付工具中获益；如果将数字金融服务教育纳入学校课程，首要的是应满足年轻人的需要。

数据保护

政策制定者应促进和支持对涉及数字金融服务的金融教育计划和用于金融知识教育的数字工具所产生的影响和有效性进行评估。应考虑运用评估和报告的标准框架，以便更好地实施结果比较，并鼓励在可能的情况下对数据作进一步研究。理想情况下，这样的框架将会借鉴国际层面现有的工具。

5.构建安全有效的同意模式

同意原则是数据隐私和金融消费者权益保护的一项基本原则。政策制定者应当加强完善同意模式，并在必要时采取重要和务实的方法予以完善。鉴于同意模式的内在局限性，应探索能满足有效且知情同意需求的替代性方法以及获得同意的创新路径。

监管机构可以鼓励行业参与者采用“从设计着手保护隐私”这一方法。简而言之，该理念是将隐私贯穿于信息系统、业务流程和网络基础设计、构建的各个阶段。“从设计着手保护隐私”的重点是采取一种主动的、预防性方法来保护用户隐私，避免用户隐私遭受侵害，[①]其七大原则是：①主动而非被动，预防而非补救原则；②以默认设置保护隐私原则；③将隐私保护嵌入设计原则；④完全实用——正和而非零和原则；⑤端对端安全——完整生命周期保护原则；⑥可见性和透明度——开放性原则；⑦尊重用户隐私——以用户为中心原则。该方法可以通过采用同意管理系统来施行，同意管理系统也使消费者的选择可以更细微、精确。

应考虑采用最少数据收集原则。监管机构可确定与风险评估有关的关键数据项，确认那些只有在特定条件才能采集与使用的数据项，或者准许行业参与者证明此类数据与风险评估的关联性。这个概念意味着只应收集最少量的数据。例如，《通用数据保护条例》（GDPR）第5条第（1）款（c）项涵盖了该原则。该条款规定个人数据应当是充分的、相关的，而且个人数据应仅限于为实现特定目的而进行数据处理所必需的数据（即‘最少数据’）”。此外，《征信通用原则》（GPCR）在“GP1”中明确，“所收集数据应当包括全部有关信息，以便使用者能够持续地充分评估和管理信用风险”。GPCR对于可共享的数据设置了限制，在处理种族人口数据等敏感问题时，该限制与可容许的目标相关联，正是这些目标构成了有关信息共享和隐私考虑的基础。

应引入分层同意概念。分层同意要求消费者为某些类型数据的处理或根据某些特定目的，做出不同类型的同意。同意模式使消费者得以决定他们选择共享的数据

① 例如，参见Deutsche Gesellschaft für Internationale Zusammenarbeit (2017). Selected Regulatory Frameworks on Data Protection for Digital Financial Inclusion. Bonn: Germany。

类型，以及他们允许哪些服务提供者使用他们的信息。当消费者采用一种同意模式时，消费者的决定也相应确定。监管机构应谨记，同意原则并不适用于某些情况和数据项（如贷款偿还违约数据）。采用“从设计着手保护隐私”方法将有助于消费者做出有关分层同意的选择。

另一种方式是，可以为同意设定时效。鉴于同意计划从未被核查或更新过，所以对一些形式的知情同意的有效性应该设置一个限制期。然而，必须承认这种做法并不能解决所有与知情同意有关的问题。在运用传统数据（即信贷偿还数据）评估风险时，该方法或许不再适用，除非消费者充分履行了自己的义务。

选择知情同意（而非相反）是监管者偏好的选项。例如GDPR提出，“未表态、预先打勾的框，或是未加选择等情形均不应……视为消费者已同意。”欲实现该特性，行业参与者可以通过明确的流程来确保消费者获得所有相关信息后自主选择。技术特性和同意管理系统将推进这一过程。

行业参与者（和数据来源方）有责任收集并保存消费者同意的有关证据。当数据需要与第三方共享时，这一点就显得尤为重要。一个同意管理系统对于完成该过程十分有帮助。虽然许多消费者对提供重要信息的同意很关注，但他们往往是在没有阅读同意条款、条件的情况下直接提供的。为了解决这些问题，可以考虑开发一些工具，它们能提供操作更简单、表示更明确和显示更突出的同意形式。这些工具很可能是基于技术的。它们不仅包括对使用标准化形式同意的要求，还包含由金融服务提供者负责记录的可使用口头形式同意选项。

政策制定者和行业参与者可采取措施确保替代性数据的预测功能得到测试和验证，保证公平使用数据，并且保证使用替代性数据开发的评分模型对少数群体或受保护群体而言是中性的。当敏感数据（例如民族、种族起源、性取向、政治立场或宗教信仰）用于评估消费者的信用状况以及模型中包含的数据是出于不同的不相容目的而收集时，需要得到消费者同意。考虑到运用替代性数据预测风险的能力和替代性决策工具的可得性，可以禁止或限制使用会产生历史歧视的替代性数据。

6.强化访问、更正、删除和反对（ARCO）的权利

在数字金融服务背景下，个人数据由多个机构保存或访问，数据也可能以不同形式储存。因此，数据访问、更正、删除和反对权在数字金融情况下尤为重要。消费者可能对哪些主体保存或能够访问数据，基于何种目的使用数据，数据在何处储

存、由谁储存，以及保存数据的性质和范围等并不知情。

至少允许消费者访问本人数据是一项普遍认可的原则，该原则在施行数据保护法的国家得到应用。同时，在一些虽未制定数据保护法，但具有数据相关产业（以收集、处理和分发数据为核心业务）的国家，这一原则也得到了应用。一般情况下，数据访问时限为1至7天。

消费者应当享有更正数据的权利。通常情况下，数据管理者应在消费者提出申请后的7至25天内做出最终处理结果。然而，当使用从开放式数据源而非封闭式网络获取的替代性数据时，应当着重强调确认数据源及数据责任人的重要性，数据责任人应对数据的准确性负责，并负责数据的更正以及答复消费者。数据的删除（清除）权与数据的被遗忘权、淘汰和有用性相关联。在封闭式网络内，信息通常有明确的保存时限，当数据被非法收集或在无法律依据情形下被进一步处理时，消费者有权申请将数据清除。

对出于特定目的对消费者信息的使用，消费者有权做出决定。此类信息使用最常见的情况是，通过采用白名单等方法，将数据用于市场营销等相关方面。然而，在一些特定情形下，针对特定类型的数据，消费者无权拒绝他人对这些数据（例如还款违约时用于评估信用风险的还款数据）进行处理。在封闭式网络内，某些数据项具有强制性，消费者因而无权进行选择，而在开放式网络内，对于数据的进一步使用，消费者拥有更大的选择余地。

7.解决数据安全问题

数据已逐渐成为一项核心资产，个人数据及身份信息被窃也成为消费者面临的主要风险。国际社会一致认可的框架安排，满足了保护数据不在未经许可情况下使用（如访问、遗失、毁坏、篡改和数据污损）的需求。在这方面，政策制定者应当鼓励采取安全措施防止数据的遗失、污损、毁坏、非法访问、篡改或滥用，并通过开展网络安全风险评估进一步强化信息技术系统，以此识别潜在威胁、采取缓释措施，并建立能最大限度降低网络事故负面影响的事故快速应对机制。政策制定者还可以通过建立规则和机制来鼓励向执法机构报告犯罪性质的事故，并促进公私机构之间的信息交流。

监管者应当鼓励金融服务提供商采取安全措施防止数据遗失、污损、毁坏、非法访问、篡改或滥用。这些安全措施还应当包括与数据违规使用沟通有关的、各方一致同意的事故应对协议。不同国家对数据违规使用沟通的时间要求不尽相同。

对于任一服务提供者或数据提供者而言，网络安全评估都应当是其整体风险管理政策和程序的一部分。在此背景下，识别潜在威胁、采取缓释措施，以及建立事故快速应对机制能够最大限度降低网络事故的负面影响。在理想情况下，各机构组织都应当指定数据安全专员（DSO）。

监管机构应当继续探索利用数据跨境流动所带来的益处。所有的数据流动（包括国内的数据流动和跨境数据流动）都应当建立相应的机制，确保数据管理者和行业参与者各司其责，并制定相应的规则和程序，确保无论数据存储于何处或已传输至何处，消费者都能够行使其权利。最后，各监管主体之间的合作协议也能够促进共同目标（与反洗钱和隐私保护框架相一致）的实现。

专栏4：对新参与者和创新中心的建议

英国金融行为监管局（FCA）设立了一个咨询单位，向为消费者开发自动化低成本金融模型的公司提供监管反馈，包括个别指导、非正式建议和对现有规则或指引的要点介绍。

日本金融厅（FSA）通过设立金融科技支持室和金融科技概念验证（PoC）中心来支持金融科技公司发展。金融科技支持室的职责是回复咨询，其中主要是对法律进行解释，它平均用不到5个工作日就可解决金融科技公司关注事宜。金融科技概念验证中心则通过在金融厅内部针对不同入选概念验证项目组建专门工作小组，为与其他相关机构合作开展测试提供场所。

意大利银行（BoI）最近成立了自己的创新中心（金融科技渠道），这是其网站上的一个专用空间，经营者可以在此提出创新性项目。成立中心的目的是开放与经营者对话的渠道，并支持其创新进程。

G20 High-Level Principles for Digital Financial Inclusion

GPFI Global Partnership for Financial Inclusion

G20 2016 CHINA

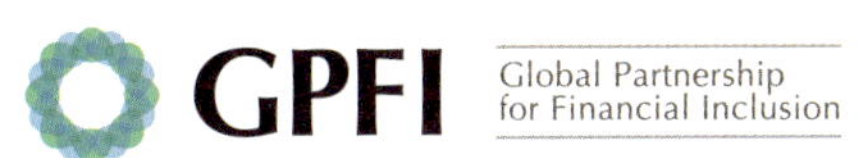

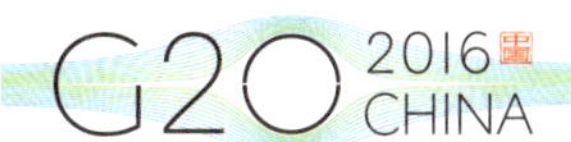

ACKNOWLEDGEMENTS

The GPFI Co-Chairs would like to acknowledge and thank the following contributors to this document:

The representatives from G20 countries, non-G20 countries, international organizations and private sector who provided inputs, advice and comments. The G20 Finance Ministers and Deputies, and Central Bank Governors and Deputies, provided important guidance through their meetings in Sanya, Shanghai, Washington, D.C., Xiamen, and Chengdu.

Patron of the GPFI: Her Majesty Queen Máxima of the Netherlands, United Nations Secretary-General's Special Advocate for Inclusive Finance for Development

Chair of the Technical Team: Dr. Tianqi Sun (People's Bank of China)

Co-Chair of the Technical Team: Douglas Pearce (World Bank Group)

Members of the GPFI Digital Financial Inclusion Technical Team, which drafted the High-Level Principles:

Alliance for Financial Inclusion: *Norbert Mumba, Robin Newnham, Kennedy Komba*

Better Than Cash Alliance: *Ruth Goodwin-Groen (core drafting team), Ros Grady (consultant, core drafting team)*

Child and Youth Finance International: *Bianca Isaincu*

Consultant Group to Assist the Poor: *Timothy Lyman, Ivo Jenik*

International Fund for Agricultural Development: *Pedro de Vasconcelos, Michael Hamp*

International Finance Corporation: *Martin Holtmann, Momina Aijazuddin (core drafting team), Loretta Michaels (consultant, core drafting team)*

Organisation for Economic Co-operation and Development: *André Laboul, Flore-Anne Messy*

People's Bank of China: *Tiandu Wang*

SME Finance Forum: *Matthew Gamser*

World Bank: *Douglas Pearce, Douglas Randall (core drafting team), Lois Quinn, Solvej Krause (consultant, analyst)*

GPFI Affiliated Partners and Industry Bodies:

Bill and Melinda Gates Foundation

GSMA

Institute of International Finance

Tianqi Sun
GPFI Co-Chair (China)

Katharina Spiess
GPFI Co-Chair (Germany)

Aysen Kulakoglu
GPFI Co-Chair (Turkey)

Preamble

The Group of Twenty (G20) recognizes the key role of financial inclusion in helping to move towards an Innovative, Invigorated, Interconnected and Inclusive World Economy. In this decade, digital finance has already successfully improved access to finance by women, the poor, the young, the elderly, farmers, small and medium enterprises (SMEs) and other underserved customer segments in both G20 and non-G20 countries. Successful business models of digital financial inclusion and new regulation and supervision approaches have emerged worldwide.

Digital financial inclusion promotes efficient interconnection among participants in economic activities. Leveraging the opportunities that technology offers to reduce costs, expand scale, and deepen the reach of financial services will be critical to achieving universal financial inclusion. In 2016, the G20 has the opportunity to shape and accelerate the use of digital mechanisms for improving financial access and inclusion. The G20 can help catalyze and inform country-led actions, with significant potential for social and economic impacts at the household, community, national and international levels.

The G20 recognizes that it is crucial to take concrete and significant actions to advance digital financial inclusion under the guidance of the G20 High-Level Principles for Digital Financial Inclusion and of international standard-setting bodies' (SSBs) principles supporting financial inclusion. Based on the specific circumstance of each country, G20 members aim at taking concrete actions to promote digital financial inclusion at their own country level.

It is also very important to strengthen international cooperation and peer exchange and learning for digital financial inclusion. The G20 is committed to further help low income developing countries (LIDCs) to take action to advance digital financial inclusion in the spirit of the 2030 agenda.

"We endorse the G20 High-Level Principles for Digital Financial Inclusion, the updated version of the G20 Financial Inclusion Indicators, and the implementation framework of the G20 Action Plan on SME Financing, developed by the Global Partnership for Financial Inclusion (GPFI). We encourage countries to consider these principles in devising their broader financial inclusion plans, particularly in the area of digital financial inclusion."

—Communiqué of the G20 Finance Ministers and Central Bank Governors Meeting
23–24 July 2016, Chengdu, China

G20 High-Level Principles for Digital Financial Inclusion

The G20 stands at an unprecedented time when our leadership has the potential to drive the growth of inclusive economies by promoting digital financial services. Two billion adults globally do not have access to formal financial services and are excluded from opportunities to improve their lives. While tremendous gains in financial inclusion have already been achieved, digital financial services, together with effective supervision (which may be digitally enabled), are essential to close the remaining gaps in financial inclusion.

Digital technologies offer affordable ways for the financially excluded—the majority of whom are women—to save for school, make a payment, get a small business loan, send a remittance, or buy insurance. The 2010 G20 Principles for Innovative Financial Inclusion spurred initial efforts and policy actions. These 2016 High-Level Principles for Digital Financial Inclusion build on that success by providing a basis for country action plans reflecting country context and national circumstances to leverage the huge potential offered by digital technologies.

PRINCIPLE 1: Promote a Digital Approach to Financial Inclusion

Promote digital financial services as a priority to drive development of inclusive financial systems, including through coordinated, monitored, and evaluated national strategies and action plans.

PRINCIPLE 2: Balance Innovation and Risk to Achieve Digital Financial Inclusion

Balance promoting innovation to achieve digital financial inclusion with identifying, assessing, monitoring and managing new risks.

PRINCIPLE 3: Provide an Enabling and Proportionate Legal and Regulatory Framework for Digital Financial Inclusion

Provide an enabling and proportionate legal and regulatory framework for digital financial inclusion, taking into account relevant G20 and international standard setting body standards and guidance.

PRINCIPLE 4: Expand the Digital Financial Services Infrastructure Ecosystem

Expand the digital financial services ecosystem—including financial and information and communications technology infrastructure—for the safe, reliable and low-cost provision of digital financial services to all relevant geographical areas, especially underserved rural areas.

PRINCIPLE 5: Establish Responsible Digital Financial Practices to Protect Consumers

Establish a comprehensive approach to consumer and data protection that focuses on issues of specific relevance to digital financial services.

PRINCIPLE 6: Strengthen Digital and Financial Literacy and Awareness

Support and evaluate programs that enhance digital and financial literacy in light of the unique characteristics, advantages, and risks of digital financial services and channels.

PRINCIPLE 7: Facilitate Customer Identification for Digital Financial Services

Facilitate access to digital financial services by developing, or encouraging the development of, customer identity systems, products and services that are accessible, affordable, and verifiable and accommodate multiple needs and risk levels for a risk-based approach to customer due diligence.

PRINCIPLE 8: Track Digital Financial Inclusion Progress

Track progress on digital financial inclusion through a comprehensive and robust data measurement and evaluation system. This system should leverage new sources of digital data and enable stakeholders to analyze and monitor the supply of—and demand for—digital financial services, as well as assess the impact of key programs and reforms.

These eight principles are based on the rich experience reflected in G20 and international standard-setting bodies' standards and guidance. They also recognize the need to support innovation while managing risk and encouraging development of digital financial products and services.

Women agents of a microcredit institution show their daily collection which is recorded in an electronic device.
Photo by Sudipto Das

Rationale For G20 High-Level Principles for Digital Financial Inclusion

The *G20 High-Level Principles for Digital Financial Inclusion* (Principles) are a catalyst for action for the G20 to drive the adoption of digital approaches to achieve financial inclusion goals, as well as the related G20 goals of inclusive growth and increasing women's economic participation. The Principles recognize the urgency of providing the financially excluded and underserved with high-quality and appropriate financial products and services. The Principles also recognize the need to use digital technologies to achieve this goal, where possible. Underserved groups—which typically include poor people, women, youth, and people living in remote rural areas and sometimes ethnic minorities—require special attention. Vulnerable groups such as migrants, elderly people, and people with disabilities may also need a particular focus. Moreover, some excluded and vulnerable groups may not have access to digital financial services or may be reluctant to adopt them and this risk needs to be proactively managed and addressed.

"Digital financial inclusion" is an evolving phenomenon. The Principles rely on the explanation in the 2016 Global Partnership for Financial Inclusion (GPFI) report on *Global Standard-Setting Bodies Financial Inclusion: The Evolving Landscape* (GPFI White Paper). It states: "*'Digital financial inclusion' refers broadly to the use of digital financial services to advance financial inclusion. It involves the deployment of digital means to reach financially excluded and underserved populations with a range of formal financial services suited to their needs, delivered responsibly at a cost affordable to customers and sustainable for providers.*"[1]

The term *"digital financial services"* covers financial products and services, including payments, transfers, savings, credit, insurance, securities, financial planning and account statements. They are delivered via digital/electronic technology such as e-money (initiated either online or on a mobile phone), payment cards and regular bank accounts.[2]

The Principles build on, and complement, the 2010 G20 Principles for Innovative Financial Inclusion.[3] They also reflect the ongoing rapid evolution in digital financial services and synthesize key aspects of the substantive guidance provided since 2010 by the G20, the GPFI, and international standard-setting bodies. Importantly, the Principles reflect the realization that access to financial services alone is insufficient. Rather, fostering widespread usage and understanding of responsible digital financial services is critical to individual, national and global welfare. The Principles also recognize the need to actively balance the promise of digital innovation with the new risks that rapidly evolving technology introduces.

An effective way to implement the Principles is through applicable national strategies and related country action plans, or other country level actions, which take into account country context and national circumstances.

A farmer uses a digital money transfer service in Qinghai Province, China.
Photo by Yunwen Li

G20 High-Level Principles for Digital Financial Inclusion—*In Action*

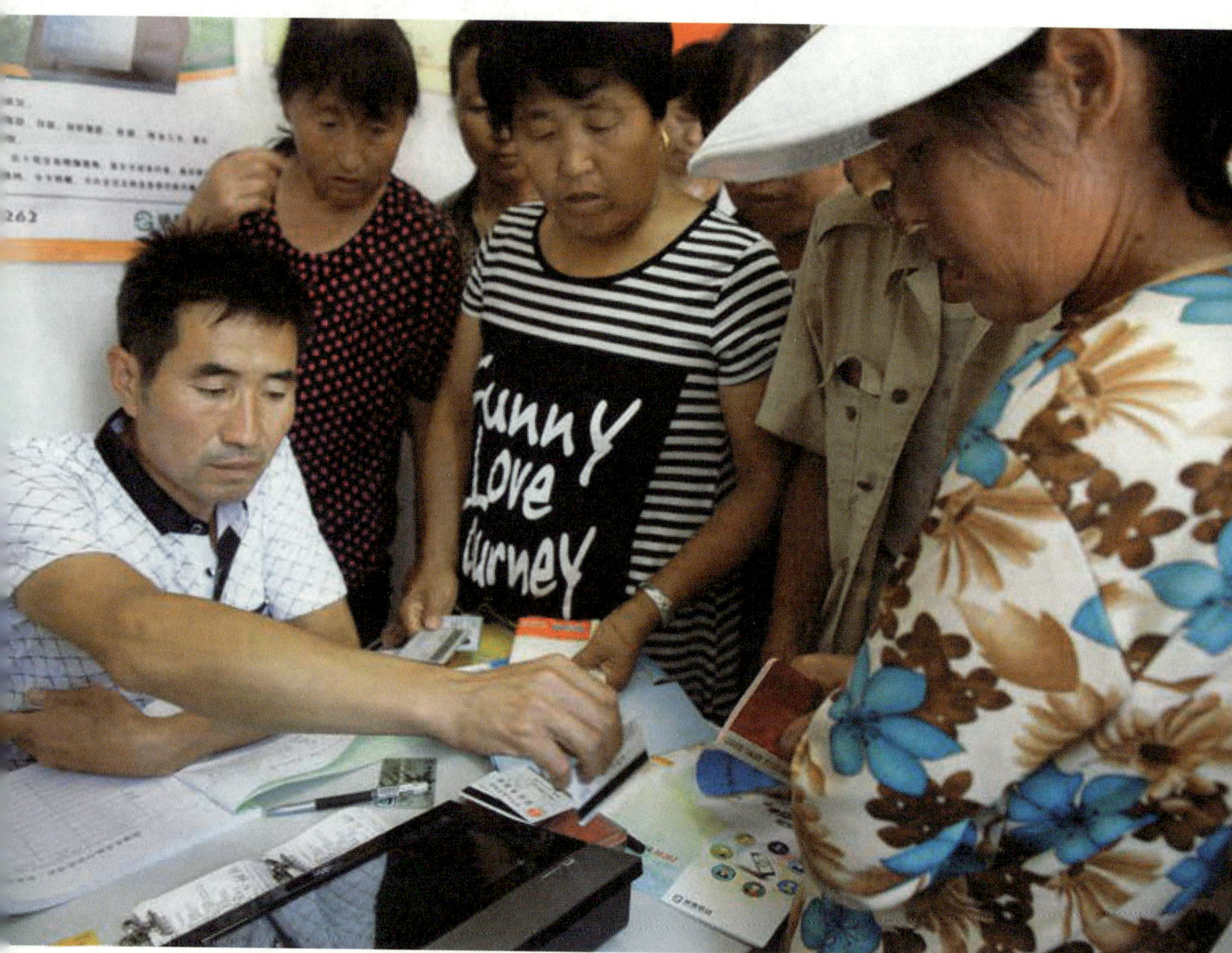

Women using a bank agent with a digital payment service in the rural area of Shaanxi Province, China.
Photo by Bo Wang

PRINCIPLE 1

PROMOTE A DIGITAL APPROACH TO FINANCIAL INCLUSION

Promote digital financial services as a priority to drive development of inclusive financial systems, including through coordinated, monitored, and evaluated national strategies and action plans.

Policy leadership and coordination across the public and private sectors are critical for expanding financial inclusion. It is important to lead by example and promote the use of innovative digital technologies to reach the financially excluded and underserved. Both steps are necessary to expand access, ownership and usage of a broad range of financial services and to reach financial inclusion targets.[4] This can be achieved through a national strategy with a clear vision and a concrete action plan that is developed in a consultative manner. It should be well coordinated, robustly monitored and evaluated, and reflect the roles of all relevant public and private-sector stakeholders. As noted in the Rationale, it is also important for stakeholders to recognize that excluded and vulnerable groups may not have access to digital financial services or may be reluctant to adopt them. This risk should be proactively managed and addressed.

"*Public and Private Sector Commitment*" is the first of the seven Guiding Principles in the 2016 *Payments Aspects of Financial Inclusion Report* from the joint task force of the Committee for Payments and Markets Infrastructure (CPMI) and the World Bank Group (PAFI Report and PAFI Guiding Principles).[5] It highlights the need for active, well-resourced, and well-coordinated actions to promote the transition from cash and checks to digital payments. The 2014 GPFI Report on "*The Opportunities of Digitizing Payments*[6]" and the 2015 GPFI Report on "*Digital Financial Solutions to Advance Women's Economic Participation*"[7] also emphasize the need for active government leadership and action in advancing digital financial services.

Examples of actions to promote digital financial inclusion include, but are not limited to, the following:

- Ensure that relevant national strategies and action plans reflect new digital models for achieving digital financial inclusion policy goals and encourage their use. They should be evidence-based and have specific objectives, measurable outcomes and clear lines of accountability, while taking account of country context and national circumstances.

- Commit to effective coordination between policymakers, central banks, financial supervisors, relevant regulatory authorities, financial ombudsmen, and others with responsibilities related to digital financial services, including telecommunications, competition, and consumer protection agencies.

- Maintain active dialogue and coordination among all key stakeholders in the digital financial ecosystem, including government, the private sector and civil society, to ensure shared understanding of digital financial inclusion goals and market conduct expectations.

- Digitize, where feasible, large-volume, recurrent payments from government agencies to consumers and small businesses. Further, provide facilities and incentives for payments to and from governments to be made digitally rather than in cash (for example, through lower fees).[8]
- Encourage and facilitate both the for-profit and the non-profit private sector to make large-volume, recurrent payments digitally rather than in cash (for example, payrolls, social benefit transfers and humanitarian aid, as well as remittances).[9]
- Encourage industry: (i) to adopt customer-centric product design approaches that focus on customer needs, preferences, and behaviors and facilitate the uptake and usage of digital financial services among the financially excluded and underserved; (ii) to make available low-cost, basic transaction accounts for the financially excluded and underserved that can enable digital payments and provide a safe place to store value.[10] Such encouragement should include clear guidance on the legal flexibility and applicability of such accounts for underserved groups, such as youth.
- Eliminate barriers to development and uptake of digital financial services—including easier access and usage of the Internet and mobile devices—as well as reform tax regimes and import restrictions that hinder the widespread uptake of new technologies.
- Work with other national authorities to remove barriers to, and promote, the smooth provision of cross-border financial services to promote digital financial inclusion.

PRINCIPLE 2

BALANCE INNOVATION AND RISK TO ACHIEVE DIGITAL FINANCIAL INCLUSION

Balance promoting innovation to achieve digital financial inclusion with identifying, assessing, monitoring and managing new risks.

The speed of innovation in digital financial services (including financial technology innovations known as "*FinTech*"[11]) over the last several years is breathtaking and holds the promise of vastly expanding the scope, reach, and sophistication of financial service design and delivery. It also offers the potential of dramatically lowering costs. Policymakers should encourage and nurture such innovation to harness the many benefits it enables, particularly for financially excluded and underserved groups. They also should recognize that rapid digital innovation introduces new risks—both individual and systemic—that need to be identified and addressed effectively and in a timely fashion. This recognition is necessary to build cyber resilience into financial markets and safeguard the financial system from illicit activities.[12]

The PAFI Report, the GPFI White Paper, and other international standard setter guidance all acknowledge that key risks may develop, or increase, through the use of digital technologies and that they need to be effectively assessed and managed.[13] Digital financial risks come in many forms. They may arise from a combination of existing and new providers, new digital technologies, reliance on agent networks, the bundling of new products across multiple service providers, and low levels of financial literacy among consumers. Digital technology risks can appear across the entire digital financial services and markets value chain, including at the operational, settlement, liquidity, credit, consumer, and anti-money laundering and combating the financing of terrorism (AML/CFT) levels. Digital technology also enables the generation and analysis of vast amounts of customer and transaction data ("Big Data"), which introduces its own set of benefits and risks that should be managed.

Examples of key actions to balance innovation and risk around digital financial inclusion include, but are not limited to, the following:

- Encourage digital innovation through market-based incentives and public-private partnerships to reach financially excluded and underserved groups in particular.
- Encourage industry to develop secure and simple user interfaces for digital financial services that make them easier to use and minimize the risk of mistaken transactions and unauthorized or illegal use—especially in relation to the needs of vulnerable groups.
- Work with industry and risk-management experts to research, identify, and assess the risks arising from the use of new digital technologies, and ensure they are effectively monitored and managed.[14]

- Establish regular knowledge-sharing mechanisms between regulators and service providers along with clear communications channels.
- Encourage regulators and industry to establish risk-management strategies that reflect the specific conditions and legal frameworks of the relevant jurisdictions. For example, this might include local Know Your Customer rules to effectively manage and mitigate identified risks rather than de-risk entire categories of customers or accounts. Regulatory guidance should also stress the importance of financial inclusion as a factor in supporting AML/CFT controls. This guidance should include clear advice about the flexibility of relevant regulations, including for the purposes of applying a risk-based approach.
- Encourage service providers to use multiple sources of digital data for evaluating consumer and small and medium enterprise (SME) creditworthiness. This approach should include appropriate safeguards while facilitating development of such data and ensuring a fair, non-discriminatory approach to its use. Examples of such alternative data sources include mobile phone use, utility payments, data enterprise registration information, and other information that can complement traditional loan repayment or insurance-related data.
- Collaborate with industry to explore the benefits that digital fiat currencies may offer to financial inclusion.
- Explore new methods for determining emerging technology risks, such as stress tests for potential cyber-related crime.

PRINCIPLE 3

PROVIDE AN ENABLING AND PROPORTIONATE LEGAL AND REGULATORY FRAMEWORK FOR DIGITAL FINANCIAL INCLUSION

Provide an enabling and proportionate legal and regulatory framework for digital financial inclusion, taking into account relevant G20 and international standard setting body standards and guidance.

If digital financial inclusion is to develop and expand in a sustainable way, providers and other market participants need a legal and regulatory framework that is: predictable, risk-based and fair; allows for new entrants; and does not impose excessive, non-risk-based compliance costs. In particular, the framework should reflect a careful assessment of the relevant risks from market, provider and consumer perspectives; provide clear market participation rules; establish a fair, and open, level playing field for market participants; and ensure a framework that can be effectively and efficiently supervised with the requisite supervisory capacity and resources.[15] The willingness to innovate and invest will be undermined without such a legal and regulatory approach, as will be the potential opportunities for financially excluded and underserved groups to access financial services. In addition, risks may not be adequately addressed.

The overall policy environment and regulatory framework should reflect a proportionate and enabling approach to regulation. This is necessary for countries to fully realize their digital financial inclusion goals, as well as the associated economic growth.[16] The recent GPFI White Paper describes the proportionality approach as involving "*. . . the balancing of risks and benefits against costs of regulation and supervision to the regulator, the supervisor and to the regulated and supervised institutions.*"[17] However, as noted in the GPFI White Paper, international standard setters have developed the concept of "*proportionality*" in varying ways.[18]

The legal and regulatory framework also needs to reflect the "*widespread understanding that financial inclusion, stability and integrity and consumer protection are not just compatible, but mutually reinforcing*" (G20 Financial Inclusion Action Plan 2014). The alignment between these objectives is particularly important in connection to digital financial inclusion given the rapid development of new business models, products, distribution channels, and digital technologies.[19]

It is equally important that supervisors of the legal and regulatory framework relevant to digital financial inclusion have the skills, capacity, and resources to effectively supervise relevant entities and the market generally. This should include the ability to understand the digital technologies involved, innovations in digital financial services markets, evolving risks, and markets. Supervisors should also be able to leverage new technologies to conduct their supervisory activities in an efficient and effective manner.[20] A risk-based approach to compliance and oversight is also needed for a proportionate approach to supervision.

Examples of key actions to develop an enabling and proportionate legal and regulatory framework include, but are not limited to, the following: [21]

- Implement a framework for digital financial inclusion that provides for market participation (including entrance requirements), prudential requirements where appropriate (e.g., for capital and liquidity), market conduct and integrity, consumer protection, AML/CFT safeguards, and insolvency. Such a framework should be technology-neutral and flexible enough to cover both new and existing service providers and product innovations (for example, through a broad definition of regulated digital financial providers and services which can be amended over time).
- This framework should also allow for piloting innovative new delivery channels, products and services, and business models, without having to immediately comply with all regulatory requirements. At the same time, such a framework should ensure fair and balanced oversight, maintaining obligations to meet AML/CFT requirements consistently with international standards, while ensuring that no participant in the pilot obtains an undue advantage. And the framework should balance the risks of digital financial inclusion with the costs of supervision and compliance.
- Promote competition and a fair, and open, level playing field for digital financial inclusion by ensuring that providers of similar digital financial services have similar rights and responsibilities regardless of their institutional type and the technology used. There should also be clear and consistent criteria for market participation (including for new and foreign entrants) and for offering specific types of digital financial services. This framework also should ensure that similar risks are regulated in a similar manner and that an appropriate risk-based approach to supervision is developed.
- Assess all areas of national and local law relevant to digital financial inclusion to identify and address areas of overlap or contradiction as well as any gaps, barriers to access, or other obstacles. These areas may include: financial services, payments systems, telecommunications, competition, discrimination, identity, barriers to excluded and underserved groups accessing digital financial services, and responsibility for agents and employees.
- Ensure a clear delineation of responsibilities among regulators for the legal and regulatory framework relevant to digital financial services and for digital financial inclusion in general.
- Build the capacity of supervisors of the legal and regulatory framework for digital financial inclusion to understand digital technologies (for example through local and international training and peer learning programs) and encourage the use of digital technologies, as appropriate, to improve their processes and capacity for supervision.
- Draft laws, regulations, and guidance relevant to digital financial inclusion in a plain and easy to understand manner, and make them easily available to industry and consumers (for example, through a publicly accessible website and other accessible channels of communication).
- Establish a sustainable mechanism among G20 members for regular communication and information exchange on digital financial inclusion legal and regulatory frameworks and related supervisory approaches, including risk management strategies and experiences.

PRINCIPLE 4

EXPAND THE DIGITAL FINANCIAL SERVICES INFRASTRUCTURE ECOSYSTEM

Expand the digital financial services ecosystem—including financial and information and communications technology infrastructure—for the safe, reliable and low-cost provision of digital financial services to all relevant geographical areas, especially underserved rural areas.

Policymakers, in partnership with the private sector, should prioritize the development of digital infrastructure as one of the foundations of their economic and social development plans.[22] Both public and private sectors increasingly rely on digital networks for the delivery of important public and private services, from health and education to communications and financial services. Particularly important to the establishment of a digital financial services ecosystem is the expansion of robust, safe, efficient and widely accessible retail payments and ICT infrastructure that provides all users with convenient, reliable points of service for sending and receiving payments and conducting other digital financial services. To the extent feasible, such infrastructure should reach the "last mile" of rural areas as well as serve major urban areas and key transit corridors. PAFI Guiding Principle 3 discusses the need for such infrastructure (including the mobile/data connectivity and power underpinning such systems).[23]

The use of digital platforms that are instantaneous and accessible to all service providers has the potential to significantly reduce the cost of digital transactions for both service providers and consumers. Such platforms potentially can sustainably process the small transaction sizes that dominate the bulk of the world's financial transactions. As such, they can change the business case dynamic in ways that encourage innovation and new players to enter the market. Open digital platforms can also improve interoperability and widen consumer choice by expanding the network of available access points for consumers and service providers to conduct transactions and provide cash-in/cash-out services. Such access points would include not just branches and agents, but also ATMs, points of service (POS) devices, mobile phones and Internet applications.

Examples of key actions to expand a country's digital financial ecosystem include, but are not limited to, the following:

- Collaborate across government agencies to ensure the basic infrastructure that supports digital financial inclusion, including telecommunications and power, is in place where needed.
- Expand broadband network/data coverage into underserved areas, using policy mechanisms such as innovative public-private partnerships, incentives for shared infrastructure programs, and targeted procurement policies.

- Modernize and expand the retail payments system infrastructure and establish open payments platforms linked to countries' clearing and settlement systems and that provide safe and efficient access to banks, non-bank financial institutions, and emerging service providers.[24]
- Encourage service providers to enable interoperability of access points and channels, further expanding the reach of consumer service access points and the overall convenience to holders of transaction accounts.
- Leverage widespread government channels—such as post offices, where applicable—for distributing digital financial services.
- Collaborate with industry to explore the potential of distributed ledger technology to improve the transparency, efficiency, security, and reach of wholesale and retail financial infrastructure, allowing for appropriate risk mitigation and safeguards.[25]
- Support the development of moveable collateral registry systems that take into account multiple forms of collateral, better reflecting the daily lives of users and broadening the base for a robust SME finance sector.[26]
- Promote the establishment and responsible use of flexible, dynamic credit reporting systems modeled on best practices as outlined by the *International Committee on Credit Reporting* (ICCR). These include relevant, accurate, timely and sufficient data, collected on a systematic basis from all reliable, appropriate and available sources, and retained for a sufficient time period.[27] The overall legal and regulatory framework for credit reporting should be clear, predictable, nondiscriminatory, proportionate, and supportive of consumer data protection and privacy rules.
- Encourage the use of innovative data sources in credit reporting systems such as data on utility payments, mobile airtime purchases, as well as use of data on digital wallet or e-money accounts and e-commerce transactions. This should be done while recognizing consumer data protection and privacy rules, and could be assisted by the customer identification systems referred to in HLP 7.

PRINCIPLE 5

ESTABLISH RESPONSIBLE DIGITAL FINANCIAL PRACTICES TO PROTECT CONSUMERS

Establish a comprehensive approach to consumer and data protection that focuses on issues of specific relevance to digital financial services.

The need for responsible digital financial practices has been widely acknowledged.[28] A sound consumer and data protection framework is essential to building trust and confidence in the acquisition and ongoing use of digital financial services, especially for consumers with limited financial literacy or the resources to absorb losses. It is especially important in a digital financial inclusion environment with rapid innovation in technology, services, providers, and distribution channels and where the volume, velocity, and variety of personal data processed increases both consumer access and risks.

Financially excluded and underserved groups, in particular, face diverse consumer risks specific to digital financial services. They include: a lack of safeguards for funds held by non-prudentially regulated providers; limited disclosure of fees, terms and conditions (for example, on a mobile phone); insufficient agent liquidity and agent fraud; confusing user interfaces that raise the risk of mistaken transactions; inadequate security of systems; irresponsible lending through digital channels; system downtime that prevents access to funds; unclear or limited recourse systems; and failure to keep personal data confidential and secure. Underserved groups also face a significant risk of discrimination.

A consumer protection framework must also take into account the volume, variety, and velocity of personal data used and processed for digital financial inclusion purposes, as well as the data's value. This includes identification, transaction, account, mobile airtime purchases, and social media data. This data can improve access, products and customer service and provide public information about financial inclusion levels. However, its use can also harm consumers (including if data is used to exclude them from the financial system).

Examples of key actions to support responsible digital financial practices to protect consumers and address related regulatory and industry self-regulatory issues include, but are not limited to, the following:

- Design a digital financial services consumer protection framework that addresses risks specific to the digital environment and reflects statistical and behavioral evidence and direct input from consumers gathered, for example, from toll-free consumer hotlines, online forums, and complaints data.
- Establish a consistent legal framework for safeguarding client funds held by non-prudentially regulated service providers (for example, though trust

accounts, pass-through deposit insurance schemes, and supplemental insurance requirements). Further, rigorously enforce rules relating to fraud affecting digital financial services and provide appropriate recourse mechanisms through targeted programs for vulnerable groups.

- Ensure consumers have convenient access to easy to understand, efficient, and free complaint resolution mechanisms that can be accessed, and operate, remotely (such as via a call center, a website or social media). They should be available from service providers and, for disputes, a third party such as a financial ombudsman.
- Develop proportionate service provider requirements for digital financial services, including: (i) clear, simple, and comparable disclosures of terms, fees and commissions; (ii) periodic account statements showing transactions and fees; (iii) toll-free customer hotlines; (iv) procedures and responsibility for unauthorized or mistaken transactions and system outages; (v) responsible and fair lending and debt collection practices; (vi) consumer guidance about how to use a digital financial service as well as security safeguards to protect against unauthorized use, disclosure, modification, and destruction of personal data; (vii) government contact details for consumer queries (such as phone numbers and websites). All consumer information should be able to be provided digitally (including over a mobile phone) and be able to be retained.
- Require digital financial service providers to train agents and employees about: product features; regulatory responsibilities; fair treatment of underserved and vulnerable groups; and recourse procedures. Training also should cover explaining disclosure documents on request, especially if the wording is in a language the consumer does not understand.
- Encourage service providers to submit periodic reports on data covering digital financial services complaints broken down by key target groups.
- Encourage providers of digital financial services to self-regulate to a higher standard than required under prevailing law (for example, through an enforceable, industry-based code of conduct).
- Develop a clear definition of the meaning of "personal data," taking account of the ability to combine different categories of information to identify a person.
- Ensure consumers of digital financial services have meaningful choice and control over their personal data—including through informed consent based on clear, simple, comprehensive, age-appropriate and brief privacy policy disclosures in relevant languages. Consumers also need to have transparent, affordable and convenient access and correction rights which can be exercised via remote and Internet-enabled access, including mobile phones and websites—or via a 24-hour call center.
- Require that data not be used in an unfair discriminatory manner in relation to digital financial services (e.g., to discriminate against women in relation to access to credit or insurance).
- Develop guidance to ensure the accuracy and security of all data related to: accounts and transactions; digital financial services marketing; and the development of credit scores for financially excluded and underserved consumers. This guidance should cover both traditional and innovative forms of data (such as data on utility payments, mobile airtime purchases, use of digital wallet or e-money accounts,[29] social media and e-commerce transactions).

PRINCIPLE 6

STRENGTHEN DIGITAL AND FINANCIAL LITERACY AND AWARENESS

Support and evaluate programs that enhance digital and financial literacy in light of the unique characteristics, advantages, and risks of digital financial services and channels.

Shortcomings in financial literacy continue to pose challenges for policymakers and service providers as they seek to expand financial services to previously excluded and underserved groups.[30] The evolution to digital delivery of financial services adds another layer of complexity for new users who may have little or no experience with digital tools, whether mobile or online. Policymakers, regulators, and service providers must all work together to ensure that such users have: access to, and awareness of, digital financial tools; simple instruction on how they work; and clear understanding of how to obtain more information as well as recourse on mistakes that may occur in this new environment of instantaneous, non-face-to-face[31] transactions. Understanding of how to use specific financial tools is complemented and enhanced by broader and deeper financial knowledge. Otherwise, there may be a further widening of inequities in access to, and use of, financial services. It is similarly important that merchants, and especially small businesses, are aware of the benefits of accepting payments and conducting transfers by digital means.

It is generally accepted that there is an urgent need to build digital and financial literacy and awareness among both consumers and merchants. This is especially the case for financially excluded and underserved groups, including people in vulnerable groups. Examples include Guiding Principle 6 *Financial Literacy* of the PAFI Report, Recommendation 5 in the 2014 Opportunities of Digitizing Payments Report entitled *Guide digital financial service providers to educate consumers and small businesses about their options to increase confidence, competence, and adoption,*[32] and the key finding concerning financial skills for women in the 2015 *Advancing Digital Financial Solutions for Women Report.*[33] The OECD/*INFE High-Level Principles on National Strategies for Financial Education*, which were endorsed by G20 Leaders in 2012, provide international guidance and policy options to develop efficient national strategies for financial education.[34]

Examples of key actions to enhance digital and financial literacy and awareness include, but are not limited to, the following:

- Identify emerging financial competency requirements arising from the digitization and bundling of financial services (for example micro credit or micro insurance made available through mobile phone offers, use of innovative data sources for credit scoring, and bundled insurance and credit products).
- Encourage development and evaluation of practical, accessible, and digitally focused financial literacy and awareness programs, particularly for underserved and vulnerable groups, to help consumers understand the

features, benefits, risks and costs of digital financial services and the need to safeguard account and security information. Further, encourage industry to share the details and results of such programs with regulators together with applicable data.

- Harness emerging high-quality digital tools to develop financial literacy and digital literacy programs that build knowledge, understanding and confidence in using digital financial services. Examples include the use of SMS questions and messages timed to inform specific consumer decisions or to remind users about their savings goals; online tools such as games to help parents teach their children about financial management; digital toolkits for tracking income and spending; online small business financial management programs; and interactive educational programs. Consumers can be particularly open to information and advice at "teachable moments" when they are making decisions with financial implications, including at 'life events' such as starting a new job, retirement, or birth of a child.
- Raise awareness among small businesses about the advantages of processing payments and transfers digitally and the features of available digital financial services.
- Promote employer and service provider-sponsored unbiased digital financial capability measures targeting currently excluded and underserved groups who may become first-time users of financial services as a result of digitization.
- Encourage informed choices by consumers by supporting the development of tools allowing consumers to compare similar digital financial products and services (such as price comparison websites).

PRINCIPLE 7

FACILITATE CUSTOMER IDENTIFICATION FOR DIGITAL FINANCIAL SERVICES

Facilitate access to digital financial services by developing, or encouraging the development of, customer identity systems, products and services that are accessible, affordable, and verifiable and accommodate multiple needs and risk levels for a risk-based approach to customer due diligence.

Governments worldwide acknowledge the importance of identity as a fundamental necessity for daily life. For approximately 1.5 billion people, the majority of them living in Asia and Africa, the inability to prove their official identity cuts them off from basic services and enjoying their full rights. It also marginalizes their participation in the economy. Evidence shows that individuals who lack official forms of identification are typically the most vulnerable people in the poorest countries.[35] As countries increasingly rely on digital networks for delivering important public and private services, the ability of consumers to remotely access those services through identification becomes acutely important.

Access to reliable identity data is critical for achieving financial inclusion goals.[36] Easier verification of customer identity supports the efforts of regulators and service providers to facilitate more efficient customer registration while meeting AML/CFT requirements. Providing online access and verification of such identity information also helps service providers streamline the customer acquisition process and reduce costs. Digital technologies, including biometrics and other forms, provide a unique opportunity to leapfrog traditional, paper-based forms of identification to build a robust and efficient identification system at a scale previously unachievable. The safety and security of such digital identification systems must also be paramount.

Examples of key actions to facilitate customer identification include, but are not limited to, the following:

- Ensure birth registration and other foundational identity systems are universal and affordable. Amend laws and regulations that inhibit or deny digital identification registration to underserved groups such as married women.
- Ensure that government identity databases—birth registration and tax IDs, for example—are made appropriately and securely available to other parts of government, subject to client consent when required by data protection laws.
- Establish an interoperable, technology-neutral national database system, where appropriate, that links relevant civil registration and identity systems and is appropriately and securely accessible to authorized parties, such as financial service providers, subject to client consent where required by data protection laws.

- Establish and promote, as necessary, new and innovative forms of identity registration and verification such as digital biometric identification products and online identity verification services, particularly for those currently lacking any form of identification. Establish acceptable open standards to manage identity, transaction and account risks.
- Implement risk–based customer identification and verification requirements to facilitate uptake of low-risk digital financial services for financial inclusion purposes, for example through tiered frameworks for customer due diligence. Such requirements should authorize identification from one or multiple state-validated sources and clearly specify the data sources that can be used for identity verification while meeting the requirements of the Financial Action Task Force for *"reliable, independent source documents, data or information."*[37]
- Establish a legal framework that protects the privacy and security of identity data and requires informed consent to use and disclose such data. This framework should also require robust recourse frameworks to allow individuals to seek redress when consent, rights or privacy have been violated.
- Collaborate with stakeholders outside government that can facilitate identification programs for excluded groups for financial inclusion and other purposes. One example would be humanitarian relief organizations and other relevant nongovernmental organizations.
- Establish clear accountability and transparency around the roles and responsibility of the public and private agencies in charge of identity management.
- Encourage development of safe and secure digital signature systems that can help facilitate authentication and validation, especially for underserved consumers.

PRINCIPLE 8

TRACK DIGITAL FINANCIAL INCLUSION PROGRESS

Track progress on digital financial inclusion through a comprehensive and robust data measurement and evaluation system. This system should leverage new sources of digital data and enable stakeholders to analyze and monitor the supply of—and demand for—digital financial services, as well as assess the impact of key programs and reforms.

Effective leveraging of digital technologies to achieve financial inclusion goals requires a comprehensive monitoring and evaluation system to track progress, identify obstacles (including gaps), and demonstrate success at both the national and program levels. Three key elements of a national monitoring and evaluation system should be adapted to reflect emerging digital models: a national results framework with key indicators and targets; the underlying data infrastructure that collects both supply- and demand-side data; and evaluation activities of key programs and reforms. Together, these elements serve to quantify and measure progress towards digital financial inclusion priorities, support in-depth analysis of financial inclusion trends and obstacles (particularly among target populations[38]), and provide reliable insights about the efficiency, effectiveness, and impact of reforms and programs. Section 5 of the PAFI report notes the importance of tracking progress towards financial inclusion goals, and provides relevant guidance.

Examples of key actions to track progress on digital financial inclusion include, but are not limited to, the following:

- Establish national key performance indicators and, where appropriate, targets for the uptake and usage of digital financial products and services. This should be done in consultation with key stakeholders, including the private sector.
- Establish or adapt financial inclusion data collection systems to cover new digital financial providers and products. For example, this should be done using demand-side surveys of individuals and firms, supply-side reporting (e.g., via offsite supervision reporting templates), and new digitally-enabled sources of data.
- Work with digital financial service providers to adapt data collection systems to provide data broken down by key priority demographic criteria, including gender, income, age and geographic location.
- Establish a memorandum of understanding among the regulatory authorities that collect data on digital financial service providers to ensure the efficient and open exchange of information.

- Establish an online data portal and/or publish regular reports to provide publicly available data on the adoption and use of digital financial services. Further, provide reports on the adoption and use of digital financial services to international agencies monitoring financial inclusion data to the extent reasonably practicable and agreed.
- Fund and encourage impact assessments of key programs and reforms relevant to digital financial inclusion.
- Monitor progress on implementation of all aspects of these High-Level Principles.

A man purchases electricity credits using his mobile phone in the village of Hogoro, Dodoma Region, Tanzania.
Photo by Jake Lyell/Alamy

ENDNOTES

1. See March 2016 Global Partnership on Financial Inclusion (GPFI) paper entitled *Global Standard-Setting Bodies and Financial Inclusion The Evolving Landscape* (page 46) (http://www.gpfi.org/publications/global-standard-setting-bodies-and-financial-inclusion-evolving-landscape). See also the Key Elements of a Digital Financial Inclusion Model in Box 8 (page 46) (http://www.gpfi.org/sites/default/files/documents/GPFI_WhitePaper_Mar2016.pdf).
2. This description of "*digital financial services*" is drawn from the 2014 GPFI Issues Paper on *Digital Financial Inclusion and the Implications for Customers, Regulators, Supervisors and Standard-Setting Bodies* (pages 1 and 2) (http://www.gpfi.org/sites/default/files/documents/Issues%20Paper%20for%20GPFI%20BIS%20Conference%20on%20Digital%20Financial%20Inclusion.pdf). See also the 2016 *Payments Aspects of Financial Inclusion Report* from the joint task force of the Committee for Payments and Markets Infrastructure (CPMI) and the World Bank Group (PAFI Report) (page 13, para. 47) (http://www.bis.org/cpmi/publ/d144.htm).
3.

G20 High-Level Principles for Digital Financial Inclusion (HLPs)	2010 G20 Principles for Innovative Financial Inclusion (2010 G20 Principles)
1. Promote a Digital Approach to Financial Inclusion	HLP 1 builds on Principle 1 "Leadership" and Principle 6 "Cooperation" of the 2010 G20 Principles.
2. Balance Innovation and Risk to Achieve Digital Financial Inclusion	HLP 2 builds on Principles 1 "Leadership," 3 "Innovation," and 4 "Protection" of the 2010 G20 Principles.
3. Provide an Enabling and Proportionate Legal and Regulatory Framework	HLP 3 builds on Principle 4 "Protection," Principle 8 "Proportionality" and Principle 9 "Framework" of the 2010 G20 Principles.
4. Expand the Digital Financial Services Infrastructure Ecosystem	HLP 4 builds on Principle 9 "Framework" of the 2010 G20 Principles.
5. Establish Responsible Digital Financial Practices to Protect Consumers	HLP 5 builds on Principle 4 "Protection" and Principle 5 "Empowerment" of the 2010 G20 Principles.
6. Strengthen Digital and Financial Literacy and Awareness	HLP 6 builds on Principle 5 "Empowerment" of the 2010 G20 Principles.
7. Facilitate Customer Identification for Digital Financial Services	HLP 7 builds on Principle 1 "Leadership" and Principle 6 "Cooperation" of the 2010 G20 Principles.
8. Track Digital Financial Inclusion Progress	HLP 8 builds on Principle 7 "Knowledge" of the 2010 G20 Principles.

4. The individual ownership of accounts is particularly important to expanding women's financial inclusion and is addressed throughout the 2015 G20/GPFI Report on *Digital Financial Solutions to Advance Women's Economic Participation* (see, for example, section 1.1) (http://gpfi.org/sites/default/files/documents/03-Digital%20Financial%20Solution%20to%20Advance%20Women....pdf).
5. http://www.bis.org/cpmi/publ/d133.pdf
6. http://gpfi.org/sites/default/files/documents/FINAL_The%20Opportunities%20of%20Digitizing%20Payments.pdf
7. http://gpfi.org/sites/default/files/documents/03-Digital%20Financial%20Solution%20to%20Advance%20Women....pdf
8. PAFI Guiding Principle 7: Large-volume, Recurrent Payment Streams
9. PAFI Guiding Principle 7: Large-volume, Recurrent Payment Streams
10. The key actions proposed for PAFI Guiding Principle 1 *Public and Private Sector Commitment* suggest that "*an explicit strategy with measureable milestones to that end*" be developed for transaction accounts for all. See also section *3.2.1.2 Transaction Account and Payment Product Features* of the PAFI Report.

11. In a letter from the Chairman of The Financial Stability Board to the G20 Finance Ministers and Central Bank Governors dated 22 February 2016, the Chairman advised that the FSB would support the objectives of the Chinese G20 Presidency in 2016 by *"assessing the systemic implications of financial technology innovations, and the systemic risks that may arise from operational disruptions."* (page 1) (http://www.fsb.org/wp-content/uploads/FSB-Chair-letter-to-G20-Ministers-and-Governors-February-2016.pdf).
12. See June 2016 *Guidance on Cyber Resilience for Financial Markets Resilience* issued by the Committee on Payments and Market Infrastructures (CPMI) and the International Organization of Securities Commissions (IOSCO): http://www.bis.org/cpmi/publ/d146.htm and the related *Principles on Financial Market Infrastructures* issued in 2012 by the then Committee on Payment and Settlement Systems (now CPMI) and the IOSCO Technical Committee: http://www.bis.org/cpmi/publ/d101.htm.
13. See, for example, PAFI Guiding Principle 2 and GPFI White Paper Part IVA *Digital Financial Inclusion—Opportunities and Risks.*
14. See Recommendation 15 concerning New Technologies in the revised 2012 Financial Action Task Force Recommendations: http://www.fatf-gafi.org/media/fatf/documents/recommendations/pdfs/FATF_Recommendations.pdf.
15. See, for example, Principles 2, 8, 9 and 25 of the Consultative Document issued by the Bank of International Settlements' Basel Committee on Banking Supervision *Guidance on the Application of the Core Principles for Effective Banking Supervision to the Regulation and Supervision of Institutions relevant to Financial Inclusion*, 2015.
16. See GPFI White Paper Recommendations 12 -18 and Parts VIA and VIB and PAFI Guiding Principle 2 Legal and Regulatory Framework.
17. GPFI White Paper, Part II, Section D, footnote 16. See also Recommendations 6 and 7.
18. Examples of the different ways the proportionality approach has been used by international standard setters include the reference in the revised 2012 *Basel Core Principles for Effective Banking Supervision* to the proportionate approach allowing assessments of compliance with the Core Principles that are commensurate with the risk profile and systemic importance of a broad spectrum of banks. The 2012 *Financial Action Task Force Recommendations* (FATF Recommendations) also refer to: enhanced due diligence measures being proportionate to the relevant risks; to effective, proportionate, and dissuasive sanctions; and to the exchange of information between supervisors being proportionate to their needs. The Financial Stability Board has also called for a proportionate approach to the regulation of shadow banking which recognizes both the relevant risks and the benefits of completion for banks (see *Transforming Shadow Banking into Resilient Market-based Financing: An Overview of Progress and a Roadmap for 2015*: http://www.fsb.org/wp-content/uploads/Progress-Report-on-Transforming-Shadow-Banking-into-Resilient-Market-Based-Financing.pdf).
19. Financial Stability Board *Global Shadow Banking Monitoring Report*, Basel, 2014 and *Thematic peer review on the implementation of the FSB policy framework for other shadow banking entities: Summarized Terms of Reference*, Basel, 2015. Basel Core Banking Principle 1 emphasizes the primary importance of the safety and soundness of the financial system, while recognizing that financial supervisors may have additional, nonconflicting responsibilities (such as financial inclusion and consumer protection).
20. GPFI White Paper Recommendations 31 to 35 and Part VIB.
21. Many of these factors are covered in the GPFI White Paper Recommendations in Part VI, or in the PAFI Report.
22. For a discussion of Financial and ICT Infrastructures see PAFI Report section 3.1.3 and for a discussion of service points and access channel networks see PAFI Report section 3.2.2.
23. See in particular PAFI Guiding Principle 3: Financial and ICT Infrastructures.
24. See PAFI Guiding Principle 3: *Financial and ICT infrastructures* for further guidance.
25. The Financial Stability Board has considered distributed ledger technology as part of its review of major areas of financial technology innovation (http://www.fsb.org/2016/03/meeting-of-the-financial-stability-board-in-tokyo-on-30-31-march/). The CPMI Committee of the Bank for International Settlements has also considered distributed ledger technology in its 2015 Report on Digital Currencies (https://www.bis.org/cpmi/publ/d137.pdf).

26. See PAFI Guiding Principle 3: *Financial and ICT infrastructures* for further guidance.
27. For background see *The World Bank Principles for Effective Insolvency and Creditor/Debtor Rights, 2016 (Principles A4 and A5)* at (http://documents.worldbank.org/curated/en/518861467086038847/Principles-for-effective-insolvency-and-creditor-and-debtor-regimes).
28. Leading examples include PAFI Guiding Principle 2: Legal and Regulatory Framework and PAFI Guiding Principle 6: Awareness and Financial Literacy; GPFI White Paper Recommendations 19 to 24 and Part IVB; and the G20 High-Level Principles on Financial Consumer Protection (http://www.oecd.org/daf/fin/financial-markets/48892010.pdf).
29. See definition of "e-money" in 2004 Committee on Payment and Settlement Systems Bank for International Settlements *Survey of Developments in Electronic Money and Internet and Mobile Payments* (section 2.1) (http://www.bis.org/cpmi/publ/d62.pdf).
30. The term *"financial literacy"* is defined as follows in the OECD/*INFE High-level Principles on National Strategies for Financial Education*, which were endorsed by G20 Leaders in 2012: "*a combination of financial awareness, knowledge, skills, attitude and behaviours necessary to make sound financial decisions and ultimately achieve individual financial wellbeing." See Atkinson and Messy (2012)*" (Footnote 4). (http://www.oecd.org/daf/fin/financial-education/OECD-INFE-Principles-National-Strategies-Financial-Education.pdf).

    The potentially broader term *"financial capability"* is defined as follows in the 2016 Basel Committee on Banking Supervision Consultative Document entitled "*Guidance on the application of the Core principles for effective banking supervision to the regulation and supervision of institutions relevant to financial inclusion*": "*World Bank (2013) defines financial capability as the internal capacity to act in one's best financial interest, given socioeconomic environmental conditions. It encompasses the knowledge, attitudes, skills and behaviours of consumers with respect to understanding, selecting and using financial services, and the ability to access financial services that fit their needs.*" (Footnote 79)

    Financial capability is mentioned as part of the quality of products and service delivery named as a key component of financial inclusion in responses to the survey the subject of the Bank of International Settlements report on *Range of Practice in the Regulation and Supervision of Institutions relevant to Financial Inclusion* (section 3.2) (http://www.bis.org/bcbs/publ/d310.pdf).
31. The 2015 G20 report on *Digital Financial Solutions to Advance Women's Economic Participation* prepared by the Better Than Cash Alliance.
32. The 2014 G20 report on *The Opportunities of Digitizing Payments* prepared by the World Bank Development Research Group, the Better Than Cash Alliance (BTCA), and the Bill & Melinda Gates Foundation.
33. https://www.betterthancash.org/tools-research/reports/digital-financial-solutions-to-advance-women-s-economic-participation
34. http://www.oecd.org/daf/fin/financial-education/OECD-INFE-Principles-National-Strategies-Financial-Education.pdf. See Principle IV**:** *Roadmap of the National Strategy: Key Priorities, Target Audiences, Impact Assessment And Resources.*
35. Target 16.9 under the Sustainable Development Goals provides: "By 2030, provide legal identity for all, including birth registration."
36. PAFI Report paragraphs 115 -117, Guiding Principle 3 Financial and ICT Infrastructures and GPFI White Paper Part IVD and Recommendation 26. See also the Key Finding in the 2015 GPFI Report on Digital Financial Solutions to Advance Women's Economic Participation concerning Government action and creation of a digital identification system.
37. The revised 2012 Financial Action Task Force (FATF) Recommendations mandate the use of risk-based customer identification requirements. See FATF Recommendation 10 and the related Interpretative Notes (http://www.fatf-gafi.org/media/fatf/documents/recommendations/pdfs/FATF_Recommendations.pdf).
38. See, for example, Priority Action 5 in the 2013 Women and Finance Progress Report to the G20 (http://www.g20australia.org/sites/default/files/g20_resources/library/G20_Women_and_Finance_Progress_report_WB_and_OECD.pdf).

A family learns how to use a mobile device to access financial services in a village in West Bengal, India.
Photo by Sudipto Das

GPFI
Global Partnership
for Financial Inclusion

G20
2016
CHINA

G20 GLOBAL PARTNERSHIP FOR FINANCIAL INCLUSION (GPFI)

Digital Financial Inclusion: Emerging Policy Approaches

ACKNOWLEDGEMENTS

This report was requested by the German G20 Presidency, and was prepared by the World Bank Group (Finance & Markets Global Practice) with substantive inputs from the following GPFI implementing partners: Consultative Group to Assist the Poor (CGAP), the Alliance for Financial Inclusion, and the Better than Cash Alliance.

The core drafting team from the World Bank Group comprised: Douglas Pearce, Loretta Michaels (consultant), Nomsa Kachingwe, and Sheirin Iravantchi.

Contributions and reviewer comments were also provided by:

- **Alliance for Financial Inclusion:** *Charles Marwa*
- **Banco Central de la República Argentina:** *Anabela Gómez*
- **Banque de France:** *Luc Jacolin*
- **Better than Cash Alliance:** *Ruth Goodwin-Groen*
- **Bill and Melinda Gates Foundation:** *SungAh Lee*
- **BMZ:** *Volker Hey*
- **Bundesbank:** *Jelena Stapf, Franziska Schobert*
- **CGAP:** *Xavier Faz, Gerhard Coetzee, Ivo Jenik, Louis de Koker (consultant), Anand Raman (consultant)*
- **Department of Foreign Affairs and Trade, Australia:** *Jayne Harries*
- **European Commission:** *Sirpa Tulla*
- **Financial Conduct Authority, UK:** *Thomas Ward*
- **GIZ:** *Albert Joscha, Wolfgang Buecker, Judith Frickenstein*
- **International Economics and Relations Directorate, Italy:** *Ricardo Settimo*
- **Ministry of the Treasury, Argentina:** *Estefanịa Campaniello*
- **People's Bank of China:** *Tiandu Wang*
- **SME Finance Forum:** *Matthew Gamser*
- **UK Department for International Development:** *Francesca Brown*
- **USAID:** *Matt Homer*
- **World Bank Group:** *Sebastian Molineus, Harish Natarajan, Massimo Cirasino, Jennifer Chien, Vyjayanti Desai, Lin Huang, Emile J. M. Van der Does de Willebois, Fredesvinda Montes Herraiz, Dorothee Delort, Timothy Kelly*

This report would not be possible without the generous support of the Netherlands' Ministry of Foreign Affairs.

Contents

Executive Summary

Digital financial services, together with effective oversight and supervision, can expand the scale, scope and reach of financial services, and are essential to closing the remaining gaps in financial inclusion. Digital technologies also offer affordable and convenient ways for individuals, households and businesses to save, make payments, access credit, and obtain insurance. In 2016, the G20's Global Partnership for Financial Inclusion (GPFI) published High Level Principles for Digital Financial Inclusion[1] (HLPs) which aimed to catalyze government actions to drive financial inclusion through a focus on digital technologies. This report outlines examples of how countries are implementing measures in line with the HLPs, with the first four over-arching HLPs providing the report structure.

High Level Principle 1 calls for promoting digital financial services as a priority to drive development of inclusive financial systems, including through coordinated national strategies and action plans. It emphasizes the need for policy leadership and coordination across the public and private sectors as critical for expanding financial inclusion, and stresses the importance of leading by example in the push for digital solutions. The report discusses below the wide-ranging, multi-faceted approaches taken by India, China, and other countries, to expand digital financial inclusion in their countries. In particular, India has made extensive efforts to expand its digital infrastructure to expand access to financial services, including through the Unique ID scheme and the Digital India program. China strongly encouraged the growth of non-bank payment players early on, particularly for the burgeoning ecommerce sector, and has made clear that it believes that digital finance can have a positive impact on traditional finance. Another common approach taken by these and many other governments to promote digital financial inclusion is digitizing Government-to-Person (G2P) payments, as illustrated by the experiences in Brazil, Turkey, and an increasing number of other countries.

High Level Principle 2 highlights that, while innovation in financial services is essential for expanding financial inclusion, it also introduces new risks – both individual and systemic— that need to be identified and effectively addressed in a timely fashion. Policymakers are addressing the innovation/risk balance through actions such as: expanded learning and information sharing between regulators and the private sector, including through "test and learn" piloting processes for introducing innovative services; new modes of engagement with industry and consumers, and efforts to better understand consumer experience around new digital distribution channels. The report outlines examples of test-and-learn approaches from the UK, the US and Kenya, as well as how insurance regulators are assessing new distribution channels such as mobile phones.

High Level Principle 3 notes that for digital financial services to flourish, there needs to be a legal and regulatory framework that is predictable, risk-based and fair; that allows for new entrants and is technology-neutral; and that does not impose excessive, non-risk-based compliance costs. Policymakers and regulators also need to ensure that the framework can be effectively and efficiently supervised with the requisite supervisory capacity and resources. Two key themes emerge: one is the increasing use of risk-based regulation and supervision, including a risk-based approach to customer due diligence (CDD) for the purposes of Anti-Money Laundering and Countering Terrorist Financing (AML/CFT). The other is a growing recognition that reporting and monitoring systems need to become more sophisticated, with a greater focus on direct linkages to financial institutions' information systems along with real-time monitoring capabilities and appropriate privacy and data protection. We discuss

[1] https://www.gpfi.org/publications/g20-high-level-principles-digital-financial-inclusion

examples of tiered regulation and CDD regimes from China, Mexico, and Tanzania, along with automated data reporting systems that are emerging out of Austria and Rwanda.

High Level Principle 4 emphasizes the need for policymakers and industry to work together to achieve a robust, open and efficient digital infrastructure, including a widely accessible retail payments system and ICT infrastructure. Areas of particular focus for national authorities include retail and online payments infrastructure that involve interoperable platforms linked to a wide range of POS, ATM and agent networks, bill payment platforms, credit reference systems, digital asset registries (particularly for movable assets) and, in some cases, the underlying communications infrastructure needed to support all these systems. The report highlights differing interoperability approaches taken in Peru and Tanzania, along with examples of credit reference systems in China and Mexico. The report also explores efforts by stakeholders in Kenya to expand merchant acceptance of digital payments instruments. Some regulators are also exploring the potential benefits, costs, and risks of issuing digital fiat currencies that could be used in a digital financial services ecosystem.

As is evident in the cases set out in this report, the increasing pace and complexity of innovation and adoption of digital technologies in the financial sector means that policy and regulatory approaches must also evolve and be tailored to country contexts. While no two countries are identical in their approach or their particular market context, there are a number of insights which can be gleaned from the examples highlighted in this report. These include:

- Proactive leadership and political will are cross-cutting success factors, including through integration and coordination across national authorities to address the range of issues relevant to harnessing digital technology.
- More progress on digital tools is needed, to help regulators do their job. As digital innovation is redefining what it is to be a service provider, financial regulators are having to take a more proactive, data-driven approach to engagement with the industry. Supervising digital financial service providers in an era of ever-increasing volumes of transactions (and increased use of fast or real time payment transactions) calls for more sophisticated and automated systems that can provide real-time monitoring and analysis.
- Promoting interoperable, open technology platforms for digital financial services helps establish a broad-based ecosystem for private and Government entities to better reach consumers and ultimately improve their financial lives. The means and timing of achieving interoperability can vary, but policymakers should make clear that it is an expectation.
- Digital identity forms an important foundation of public digital infrastructure and opens the door for access to services across the economy – including beyond financial services. National governments need to prioritize availability of robust and easily verifiable digital ID, whether biometric or other types of data-based forms, which can be used to facilitate access to digital financial services. There are valid concerns about privacy and civil liberties to be addressed, and emerging examples of effective ways to oversee issues such as data security, quality of service and network reliability.

1. Introduction

In recognition of the importance of new technologies and business models for expanding financial inclusion, the G20 developed the 2010 Principles for Innovative Financial Inclusion which spurred policy actions and national efforts towards facilitating innovation in financial services. Building on the 2010 Principles, the 2016 G20 High Level Principles for Digital Financial Inclusion (HLPs), produced by the G20's Global Partnership for Financial Inclusion (GPFI),[2] aimed to catalyze government actions to drive financial inclusion through a focus on digital technologies, and to provide a basis for country action plans and initiatives reflecting country context and national circumstances (see Box 1 for the headline HLPs).

The G20 HLPs set out suggested actions that countries can pursue to promote digital financial inclusion. Many countries are now implementing measures in line with the HLPs, including the introduction of country strategies to increase the use of digital financial services, efforts to foster innovation and manage potential risks through test-and-learn approaches, and the expansion of digital infrastructure, such as interoperable service platforms and information databases.

This report highlights such actions, with a focus on the roles of policymakers and regulators highlighted in the first four HLPs. HLPs 5 through 8 are addressed by other cross-agency GPFI implementing partner initiatives, such as the Responsible Finance Forum,[3] and the Identity for Development (ID4D[4]) program, and are therefore not discussed in this report. The report also summarizes insights from the selected cases, and notes where there are apparent implementation gaps. It is hoped that the country cases and analysis will help stimulate ideas, dialogue and information-sharing among policymakers across G20 and non-G20 countries.

The examples outlined in the report are not intended to be considered "best practice," as the use of digital technologies for financial inclusion is fast-evolving. Many of the profiled examples reflect actions under several HLPs, which indicates the wide-ranging nature of both opportunities and constraints for harnessing digital technologies to expand financial inclusion. There is no one-size-fits-all approach, but some common themes emerge from the examples covered in this report.

GPFI implementing partners actively support measures, consistent with the HLPs, to increase access and usage of financial services through new technologies. GPFI implementing partners which provide support to policy reforms and other measures taken by national authorities include the World Bank Group (World Bank and IFC), the Consultative Group to Assist the Poor (CGAP), the SME Finance Forum, the Alliance for Financial Inclusion (AFI)[5], and the UN-housed Better Than Cash Alliance (BTCA). The UN Secretary-General's Special Advocate for Inclusive Finance for Development, Her Majesty Queen Maxima, as patron of the GPFI, is also an influential proponent of actions which are consistent with the HLPs. The global Standard Setting Bodies (SSBs), with the support of the World Bank[6] and the GPFI,

[2] www.gpfi.org
[3] https://responsiblefinanceforum.org/
[4] http://www.worldbank.org/en/programs/id4d
[5] http://www.afi-global.org/working-groups/digital-financial-services-working-group
[6] http://www.worldbank.org/en/topic/paymentsystemsremittances/brief/pafi-task-force-and-report

are increasingly providing guidance and principles to guide national financial regulators in harnessing innovation and technology safely.[7]

Box 1. 2016 High Level Principles for Digital Financial Inclusion

- **Principle 1. Promote a Digital Approach to Financial Inclusion:** Promote digital financial services as a priority to drive development of inclusive financial systems, including through coordinated, monitored, and evaluated national strategies and action plans.
- **Principle 2. Balance Innovation and Risk to Achieve Digital Financial Inclusion:** Balance promoting innovation to achieve digital financial inclusion with identifying, assessing, monitoring and managing new risks.
- **Principle 3. Provide an Enabling and Proportionate Legal and Regulatory Framework for Digital Financial Inclusion:** Provide an enabling and proportionate legal and regulatory framework for digital financial inclusion, taking into account relevant G20 and international standard setting body standards and guidance.
- **Principle 4. Expand the Digital Financial Services Infrastructure Ecosystem:** Expand the digital financial services ecosystem—including financial and information and communications technology infrastructure—for the safe, reliable and low-cost provision of digital financial services to all relevant geographical areas, especially underserved rural areas.
- **Principle 5. Establish Responsible Digital Financial Practices to Protect Consumers:** Establish a comprehensive approach to consumer and data protection that focuses on issues of specific relevance to digital financial services.
- **Principle 6. Strengthen Digital and Financial Literacy and Awareness:** Support and evaluate programs that enhance digital and financial literacy in light of the unique characteristics, advantages, and risks of digital financial services and channels.
- **Principle 7. Facilitate Customer Identification for Digital Financial Services:** Facilitate access to digital financial services by developing, or encouraging the development of, customer identity systems, products and services that are accessible, affordable, and verifiable and accommodate multiple needs and risk levels for a risk-based approach to customer due diligence.

Principle 8. Track Digital Financial Inclusion Progress: Track progress on digital financial inclusion through a comprehensive and robust data measurement and evaluation system.

[7] A financial regulator task force chaired by the World Bank and the Committee on Payments and Market Infrastructures (CPMI) produced the 'Payment Aspects of Financial Inclusion' framework and guiding principles in 2016. A 2016 GPFI report outlined other SSB initiatives: http://www.gpfi.org/sites/default/files/documents/GPFI_WhitePaper_Mar2016.pdf

2. Emerging Policy and Regulatory Approaches to Digital Financial Inclusion

Financial inclusion involves multiple stakeholders, from policymakers and regulators to private industry, including employers, educational systems, communities and individuals. The responsibility of policymakers and regulators in this context, as set out in the HLPs, is to ensure that an open and enabling environment for financial services, from predictable laws and regulations to sound and accessible physical infrastructure, is in place while protecting consumers.

2.1. HLP 1: Promoting a Digital Approach to Financial Inclusion

High Level Principle 1 calls for promoting digital financial services as a priority to drive development of inclusive financial systems, including through coordinated and monitored national strategies and action plans. It emphasizes the need for policy leadership and coordination across the public and private sectors as critical for expanding financial inclusion, and stresses the importance of leading by example in the push for digital solutions.

There is broad global agreement on the importance of digitizing financial services, including to expand financial inclusion, as evidenced by the efforts and public statements of both global and national policymakers. There are a growing number of countries adopting national financial inclusion strategies that place a strong emphasis on the use of digital financial technologies (see Box 2 for examples). The 2016 Progress Report of the Maya Declaration indicated that 'digital financial services' featured in the top three thematic areas for targets and commitments made by AFI member countries in Sub-Saharan Africa and Asia.[8] National governments and large institutions are increasingly committing to digitization of their large government payment streams.[9]

Box 2. National Financial Inclusion Strategies with a Digital Focus

Pakistan launched its NFIS in 2015 with the vision to ensure individuals and firms can access and use a range of quality payments, savings, credit and insurance services which meet their needs with dignity and fairness. The NFIS emphasizes that "the vision aspires to having universal access to formal accounts, not limited to simply traditional savings and checking accounts but would also include digital transaction accounts (DTAs) such as branchless banking accounts." In addition, the Pakistan NFIS framework for action highlights DTAs as a key driver for financial inclusion, and explicitly outlines actions for expanding access to DTAs and expanding the scale and viability of DTAs through digitizing government payments.[10]

The NFIS launched by **Tanzania** in 2014 included, as core enablers for financial inclusion, the need for a "robust e-payments platform" as well as a "robust electronic information infrastructure for individual and business profiles, credit history and collateral."[11] Actions related to building these enablers included developing regulations for mobile financial services, supporting market efforts for achieving payments interoperability, and

[8] 2016 Maya Declaration Report. Available at: http://www.afi-global.org/publications/2359/The-2016-Maya-Declaration-Report

[9] As of the end of 2016, the Better Than Cash Alliance counted 54 members that had committed to BTCA's digital payment principles. https://www.betterthancash.org/news/newsletters#filters

[10] Pakistan National Financial Inclusion Strategy 2015. Available at: http://pubdocs.worldbank.org/en/232671435258828008/Pakistan-National-Financial-Inclusion-Strategy-2015.pdf

[11] Tanzania National Financial Inclusion Strategy 2014 –2016. Available at: http://www.afi-global.org/sites/default/files/publications/tanzania-national-financial-inclusion-framework-2014-2016.pdf

implementing risk-based customer due diligence (CDD) among other actions (further discussed in Section 2.3).

In the **Philippines**, the NFIS launched in 2015 also takes note of the role of technology and other innovations in reaching the financially excluded. The NFIS also includes as a regulatory strategy, promoting interoperability in technology-based solutions, including in retail payments and G2P payments.[12]

In **China**, the Plan for Promoting the Development of Financial Inclusion launched at the end of 2015 outlines an ambitious agenda for improving the availability, uptake, and quality of financial products and services, with a clear focus on digital technology. It encourages digital innovations in financial products and service, the usage of new technology (such as big data and cloud computing) in financial institutions, and employing internet as a key tool for achieving accessibility and affordability of financial services.[13]

In **Mexico**, the National Financial Inclusion Policy was approved by the National Financial Inclusion Council in June 2016. One of its main objectives is to harness technology to connect low-income individuals to the financial system through a regulatory framework that allows innovation and fosters soundness and stability of the financial system. In this respect, the Policy defines a set of actions aimed at using technological innovations to improve financial inclusion, including, among others, a thorough revision and updating of the current regulatory framework to allow the entrance of new finance providers and the provision of financial services through new channels, the promotion of mechanisms that reduce usage of cash and increase usage of digital financial products and services, and fostering interconnectivity of digital financial services.[14]

Other NFIS also recognize the importance of technology and digital financial services in reaching the unbanked and underserved market, and some strategies currently under preparation (for example, Zambia and Jamaica) are actively incorporating digital aspects of financial inclusion into their strategies.

Public strategies and commitments, of course, need to be followed up by concrete actions that encourage innovative, appropriate product offerings by service providers along with faster, easier and safer uptake by users. Such policy actions should not only promote usage, but also help remove or mitigate issues that hinder access to financial services. India and China have implemented wide-ranging initiatives in recent years, and are prominent cases covered in this section, and in the report more broadly. A common HLP1-consistent approach taken by governments to promote digital financial inclusion is digitizing Government-to-Person (G2P) payments, as illustrated by the experiences in Brazil, Turkey, and an increasing number of other countries.

The cases set out in this section illustrate the need for strong policy leadership and effective coordination across financial sector regulators and policymakers, ICT regulators, national ID authorities, payments service providers, and other relevant stakeholders, in order to ensure that the regulatory framework and infrastructure ecosystem are conducive to digital financial inclusion. Clarifying the policy priorities for, and approach to, supporting digital financial services, through issuing Guidelines or developing a strategy for digital financial inclusion, can be effective in catalyzing and informing actions by a wide range of stakeholders.

The India Stack: A Multi-Stakeholder Approach to Digital Financial Inclusion

A prominent country example that reaches across all the HLPs, but especially HLP 1, comes from India. As part of the "Digital India Programme," which was formally launched in July 2015, the Government of India embarked on several initiatives aimed at expanding the digital

[12] Philippines National Financial Inclusion Strategy 2016. Available at: http://www.bsp.gov.ph/downloads/publications/2015/PhilippinesNSFIBooklet.pdf

[13] http://pubdocs.worldbank.org/en/911391453407695993/CHINESE-Advancing-Financial-Inclusion-in-China-Five-Year-Plan-2016-2020.pdf; http://www.cbrc.gov.cn/EngdocView.do?docID=14667AC65F6444079F404024229CD810

[14] Mexico National Financial Inclusion Policy 2016. Available (in Spanish) at: http://www.gob.mx/cms/uploads/attachment/file/110408/PNIF_ver_1jul2016CONAIF_vfinal.pdf

economy, including facilitating digital financial inclusion.[15] Observers have dubbed the combination of the many technology initiatives undertaken by both Government and non-Government stakeholders, including those pre dating the launch of the Digital India programme, the "India Stack" (see Box 3). Core elements of the stack focus on generating greater efficiency in the delivery of G2P social transfers, e.g., subsidies and social cash transfers, as well as on removing barriers to financial access, including limited access to formal ID documentation, bank branches or agents, and to credit for micro-entrepreneurs and SMEs.

Box 3. Elements of the India Stack

The India Stack is an open digital infrastructure platform that makes use of open Application Programming Interfaces (APIs)[16] to promote "presence-less, paperless, and cashless delivery" of services across different sectors of the economy.[17] The India Stack is built on four technology layers:

- *Presence-less layer* which leverages India's Aadhaar unique identification and authentication system to enable remote and real-time identification and verification of individuals and businesses;
- *Paper-less layer* which is comprised of a "Digital Locker" and "Digital Signature" (or e-Signature) and enables entities to share documents and enter into contracts digitally and remotely;
- *Cash-less layer* which is based on the recently developed Unified Payments Interface and which allows for real-time and interoperable payments across all bank accounts and mobile wallets. Transactions can be stored, and transaction histories shared, for example, with credit providers to enable alternative credit-scoring models; and
- *Consent layer* which, while not yet complete, will enable individuals to share data of their choosing, or to allow time-bound and identity-verified access to their data, but only with their consent.

While the India Stack is itself an innovative platform approach that can significantly expand access to digital financial services, it builds on the initiatives undertaken by several Government departments, as well as by other public authorities and non-government stakeholders. Initiatives undertaken by the Government and other public authorities include:

- In 2009, the Unique Identification Authority of India (UIDAI) launched the Aadhaar ID scheme, which has provided a unique biometric identity to over 1 billion people. The ID scheme captures biometric information from individuals, including iris scans and thumbprints, and issues a unique 12-digit ID number to each individual.[18] The UIDAI has also developed an e-KYC platform based on the Aadhaar ID database;
- In 2014, the Government launched the Pradhan Mantri Jan Dhan Yojana (PMJDY) scheme, to provide basic bank accounts to all Indians above the age of 10 years,[19] largely for the disbursement of welfare benefits, but also to facilitate access to a broader range of financial services. By February 2017, the PMJDY scheme had registered 273.9 million bank accounts;[20]

---

[15] The Digital India Programme builds on e-Governance initiatives introduced in the 1990s, and the National e-Governance Plan launched in 2006. http://digitalindia.gov.in

[16] *Application Program Interface* (API) is a set of routines, protocols, and tools for building software applications. An API specifies how software components should interact. An open API allows for vendor neutral access to technology platforms.

[17] http://indiastack.org/about/

[18] https://uidai.gov.in/new/

[19] http://pmjandhanyojana.co.in/

[20] https://www.pmjdy.gov.in/account

- In 2015, the Controller of Certifying Authorities (CCA), under the Ministry of Electronics and Information Technology, launched e-Sign to enable Aadhaar holders to digitally sign a document;[21] and
- Also in 2015, the Reserve Bank of India (RBI) licensed new categories of financial institution, namely payment banks and small finance banks, to further expand access to transaction accounts;
- In 2016, the National e-Governance Commission, under the Ministry of Electronics and Information Technology, launched the Digital Locker (DigiLocker) platform to facilitate digital issuance and verification of documents;[22] and
- Also in 2016, the Ministry of Finance issued a Cabinet Note to provide guidelines for the promotion of card and digital payments, as well as to coordinate various Government initiatives aimed at encouraging digital transactions.[23] A Committee on Digital Payments (also referred to as the Watal Committee)[24] was established to review the digital payments framework in India, and to provide further recommendations to stimulate the growth of digital payments.[25]

Non-government initiatives that have supported the development of the India Stack, and have contributed to digital financial inclusion, include:

- The National Payments Corporation of India (NPCI) launched the Aadhaar Payments Bridge and Aadhaar Enabled Payments System in 2011, which uses the Aadhaar ID as a central key for electronically channeling Government benefits and subsidies;[26] and
- The Indian Software Product Industry Roundtable (iSPIRT), a non-governmental organization aimed at promoting the Indian software industry, was established in 2013 and has been instrumental in promoting the development of APIs and supporting systems for the India Stack.

The coordinated cross-government approach taken to developing the foundations of the India Stack has not only resulted in a significant increase in the number of individuals with access to digital transaction accounts and other financial services[27] as indicated above, but it has also enabled the Government to digitize the delivery of subsidies and social welfare payments, resulting in estimated savings of close to Rs 50 billion (USD 750 million) as of December 2016.[28]

Authorities still face challenges, of course, in leveraging the India Stack for financial inclusion. For example, last-mile challenges of delivering services in rural/remote areas remain, with continuing low density of banking correspondent or agent networks.[29] At the same time, newly-licensed MNO-led payment banks face challenges in re-orienting their agent networks, long used to providing airtime and SIM registration services, to providing financial services.[30]

---

[21] http://cca.gov.in/cca/?q=eSign.html
[22] https://digilocker.gov.in/
[23] http://dea.gov.in/sites/default/files/Promo_PaymentsMeans_Card_Digital_0.pdf
[24] http://dea.gov.in/sites/default/files/Constitution_Committee_digitalpayments.pdf
[25] http://www.finmin.nic.in/reports/watal_report271216.pdf
[26] http://www.npci.org.in/
[27] Through the PJMDY accounts, the Government of India also provides insurance and pensions to individuals.
[28] https://dbtbharat.gov.in/
[29] http://indiabudget.nic.in/es2015-16/echapvol1-03.pdf
[30] http://www.cgap.org/blog/how-india%E2%80%99s-new-payments-banks-stack

China: Promoting Digital Financial Services

A country that has focused particular attention on promoting digital financial solutions is China, and its digital finance sector has expanded rapidly in recent years. The Chinese regulatory authorities allowed space for the nascent industry to innovate and grow, with the prior development of electronic payments and e-commerce through entities such as China Union Pay, Alibaba and wholesaler DHGate all enabling the incorporation of merchants into an extensive digital ecosystem. It was not until 2010 – six years after the launch of Alipay – that the People's Bank of China (PBOC) issued key regulations addressing non-bank payment services, setting out licensing requirements and procedures covering topics such as minimum capital requirements and investor requirements. Five years later, in July 2015, China's four financial regulators, the Ministry of Finance and several other agencies, jointly issued the *Guidelines on Promoting Sound Development of Internet Finance* ("Guidelines"),[31] establishing six goals for the internet (digital) finance[32] sector:

- Promoting innovation via internet finance platforms, products, and services and encouraging existing financial institutions to adopt new technology;
- Encouraging cooperation between financial institutions and technology companies;
- Improving access to capital for internet finance firms through promoting venture capital, SME finance, and public listings;
- Reducing administrative approvals and other barriers to development and providing an enabling regulatory environment;
- Implementing an appropriate tax system for firms in the industry that benefits small firms and encourages investment in new technology; and
- Encouraging the participation of internet finance companies in the development of a national credit information infrastructure.

In so doing, the Chinese government clarified its position on the development of internet finance, i.e., that promoting new financial technologies can positively impact traditional finance. It also balanced promotion of digital finance with new guidelines for reducing emerging risks such as fraud, money laundering, illegal fundraising, and the unauthorized disclosure of users' personal information. The Guidelines further clarified the regulatory mandates of different financial regulators with respect to Internet finance. PBOC is responsible for the regulatory oversight of Internet-based payments; the China Banking Regulatory Commission (CBRC) is responsible for oversight of online lending, Internet-based trust products, and Internet-based consumer finance; the China Securities Regulatory Commission (CSRC) is responsible for oversight of equity-based crowd-funding and Internet fund business; and the China Insurance Regulatory Commission (CIRC) is responsible for oversight of Internet insurance.[33]

The PBOC subsequently issued rules, "Administrative Measures for Internet Payment Services of Non-Banking Payment Institutions," in December 2015 for the internet payments industry following the release of the guidance document for public comment, setting out new rules on CDD, online payments usage, daily payments values, transaction values in function of verification, disclosure, etc. These rules went into effect in July, 2016. (See HLP 3.)

---

[31] http://www.pbc.gov.cn/goutongjiaoliu/113456/113469/2813898/index.html (in Chinese)

[32] China uses the term internet finance to encompass digital financial services

[33] Joint PBOC - World Bank Report (forthcoming): "Towards Universal Financial Inclusion in China: Models, Challenges, and Global Lessons".

In the years leading up to China's Guidelines and new rules on Internet Finance, it was also making a concerted effort to expand digital points of service in rural areas. In 2010, the PBOC launched a pilot program to test withdrawal services for farmers using bankcards and point-of-sale (POS) devices, and in 2014 allowed users to add remittances and bill payment services. In order to promote electronic payments and e-commerce in rural areas, PBOC has also made efforts to encourage resource-sharing between withdrawal service points and e-commerce outlets in rural areas. By the end of 2016, the number of rural withdrawal service points across China had reached 983,400, covering more than 500,000 (or over 90% of) administrative villages. In 2016, these service points conducted a total of 255 million payment transactions, amounting to RMB 120B.

Digitizing Government-to-Person Payments: Brazil, Mexico, and others

A far-reaching and catalytic example is the shift towards digitizing G2P payments, and in particular social safety net or social cash transfers. Many countries now have initiatives to deliver G2P payments using electronic means, and country cases are widely documented.[34] For example, in Brazil, the Bolsa Familia conditional cash transfer program reaches nearly 14 million households through an electronic benefit card, and was initiated back in 2003;[35] while in Mexico, the Federal government has centralized its payments and increased the share of these that are provided digitally, including some social benefits, through transaction accounts.[36] Other countries that have shifted or are in the process of shifting from cash to electronic G2P payments include Pakistan, South Africa, Kenya, Uganda, India, Nepal, Haiti, Colombia, Bangladesh and several others.

Digitizing government payments is a catalytic means of promoting digital financial services, but is also a wide-ranging endeavor that requires careful planning. Where such initiatives have been successful, there has been concerted effort by policymakers to adopt a coordinated approach, including with NGOs and donors as well as with private sector service providers. Insights from the implementation of well-established initiatives, such as in Brazil and Mexico, suggest that:

- Successful G2P initiatives are often one element of a larger plan to digitize and centralize Government payments and to promote the use of electronic payments in the economy;
- Building internal automated systems for managing social welfare programs should be conducted in parallel, if not before, the rollout of digital G2P payment programs;
- Adequate design of products in which beneficiaries receive G2P transfers is critical for beneficiaries to actively use digital devices to make and receive payments and transfers with the funds they receive in their accounts, instead of only cashing out such funds the moment they receive them;

[34] The forthcoming G20 GPFI "Guidance Note on Building Inclusive Digital Payments Ecosystems" will be a valuable further reference.

[35] IDB (2015). How Does Bolsa Familia Work? Best Practices in the Implementation of Conditional Cash Transfer Programs in Latin America and the Caribbean. Available at: https://publications.iadb.org/bitstream/handle/11319/7210/How_does_Bolsa_Familia_Work.pdf?sequence=5

[36] For instance, while all of the registered beneficiaries of the main conditional cash transfer program in the country (PROSPERA – formerly) are opened a bank account when they enroll into the program as of, April 2017 about 81 percent receive a program-related debit card with limited functionality which can only be used as an identification tool to receive their corresponding transfer in cash from government agents. The remaining 19 percent do receive a fully functional debit card, which they can use to access their program-related deposits in a standard way so that they can make payments or cash withdrawals with their card. Likewise, about 50 percent of all old-age transfers recipients receive their transfers fully in cash, while the remaining 50 percent receive them in a standard bank account, and they can access these funds with a standard debit card.

- Building a digital ecosystem that reaches beneficiaries where they live and work, including ATMs, POS devices and incentivizing merchant acceptance of digital payments, including online payments, is key; and
- Coordinated efforts to raise financial awareness and capability are needed to empower beneficiaries, especially women who may lack control of their own cellphones, to use new digital financial services beyond the receipt of G2P payments.

2.2. HLP 2: Balancing Risk and Innovation to Achieve Digital Financial Inclusion

High Level Principle 2 highlights that, while innovation in financial services is essential for expanding financial inclusion, it also introduces new risks – both individual and systemic— that need to be identified and effectively addressed in a timely fashion. Policymakers need to encourage and nurture innovation to harness the many benefits it enables, particularly for financially excluded and underserved groups. They also need to recognize that new risks will be an inevitable element of such innovation and that both old and new risks need to be addressed and mitigated. This recognition that not all risk can be eliminated is increasingly important as global policymakers focus on building cyber resilience into financial markets and work to safeguard the financial system from illicit activities.

Policymakers are addressing the innovation/risk balance through actions such as: learning and information sharing between regulators, development of digital supervision tools for regulators, engaging with private sector innovators, and finding new modes of engagement with industry and consumers.

Cases are emerging of regulators working with industry to design new tools and processes that not only streamline companies' compliance requirements, but essentially redesign how the regulators collect and monitor the data. (This is discussed in more detail under HLP 3.) More commonly, many regulators are revisiting how they regulate some financial services in light of the new digital distribution channels that service providers are using, by revising existing rules and/or, in the case of some new categories of services, choosing to allow limited pilots before making any regulatory decisions.

The rapid pace of growth in digital financial services requires regulators and policymakers to be proactive in engaging with industry to ensure that while new innovations expand the reach of financial services to new market segments and through new channels, potential risks to consumer protection, inclusion, market integrity and investor confidence, and financial stability are sufficiently addressed.

The examples illustrated in this section highlight that there are multiple and various approaches that regulators can take to balancing the risks and benefits of innovation for digital financial inclusion. Some regions like the EU are conducting public consultations and establishing task forces on how to address the topic.[37] Others are choosing to create a framework for experimentation, whether through the existing regulatory regime, a newly structured test and learn environment or through informal engagement processes, that can enable the development of digital financial services that meet the needs of customers, while at the same time limiting potential risks.

[37] https://ec.europa.eu/info/files/consumer-financial-services-action-plan-better-products-more-choice_en

Test and Learn Approaches in Kenya, USA and UK

One of the biggest changes for regulators in this new digital environment is how they interact with the industry they oversee and the consumers who are served by that industry. The speed of innovation in financial services, both in terms of product design as well as the types and numbers of new players involved, has introduced risks that challenge traditional approaches to the key regulatory objectives of financial stability, integrity, customer protection and financial inclusion.

A prominent example of how regulators are responding to new digital services innovation is the development of regulatory piloting efforts, for allowing new services to be introduced or tested, including those that might not fit into traditional oversight categories. The overall concept of allowing for such "testing" is not new. Notably, the Central Bank of Kenya (CBK) allowed mobile operator Safaricom to introduce its M-Pesa mobile payment service in 2007, without a regulatory framework yet in place.

The test and learn concept is now being tried in multiple countries for digital technologies in the financial sector. In the UK, a "Regulatory Sandbox" was established by the Financial Conduct Authority (FCA), under the auspices of their Project Innovate program. The FCA's Sandbox is intended not as a way to avoid or negate regulation, but to provide a safe space for firms to test innovative products, services, business models and mechanisms of delivery, while ensuring that consumers are adequately protected.

At the same time that the FCA's Project Innovate was getting started, the US Consumer Financial Protection Board (CFPB) was embarking on a similar initiative. The CFPB's Project Catalyst "encourage[s] consumer-friendly innovation in markets for consumer financial products and services" by providing several unique engagement opportunities for innovators.[38] For example, the CFPB regularly conducts informal "office hours," and recently announced a public inquiry[39] into alternative credit data to expand access to credit for underserved customers. The CFPB also lets innovators conduct pilot programs in a sandbox-like setting, so new ways of meeting regulatory or disclosure requirements can be studied jointly by both the agency and the company.

The pilot programs are viewed as a valuable learning mechanism for the CFPB. As part of the pilots, they are provided significant amounts of data. This has spillover effects to other policy efforts by advancing the CFPB's understanding of consumer behavior and financial innovation, including whether or which aspects of innovations may be beneficial to certain segments of consumers. Another US regulator, the Office of the Comptroller of the Currency (OCC), in 2016 launched a "Responsible Innovation" initiative and has indicated that they intend to make national (as opposed to state-level) banking charters available to fintech companies, among other pro-innovation activities.[40]

Since the UK and US announcements regarding the launch of testing frameworks, a number of jurisdictions have also launched their own initiatives (Australia, Hong Kong, Malaysia, Singapore, Thailand, United Arab Emirates) or announced an intention to establish one soon (Indonesia, Kenya, Switzerland). Low and middle-income countries are also establishing sandbox-like programs aimed at promoting fintech innovation, often with the aim of expanding financial inclusion, particularly into unserved rural areas. It's not just bank regulators looking at this concept, either; insurance regulators are also taking a test and learn

---

[38] http://www.consumerfinance.gov/about-us/project-catalyst/

[39] https://www.consumerfinance.gov/about-us/newsroom/cfpb-explores-impact-alternative-data-credit-access-consumers-who-are-credit-invisible/

[40] https://www.occ.treas.gov/topics/bank-operations/innovation/index-innovation.html

approach. In Ghana, for example, the National Insurance Commission (NIC) allows mobile-insurance products to be tested on a case-by-case basis, checking the commercialization agreements between the MNO, the Technical Service Provider and Insurer in advance and closely monitoring activities thereafter.

While approaches to test and learn vary by name and design, most of them share a similar objective: creating a framework for experimentation and innovation in a small-scale, controlled environment to promote the growth and competitiveness of the (innovative) financial sector in favor of consumers. Two common attributes of test and learn approaches are:

- Structured communication between the regulator and the firm operating in the test and learn environment (sometimes called the "sandbox entity") in which the regulator advises the sandbox entity on legal and regulatory requirements and, in some cases, issues temporary exemptions and waivers; and
- The monitored testing of innovations under a controlled environment.

The issue of regulatory capacity to properly oversee such programs will be critical. The capacity to balance risk and innovation to achieve digital financial inclusion, while ensuring financial stability, integrity and consumer protection is crucial for regulators. Regulators who are contemplating a regulatory sandbox or 'greenhouse' should therefore carefully consider all the options available and compare their costs and overall benefits, as well as compatibility with the existing legal and regulatory framework, and their capacity to implement. As they strive to encourage innovation through such methods, regulators also need to take care to avoid creating market-distorting excessive 'first mover' advantages. Setting timely constraints on the experimental phase in advance might help to limit those distorting effects.

Box 4. UK Financial Conduct Authority's Regulatory Sandbox

The UK's FCA wanted to encourage innovation in financial services, in order to promote more effective competition. It therefore wanted to encourage firms to develop creative solutions in a controlled environment of lowered regulatory requirements. The FCA felt that without providing some degree of official regulatory sanction for such piloting, industry players would not invest the time and resources needed for developing innovative services. A safe testing environment, or "sandbox," would enable a test-and-learn approach to new and innovative services, but within the confines of approved pilot parameters, oversight and information sharing that would allow flexibility but limit risk. In designing the program, the FCA sought to address two main challenges— how to deliver a sandbox that lowers barriers to testing within the existing regulatory framework; and how to ensure that the risks from testing novel solutions were not transferred to consumers.

The resulting Sandbox program is aimed at both "unauthorized" (i.e., unregulated) businesses that need authorization before testing their services, as well as authorized firms looking for clarity around applicable rules before testing an idea that does not easily fit into the existing regulatory framework. In the case of unauthorized firms, they can be granted restricted authorization that only allows them to test their ideas. These firms still need to apply for authorization and meet threshold conditions, but only for the limited purposes of the sandbox test.[41] For authorized firms, the Sandbox has three tools: individual guidance; waivers or modifications to the FCA's rules where the rules are deemed burdensome (but not waivers to national or international law); and/or, in selected cases, no enforcement action letters (NALs). Such letters would only be issued where the FCA feels it is unable to issue individual guidance or waivers but believes it is justified in light of the particular circumstances and characteristics of different sandbox tests. The letter would only apply for the duration of the sandbox test, only to FCA disciplinary action and will not limit any liabilities to consumers.

The FCA set out specific criteria which have to be met by firms as a prerequisite for entry to the sandbox:

[41] https://www.handbook.fca.org.uk/handbook/COND.pdf

- **Genuine Innovation**. Is the new solution genuinely novel, or significantly different to existing offerings?
- **Consumer Benefit**. Is there a good prospect of identifiable benefit to consumers? This criterion has to be met throughout the 6-month period of testing.
- **Is the Firm in Scope**? Is the new solution designed for, or supportive of, the financial services industry?
- **Need for Sandbox Testing**. Is there a genuine need for testing within the sandbox framework?
- **Readiness to Test**. Is the proposition at a sufficiently advanced stage of preparation to warrant live testing?

In November 2016, the FCA announced that out of 69 applications, it had accepted 24 applicants to the first cohort of its sandbox program. The 24 fintech firms selected came from a diverse range of countries, including Singapore, Denmark, USA and Canada, included both incumbents and new players, and covered a broad range of sectors such as payment and blockchain firms, retail banking, mortgages and insurance, advice, profiling and disclosure, international public offerings, and digital identity.

Access to insurance expanded through digital channels

There is increasing attention on the potential to harness digital technologies to expand access to insurance, including through alternative digital channels such as mobile network operators (MNOs). For most MNO offerings, insurance is often provided only as a means of attracting new customers and encouraging customer loyalty, although many products are evolving from the loyalty approach to freemium and paid products. Africa in particular has seen significant growth via these channels, with five out of seven high-growth products launched between 2011 and 2014 being distributed via MNOs. In terms of specific products for the non-G20 countries we are focusing on in this report, life, accident and health micro-insurance constitute the majority of the market, although there are regional variations (e.g., in Asia, life and personal accident dominate, while in Latin America, credit life has long been the dominant product).[42] Most initial mobile-insurance product offerings started out as simple life and accident covers, but over time these became increasingly diverse, and some schemes now include personal accident, agriculture, and hospitalization covers, among others, often as bundled risks.

While MNOs are playing an increasingly significant role in micro-insurance offerings, they are so far largely acting as distribution channels, often in partnership with Technical Service Providers (TSPs) such as BIMA and MicroEnsure, leaving commercial insurers as the dominant risk carriers. TSPs play a crucial role in mobile-insurance partnerships and assume key functions across the insurance value chain. In some cases, all functions except underwriting (with the insurer) is outsourced to a TSP. In cases such as these, with multiple players involved, insurance regulators are seeking to provide greater oversight through increased cooperation and collaboration with telecommunications regulators.

For example, in Ghana, the Deutsche Gesellschaft für Internationale Zusammenarbeit (GIZ) GmbH on behalf of the German Federal Ministry for Economic Cooperation and Development (BMZ), supported the National Insurance Commission (insurance regulator) to conduct a detailed risk assessment of the mobile insurance landscape and developed a risk framework to improve the regulatory guidelines for mobile insurance products. The assessment resulted in the National Insurance Commission (insurance regulator) entering into a memorandum of understanding (MOU) with the Bank of Ghana (central bank) and the National Communications Authority (telecommunications supervisor) to approve micro-

[42] For further information, see
https://a2ii.org/sites/default/files/field/uploads/lessons_from_a_decade_of_microinsurance_regulation_a2ii_nov_2016.pdf

insurance distribution agreements between the MNO and the insurer.[43] Furthermore, the National Insurance Commission drafted Market Conduct Rules for Insurers and Corporate Agents, which balances the regulation of market development to protect policy holders and mobile network subscribers against the maintenance of conducive market development incentives. In a few markets, however, MNOs are seeking their own micro-insurance licenses, sometimes as partnerships with TSPs or directly with insurance providers[44]: MNOs BIMA-Milvik in Cambodia and Vodacom SA in South Africa, respectively, have set up as commercial insurers offering micro-insurance.[45] These types of players are a relatively recent market phenomenon, and it will be interesting to see whether MNOs and regulators favor this approach over MNOs playing a distribution-only role.

2.3. HLP 3: Creating an Enabling Legal and Regulatory Framework

High Level Principle 3 notes that for digital financial services to flourish, there needs to be a legal and regulatory framework that is predictable, risk-based and fair; allows for new entrants and is technology-neutral; and does not impose excessive, non-risk-based compliance costs. Policymakers and regulators also need to ensure that the framework can be effectively and efficiently supervised with the requisite supervisory capacity and resources.

There have been a number of positive developments in recent years aimed at expanding the breadth and reach of services for the unbanked through regulations that encourage innovation and open up a greater role for new, non-bank players. This is seen for example in digital payments, agent banking, and separating intermediation from payments. Many observers have termed these developments a "functional" approach to regulation, with a focus on the services in question as opposed to the type of entity providing the service (i.e., an "institutional" approach).

A prominent early example of this approach is the European Union's Payment Services Directive (PSD), adopted in 2007 and updated with PSD2 in 2015, aimed at easing market entry for new payment players, improving transparency, and harmonizing EU member state regulations to further promote competition and innovation by opening the European retail payment market to emerging fintechs, and improve consumer protection.[46] In particular, PSD2 introduced graduated requirements for payments players proportionate to the size of business and scale of risks, in order to support innovation while adequately protecting consumers.

Another regulatory development aimed at expanding the reach of financial services is the adoption of the risk-based approach by the Financial Action Task Force (FATF) requiring the calibration of AML/CFT regulatory, compliance and oversight measures to mitigate the actual risk posed by providers, customers, products and services. While there are many facets to the risk based approach, a common method of adopting it within a financial inclusion framework is through the use of tiered Customer Due Diligence (CDD) regimes, which allow for increasing levels of CDD as the functionality of products and services increases. Functionality, in turn, can be controlled through maximum balance and transaction limits as well as usage restrictions.

In addition, as non-bank payment service providers expand their activities, regulators are rethinking how they oversee and supervise these entities. Non-bank digital payments services

---

[43] http://www.ghananewsagency.org/economics/care-international-focuses-on-improving-financial-inclusion--110343
[44] https://a2ii.org/sites/default/files/field/uploads/lessons_from_a_decade_of_microinsurance_regulation_a2ii_nov_2016.pdf
[45] BMZ 2015, Wiedmaier-Pfister and Leach
[46] https://ec.europa.eu/info/business-economy-euro/banking-and-finance/consumer-finance-and-payments/payment-services_en

are not new as such, given the long-standing use of limited purpose stored-value cards, or the advent of payment companies like PayPal in 1998. But these earlier electronic payment services tended to be supported by either closed-loop systems, in the case of store cards or transit system payment cards, or relied on direct linkages to bank accounts, as in the case of PayPal. What is new is the broad acceptance and recognition of non-bank players for the provision of open-loop payments and transaction accounts using digital means. The rapid growth of general purpose reloadable prepaid cards, particularly in the US, and the use of mobile money systems in many parts of the world, especially Africa, has demonstrated to regulators the massive, untapped demand for simple, low-cost, easy-to-use transaction accounts that don't require users to open traditional bank accounts. It has also led to a gradual rethink of how to best bring the unbanked into the formal financial services market, from the traditional focus on microcredit and group savings to the provision of personal transaction accounts utilizing electronic funds, or "e-money." A number of countries have instituted guidelines around the use of e-money over the last ten years, and the trend will no doubt continue.

Two key themes that emerge are the increasing use of risk-based regulation and supervision, including the risk-based approach to CDD, and a growing recognition that reporting and monitoring systems need to become more sophisticated, with a greater focus on direct linkages to financial institutions' information systems (where feasible) along with real-time monitoring capabilities and appropriate privacy and data protection.

An example of new risk-based regulation for digital financial services is a recent set of moves by the PBOC, which issued new rules at the end of 2015 governing online payments by non-banks, "Administrative Measures for Internet Payment Services of Non-Banking Payment Institutions".

Box 5. Tiered Regulation and Industry Self-Regulation

Effective July 2016, China's new rules tighten the CDD requirements for non-bank payments, with three tiers established, including real-name registration of all accounts and increasing levels of scrutiny as transaction levels increase. Perhaps most intriguing in the new rules is the concept of tiered regulation of payment platforms. There is greater scrutiny on the verification methods used by the platforms for identification, with tighter methods being awarded higher ratings by the PBOC. The PBOC will rate each payment platform based on their own analysis and categorization scheme, and platforms with higher ratings will have fewer restrictions, whereas platforms with lower ratings will face extra scrutiny from regulators. Another advantage for platforms with higher ratings is that daily limits for users could be increased by up to double the standard limit as defined in the regulations. (Annual limits remain unchanged by the tiered system.)

Along with instituting new rules for digital payments providers, the PBOC supported the establishment of the China National Internet Finance Association (NIFA) as a way to self-police the industry. Guided by the PBOC and registered as a "national Level One association" under the Ministry of Civil Affairs, the group has 408 member institutions, including banks, securities companies, funds, insurance, trusts and consumer finance companies, and non-bank payment service providers, along with other related organizations, such as guarantee companies, credit services and Internet peer-to-peer lending companies. The charter of the association includes establishing industry standards and operational rules by sub categories, promoting information sharing and communication within the industry, defining self-regulatory content and penalty mechanisms, and strengthening the legal and compliance culture of the industry. In September 2016, the NIFA also launched their Credit Information Sharing platform to capture and share customer data, without sharing the underlying individual customer information. When the system receives a request, it will send a query out to all members and collate the data, without divulging the source of the data, thus protecting competitive information.

Tiered CDD Regimes

As mentioned above, an important manifestation of the risk based approach for digital financial inclusion is the tiered Customer Due Diligence (CDD) regime.[47] CDD is the process of identification and verification of individuals and businesses undertaking financial transactions, including ongoing customer due diligence and monitoring of transactions, in order to detect transactions that may involve illicit financial activities, such as money laundering or the financing of terrorism. National authorities increasingly recognize that appropriate and proportionate CDD systems are an important factor in staving off de-risking trends.

While the critical importance of an effective CDD regime is clear, there is acknowledgement that stringent CDD rules have at times prevented poor and rural users from accessing formal financial services. The traditional rules for opening new deposit accounts often entail a number of requirements that poor people find hard to meet (e.g., the need to verify identity and provide proof or address and source of income). In addition, CDD requirements may be costly, especially in relation to low margin clients (e.g., where they entail handling paper-based forms, conducting a personal interview, or expensive software to monitor transactions). Policymakers and regulators now recognize that lower risk transactions, such as low-value payments, can be subjected to simplified CDD rules without jeopardizing anti-money laundering and countering terrorist financing (AML/CFT) objectives. Using a tiered approach with increasing CDD requirements for increased product functionality helps to mitigate risks efficiently, while also bringing low income consumers into the formal financial sector.[48]

While regulators have been mulling the issue of appropriate simplified CDD for some time (South Africa's tiered approach dates back to the adoption of Exemption 17 in 2002, which allowed banks to drop the proof of address requirements for a basic account with limited functionality),[49] formal SSB recognition of the concept only goes back to June 2011 when FATF issued its first financial inclusion guidance paper,[50] since revised in 2013.[51] Since then, a number of countries (AFI reports that this includes 42 of its members)[52] have started adopting formal tiered CDD regimes.

Two notable examples in establishing formal tiered CDD regimes are Mexico and Tanzania. In 2011, Mexico approved a tiered scheme for opening deposit accounts at credit institutions. The scheme offers a model for inter-agency coordination, as it involved the relevant departments at the central bank, the Ministry of Finance and the banking regulator. This scheme entails 4 levels – three low-risk accounts, and the traditional current account – and provides for flexible account opening requirements for low-value, low-risk accounts that increase progressively as transaction values increase. Perhaps most notable at the time were the introduction of "Level 1" requirements, exempted from identity verification requirements on the basis of the low level of risk, which allowed for non-face-to-face account opening for low value debit card-based e-wallets. Although identities of users are not verified, transactions are closely monitored for suspicious activity. The scheme also allowed for

[47] The terms "Know Your Customer" (KYC) and CDD are often used interchangeably in practice, though the FATF recommendations refer to CDD.
[48] http://www.fatf-gafi.org/media/fatf/documents/reports/AML_CFT_Measures_and_Financial_Inclusion_2013.pdf
[49] http://www.cgap.org/sites/default/files/CGAP-Focus-Note-AML-CFT-Strengthening-Financial-Inclusion-and-Integrity-Aug-2009.pdf;
[50] FATF Anti-Money Laundering and Terrorist Financing Measures and Financial Inclusion (June 2011) at http://www.fatf-gafi.org/media/fatf/content/images/AML%20CFT%20measures%20and%20financial%20inclusion.pdf.
[51] See also FATF's Forty Recommendations at http://www.fatf-gafi.org/media/fatf/documents/recommendations/pdfs/FATF_Recommendations.pdf
[52] www.afi-dataportal.org

outsourcing CDD elements to third parties and paperless record-keeping. Over 10 million new accounts were opened in the two years following the new rules, with the large majority of them initially registered as Level 1 accounts.[53]

In 2015, after much consultation, Tanzania established its own tiered CDD regime for mobile money, encompassing three tiers: Tier 1, for basic electronically registered accounts, requiring only a registered phone number; Tier 2 which requires both a registered phone number as well as in-person confirmation - and a copy- of an acceptable national identity document; and Tier 3, which is aimed at SMEs and includes not just the full CDD of Tier 2 but also tax ID and VAT registration numbers along with business license numbers. While the new system is considered a good approach for expanding mobile money, the Tanzanian banking sector continues to operate under its traditional, more stringent, CDD requirements. Given the ongoing convergence of the mobile money and traditional banking sectors, not to mention the growing interest by banks in establishing simplified basic accounts, Tanzania's simplified CDD regimes need to be aligned.

These are just a couple of examples of what is a growing trend amongst regulatory regimes, aimed at making it easier for financial institutions to open accounts for previously excluded market segments, where risk is considered to be sufficiently low. Financial regulators increasingly see, however, that weak (or non-existent) official identity systems are major barriers to the inclusion of all members of society. Some of these regulators are therefore taking measures to address the problem by introducing special purpose identity systems, which can be useful in the interim in the absence of universal coverage ID schemes.

ID as a critical facilitator of digital financial inclusion

Policymakers, donors and other stakeholders worldwide are recognizing the need to develop comprehensive ID programs to enable access to financial services, as well as to multiple other types of services. The Principles on Identification for Sustainable Development[54], launched by the World Bank-hosted Identification for Development initiative or 'ID4D',[55] and endorsed by more than 15 global organizations, ranging from development agencies to think tanks and industry groups[56], set out guidance to help facilitate the development of robust and inclusive digital ID systems.

Notable examples of the enormous potential of digital IDs to unlock access to financial services include Pakistan's eID system and India's Aadhaar system (as discussed in Section 2.1). In Pakistan, the National Database and Registration Authority (NADRA) developed the Computerized National Identity Card (CNIC) which incorporates biometric information to provide a unique identity number to citizens. Roughly 99 per cent of the adult population has been registered with a CNIC card. Initiatives to integrate the CNIC with financial services have been underway for several years, including links to entry-level transaction accounts,

[53] By December 2016, there were 14.7 million Level 1 accounts, 19.5 million Level 2 accounts, 0.4 million Level 3 accounts; and 94.4 million traditional current accounts in the country (Banco de México, 2017). Population estimates at that time of people of 15 years and older were about 90 million (CONAPO).

[54] "Principles on Identification for Sustainable Development: Toward the Digital Age", 2017. (http://documents.worldbank.org/curated/en/213581486378184357/pdf/112614-REVISED-PUBLIC-web-final-ID4D-IdentificationPrinciples.pdf)

[55] http://www.worldbank.org/en/programs/id4d

[56] See page 2 of the "Principles on Identification for Sustainable Development: Toward the Digital Age" report for a complete list of endorsing organizations.

social benefit payments, electronic credit information bureaus, and most recently to e-payment facilities.[57]

In countries where full coverage of the national ID has not yet been achieved, various interim approaches have been taken to develop "special purpose" ID systems within the financial services sector. An example of a special purpose ID system is Nigeria's Bank Verification Number (BVN). Nigeria does not issue unique identity numbers at birth, and therefore grapples with establishing a unique national identifier. Citizens can obtain one of three forms of official ID – passport, driver's license, or voting card – but these systems use different forms for registering and because the systems aren't uniform or centrally verified, people can use different names for each or even open multiple identity accounts.

Because of this situation, and the likelihood that it will take many years to fully rectify, the Central Bank of Nigeria (CBN) decided to work with the banking industry to set up the BVN. To obtain a BVN, individuals can go to BVN enrollment centers, which include all bank branches, for free enrollment and submit their 10 finger-prints, facial picture, name and address, which is then submitted to a central matching system. Once the biometrics are checked to prevent multiple accounts, the person is then issued an 11-digit number against the biometric record.

So far, the BVN has proven to be an effective, if limited, form of ID for the financial industry. Users can obtain a BVN without necessarily opening an account, but they can't open an account without the BVN. The BVN is also starting to be used for non-bank services, such as agricultural subsidies. The system is still evolving, and policymakers are now working to link the BVN database into the Nigerian social security system (NIMC) so that people don't have to re-enroll into NIMC once they obtain a BVN. There is also an intention to link the BVN to credit bureaus and non-bank financial institutions such as microfinance banks, in part through an API for direct interface and validation. And while there is no current requirement for non-bank financial institutions to use the BVN, the CBN is in the process of formulating guidelines to mandate use of the BVN.

Another example of a central bank establishing a financial identity system is in Uganda, where a specialty ID system used in matching of credit data profiles in the financial sector will ultimately be replaced by a national ID scheme which aims for universal coverage. The initial Financial Card System (FCS) is being wound down by the Bank of Uganda as the National Identification and Registration Authority (NIRA) is rolling out a national ID card. So far, NIRA has issued over 20 million cards, compared to the 1.4 million FCS smart cards issued. The smart cards won't disappear entirely, as the vendor is working with NIRA to match the FCS card numbers with new national ID numbers, but going forward the National ID number will ultimately become the key identifier in financial sector transactions.

It is important to note that the examples noted in Nigeria and Uganda are innovations taken by financial regulators in the face of insufficient, or complete lack of, national ID systems, and not necessarily recommendations for addressing national identity challenges. Policymakers need to establish robust national identity systems for a host of reasons, not just inclusion, as set out in HLP 7. While sectoral approaches like Nigeria's and Uganda's might

[57] "Leveraging ID Systems for Financial Sector Development", 2017 (forthcoming). Report by Consult Hyperion prepared for the World Bank Group's ID4D initiative, and Finance & Markets Global Practice.

be useful for limited purposes, they can be inefficient in the overall context of national ID programs unless standards can be agreed upon that allow for evolution and incorporation into national ID solutions.

Leveraging Technology to Build Oversight Capacity: Austria and Rwanda

A growing theme among regulators is the need to develop and/or update reporting and monitoring systems, particularly in the face of increasing regulatory requirements and evolving digital financial services. While all central banks employ some form of information system for linking to their bank clients, the development of systems and capacity to track and oversee non-bank players such as digital payments providers, often lags behind the rate of industry growth. In many cases, regulators are still relying on self-reporting by industry, or on infrequent and paper or Excel-based reporting. Such relatively rudimentary approaches are inadequate for properly monitoring the volume of digital transactions of today's payments industry, and the pace of change in terms of products, delivery mechanisms, and providers.

A critical element of automating the process for collection, aggregation and analysis of data is the use of standardized reporting formats, which are easily extensible and portable across systems and make use of well-defined taxonomy and meta-data. There is a worldwide shift towards eXtensible Markup Language (XML) for message and data exchanges. Extensible Business Reporting Language (XBRL) was developed for the reporting of business results, corporate announcements and balance sheet data to capital market regulators and market data providers. This is now being widely adopted by banking sector regulators.

Many regulators in advanced economies have already updated (or are in the process of updating) their market monitoring systems, in many cases working closely with industry to develop regulatory technology, or 'RegTech', systems for improved reporting and compliance. RegTech[58] also helps regulators collect, analyze and monitor market data, as well as identify consumer pain points. To be sure, developed country regulators still struggle with legacy systems, and the pace of reporting and monitoring modernization occurring in emerging markets is often behind where it needs to be given the rate of growth in digital financial service providers, with notable exceptions (e.g. see Box 6).

Box 6. Automating Regulatory Reporting and Supervision

Some central banks have embarked on initiatives aimed at enhancing internal systems and processes for regulatory reporting and off-site supervision, in a bid to shift away from template-based approaches towards real-time, input-based approaches that enable greater efficiency in the collection of data and information from banks and non-bank financial institutions. The "input-based" approach leverages new technologies (or "regtech") that enable regulators to capture more granular data on financial sector activity, including on activity by new market entrants, or related to new digitally-enabled delivery mechanisms or products, while reducing the reporting burden on regulated institutions.[59]

For instance, the **Austrian** central bank, Oesterreiche Nationalbank (OeNB), in collaboration with the banking industry, introduced a new software platform to streamline the data collection and regulatory reporting process for banks in Austria. The software platform, known as 'Aurep,' provides a direct interface between the IT systems of the OeNB and banks, enables the OeNB to capture granular data automatically via the platform. Importantly, 'Aurep' also acts as a buffer between the OeNB and banks, such that banks upload standardized

[58] Regtech as referred to here is the design and deployment of technology-enabled solutions for the collection, analysis and usage of data to: (i) improve market oversight, (ii) reduce the cost of compliance, (iii) develop smarter, proportional, risk-based regulation, and (iv) increase consumer trust, financial health, and participation in the system.
[59] BearingPoint Institute (2015) https://www.bearingpointinstitute.com/en/regulatory-reporting-are-we-headed-real-time

data sets (basic cubes) as prescribed by OeNB onto the platform, but retain control of commercially sensitive information. The platform can then transform the basic data sets into the formats required by various departments within the OeNB. This new reporting system significantly reduces the compliance burden for regulated banks, and also ensures greater consistency and quality of data disseminated internally within the OeNB. Whether or not OeNB plans to extend this platform to include reporting by non-bank financial players remains to be seen.

In **Rwanda**, the National Bank of Rwanda (BNR) is in the process of implementing an automated financial reporting and supervision system for the collection, analysis and dissemination of data from regulated banks and non-bank financial institutions. The system not only aims to streamline data collection and reduce the regulatory reporting burden for financial institutions, but it also aims to provide BNR with additional, more granular data to track progress on financial inclusion. The system will allow BNR to automatically pull data from financial institutions' core MIS (for those that have them), thus improving the accuracy, integrity, and timeliness of offsite reporting data.

With support from the World Bank, new reporting templates have been designed to improve the scope, consistency, and quality of data, including financial inclusion indicators– such as target market segments, gender, geographic location, among others. All licensed banks have been on-boarded onto the system, while some MFIs are submitting the new templates in Excel format. Related reforms are ongoing to establish core MIS in Savings and Credit Cooperatives (SACCOs) to ensure that they too can participate in the new system.

The cases set out in this section illustrate the need for a legal and regulatory framework that is proportionate, risk-based, and that creates a conducive environment for digital financial inclusion. Tiered CDD regimes, for example, can expand access to financial services by lowering the documentation barriers facing individuals as well as lowering the costs of compliance for financial service providers. As digital financial services and delivery mechanisms become more complex, building the capacity to adequately supervise and regulate the market will become critical. Regulators can leverage technologies to enable them to better monitor and supervise the market, while keeping pace with new developments.

2.4. HLP 4: Expanding the Digital Financial Services Infrastructure Ecosystem

High Level Principle 4 emphasizes the need for a robust, open and efficient digital infrastructure, including a widely accessible retail payments system and ICT infrastructure, to enable the broad delivery of digital financial services. This particular HLP calls for policymakers to work closely with the private sector to ensure that the entire ecosystem for digital financial services runs smoothly and seamlessly, from voice and data networks, including the various digital points of service that consumers rely on such as POSs and ATMs, to the power and transport systems that underpin these networks. Because the provisioning and ownership of the entire digital financial ecosystem will necessarily be made up of a combination of public and private resources, policymakers have to walk a fine line between the options of relying solely on private investment, public spending on infrastructure where needed, targeted subsidies where merited, and/or legal mandates to service providers where it's deemed necessary for the public good.

Areas of particular focus for national authorities include retail and online payments infrastructure that includes interoperable platforms that link to a wide range of POSs and ATMs, agent networks, bill payment platforms, credit reference systems, digital asset registries (particularly for movable assets) and, in some cases, the underlying communications infrastructure needed to support all these systems. Some regulators are also exploring the potential benefits, costs, and risks of issuing digital fiat currencies that could be used in a digital financial services ecosystem, and would combine the benefits of private virtual currencies with the stability and consumer protection afforded by the central bank issuer.

The examples set out in this section highlight that achieving digital financial inclusion will require regulators and policymakers, in collaboration with private sector stakeholders, to develop a robust digital infrastructure ecosystem – including ICT, credit information, and payment systems infrastructure – that is accessible and interoperable. Public investments in ICT infrastructure, such as in Peru and Zambia, can go a long way in establishing the foundations for digital financial inclusion. Furthermore, promoting the use of electronic payments, through reforms to the payments system, driving merchant acceptance of digital payments and expanding access channels to rural and remote areas, will contribute towards increased uptake of digital financial services.

Payments Infrastructure and Credit Reporting Systems: China

Some countries are undertaking broad national initiatives to expand their financial infrastructure ecosystems, such as India, discussed earlier. Another ambitious program is found in China, driven in part by that country's rapidly growing e-commerce sector. Much of China's progress in advancing digital financial inclusion can be attributed to the efforts undertaken in recent years to strengthen the country's financial infrastructure through an integrated city and rural approach.[60] The People's Bank of China (PBOC) in collaboration with other stakeholders established a comprehensive and robust national payments system infrastructure in China. Meanwhile, government authorities prioritized the development and maintenance of a sound payments infrastructure in rural areas, which facilitated growth in physical access networks, improved diversity and efficiency of payment products, and allowed for the digitization of government-to-person (G2P) transfers. The key elements of the program include the following:

- Starting in 2002, PBOC developed a number of interbank clearing systems, including the China National Advanced Payment System (CNAPS), China Domestic Foreign Currency Payment System, and local clearing systems, to support the application of negotiable instruments, payment cards, and other payment instruments;
- China UnionPay was established (also in 2002) to develop and operate the inter-bank card information exchange system, to promote the interoperability of bank cards. UnionPay now forms the backbone for the interoperability for agents and payment cards, and also provides the rails on which Alipay and other online payment platforms operate.
- PBOC operates the Internet Banking Payment System (IBPS) which offers near real-time inter-bank direct credit and debit transfers for internet banking initiated transactions. Rural credit cooperatives (and other rural financial institutions) and city commercial banks have created systems for their respective members and these are connected to PBOC's systems which thereby enables transactions between the rural banks and the other nationwide banks;
- Coordination of China's payment systems infrastructure has been strengthened through the establishment of the China Payment and Clearing Association in 2011; and

[60] Joint PBOC - World Bank Report (forthcoming): Towards Universal Financial Inclusion in China: Models, Challenges, and Global Lessons

- In August 2014, the PBOC's "Guidelines on Comprehensively Promoting and Deepening the Development of Payment Service Environment in Rural Areas" was formally issued, to further expand coverage of payment service systems.

The PBOC also established the Fundamental Database for Financial Credit Information and set up the Credit Reference Center (PBOC-CRC), a public credit registry that collects data from a wide range of financial institutions, including banks, rural credit cooperatives, trust companies, consumer finance companies, auto finance companies and micro-finance institutions, financing guarantee companies, financial leasing companies, insurance companies and securities companies.

Box 7. Credit Reference Center

First conceived in 2006, the CCRC's mandate is to establish, operate and maintain the national centralized commercial and consumer credit reporting system. Financial institutions are able to access records from the system, which also supplements financial data provided with public information in the areas of social security payments, housing provident fund payments, administrative penalties and awards related to environmental protection, tax arrears, court judgments and bureaucratic actions, etc.

The CCRC covered 910 million individuals by the end of 2016,[61] including 430 million with a borrowing history, and 22.1 million legal entities, including 6.36 with a borrowing history. The registry receives positive and negative information for all relevant credit products at any value. It not only collects data from traditional sources, such as regulated lending institutions and public domain, but also from alternative data sources, including utilities and telecoms.

PBOC continues to develop the credit reporting system in China, and strengthen the cooperation between CRC and other credit bureaus. This further contributes to China's credit reporting system which, with an annual inquiry volume of about 500 million, is now the largest in the world.

Interoperability: Tanzania and Peru

An issue that policymakers are paying greater attention to with regard to financial infrastructure that enables digital financial services, is interoperability of services across service providers and points of service, including agents.[62] This issue is of particular importance to national efforts to broaden the reach of financial services into previously underserved, often rural areas, through digital technologies and delivery mechanisms. The economics of reaching rural customers makes it unrealistic for all service providers to set up agents in all geographic areas, but at the same time policymakers want to ensure some level of competition and customer choice in financial services. One means of achieving that goal is to promote interoperability of financial service providers, so that customers can interact with other customers or merchants that they need to reach, without being required to open multiple accounts.

Policymakers have tended towards one of two approaches to interoperability: encourage industry players to enable it on their own, in some cases with the promise to mandate it if industry does not get there fast enough, or come up with their own government-led solutions. A recent example of industry-led mobile money interoperability was seen in Tanzania, where the four leading MNOs, supported by the IFC, worked together over the course of a year to agree payment scheme rules including exchange fees, dispute resolution and settlement

[61] PBOC data.

[62] Some regions, such as SADC, are also exploring the issue of regional interoperability; cross-border interoperability is not addressed in this report.

arrangements. The Bank of Tanzania supported the discussions and was kept informed on how the discussions were proceeding, so that by the time an agreement was finalized, all parties involved, including the regulator, were fully informed and in support of the arrangement.

The impact of this approach has been shown in the growth of cross-operator transactions since the scheme was facilitated (specifically, transactions between mobile money customers using different service providers): from an average of under 100,000 transactions per month in October 2014 when the new scheme began, cross-operator P2P transactions in Tanzania are now up to 4 million per month, and growing almost 15% a month.[63] These cross-operator transactions now make up about a quarter of all transactions, and this growth was achieved before the operators themselves had even kicked off any marketing campaigns announcing the new interoperability rules. Schemes such as Tanzania's, which start with existing infrastructure and make it interoperable through industry-agreed rules, have generally proven to be the most successful and enduring solutions for achieving interoperability.

In other cases, policymakers are choosing to support centralized solutions, either on their own in the form of national switch platforms or by encouraging industry to develop its own centralized solution. A prominent recent example of the latter is Modelo Peru, the multi-stakeholder effort in Peru to establish interoperability amongst all the country's financial actors and expand access to the 71 percent of Peruvians who lack access to a bank account, particularly in rural areas. Modelo Peru[64] has been lauded as an example of national interoperability, with many different players coming together to create one seamless payments ecosystem. (See Box 8.)

Box 8. Modelo Perú

Launched in February 2016 and spearheaded initially by the Bankers' Association of Peru (ASBANC), Modelo Perú is an effort to establish an interoperable nationwide payments platform. Critically, the effort had the strong support of government officials and the banking supervisor SBS (Superintendencia de Banca, Seguros y AFP) as well as the Central Bank of Peru, which helped convince non-bank players like the MNOs to join. The support from regulators and the government included the 2013 National Law for Electronic Money, which helped to set the ground rules for this new ecosystem.

The platform itself, branded Bim (Billetera Móvil), brings together over 30 financial institutions, government, telecommunications companies, and large payers and payees into a shared payments infrastructure. Its goal is to expand banking access to both banked and unbanked Peruvians and, importantly, aims to reduce the transactions costs associated with cash for both financial service providers and other businesses.

The main product offered by the platform is an interoperable e-wallet, co-branded Bim, that can be accessed on mobile phones using USSD or SMS-based means, thus making it available to all mobile phones. New users do not need a preexisting bank account, access to internet on their mobile, or even calling credit on their phone accounts. They can sign up and open an electronic wallet directly on their phones or at any of the more than 8,500 physical points of sale nationwide already operating with Bim. The process for opening accounts requires only that the new user provide a personal national ID number and code, select a personal passcode, and choose the financial institution to house the individual's account. Initially issued by 9 institutions, including 3 MNOs, the e-wallets can be used at any Bim-branded store or agent for payments or cash-in/cash-out, and can also be used to receive payments as well, both P2P as well as government payments.

Pagos Digitales Peruanos (PDP), the company set up to run the Bim platform, has a unique shareholding structure, with 51 percent ownership controlled by a non-profit entity set up by ASBANC, and the remaining ownership held by 33 participant shareholders who purchased shares of 2.45 percent each at launch. The company sets the scheme rules for the platform and acts as a service provider to all e-money issuers in the country.

---

[63] Bank of Tanzania data

[64] http://www.centerforfinancialinclusion.org/publications-a-resources/browse-publications/794-modelo-peru-cfi-brief

The scheme's managers have estimated that the platform needs a minimum of 1 million active users, or 3 million transactions per month, for the system to break even operationally. By the end of 2016, they had reached 240,000, somewhat below their initial target of 300,000 for the year. The system faces some challenges at this point, particularly around transaction numbers, rural coverage, and integrating Bim into existing bank and merchant POS systems, but PDP is committed to addressing these challenges in order to create volume and scale and become a truly unified national payments system.

Mexico's Transactional Database

The Central Bank of Mexico (Banco de Mexico) has developed a database to provide banks with an overall picture of their customers' transactions across borders, with the goal that this open and efficient digital infrastructure will strengthen industry's AML/CFT efforts and help mitigate the effects of de-risking. The database contains transactional information about client and other users' transfers abroad.

Beginning in March 2016, banks started daily reporting of: basic client information; recipient bank and beneficiary name; and information about the outbound transfer (amount, currency and reason for the transaction). In exchange, banks will receive aggregated data on their clients' status in the financial system, subject to their clients' authorization. The Central Bank anticipates also incorporating information about inbound international transfers to the database in the future.

Anticipated benefits of the national database include: data validation; aggregated data about customer transactions throughout the financial system; and access to this data by national authorities. Based on this data, banks will be able to build transactional indexes that can help map the nature of client activity. This should help facilitate detection of customer transaction anomalies. Additionally, banks will have the required information to know their customers based on their overall activities, rather than their activities with only one bank. The Mexican Secretariat of Finance and Public Credit (SHCP) has issued regulations mandating the incorporation of this data in risk analyses performed by banks.

Tentatively, 145 data points are planned to be shared with participant banks, based on data reported in the previous year, such as the countries where money was sent, the number of banks from which transfers were made and/or received, the total number of transfers, the number of days in the period during which a transfer was made, etc.

Once the data sharing platform is launched in 2017, banks will be able to access customer data on demand for the previous 360 days of reporting. The platform will allow banks to explore both individual and aggregated customer data by client segment. Anticipated uses include on-demand inquiries when clients solicit new international transfers. As the platform will be updated daily, this should facilitate a more comprehensive and up-to-date risk assessment.

Databases such as Banco de Mexico's are examples of data sharing in support of smoother functioning of financial markets along with improved AML/CFT oversight. An important next step for policymakers to consider is opening up other useful sources of data beyond credit registries, such as government databases, along with more linkages to non-bank financial institutions including fintech companies, in order to expand opportunities for more of the unbanked to participate in the financial system. While the potential benefits of greater data availability can be extensive, however, data privacy and protection safeguards will remain critical elements of such efforts.

Expanding Merchant Acceptance of Digital Payments: Kenya, Mexico and Argentina

An important component of expanding a digital payments ecosystem is enlisting a large merchant base that can accept those digital payments. For purposes of targeting the financially underserved, it is especially critical to include small merchants who are located in and cater to low-income communities. Such merchants are not typically going to employ the standard point-of-sale (POS) systems that accept bank credit cards, so finding affordable solutions for those businesses to accept simple digital card and mobile payments is necessary. At the same time, if there are multiple payment options available to customers, the typical small merchant must decide which type to accept and therefore which POS system to buy. In the face of such decisions, many merchants, understandably, simply choose to stick with cash.

One innovative company in Kenya chose to offer a low cost payment system to small merchants that allows them to accept a number of different payment options, without having to purchase new POS terminals. Kopo Kopo launched its merchant services in early 2012, and offers a web-based platform, accessible via Android, desktop, SMS and USSD, that enables small and medium enterprises (SMEs) in emerging markets to accept, process, and manage multiple mobile money payments. Kopo Kopo is now Safaricom's largest merchant aggregator, and one of the largest merchant aggregators in Sub-Saharan Africa. The regulator in this case, the Central Bank of Kenya, was aware of Kopo Kopo's activities but chose to let them operate as any other value-added service in the market, rather than as a regulated entity. The CBK's view was that the mobile money operator was responsible for its relationships with its merchant partners. Allowing the entrance of new and diverse players like Kopo Kopo, who viewed SMEs and poor customers as their main clients, was an important element in enabling the growth of the digital payments ecosystem across all income levels.

Another innovative start-up, Tienda Pago in Latin America, is focusing on facilitating transactions between retailers and suppliers. Suppliers receive large volumes of cash on a frequent basis from retailers (an inconvenience on their part) and are interested in business solutions that can reduce this pain point and decrease operational costs. These same suppliers leverage their strong merchant relationships and existing distribution models to coordinate bringing payment solutions to retailers, partnering with traditional payment service providers (PSPs). A joint-venture led by Grupo Bimbo, a bakery company based in Mexico, is one example of a non-traditional payment actor partnering with a large bank and a payments processing firm (Blue Label Technologies) to install card-accepting machines, reaching tens of thousands of small convenience stores across the country.[65]

In August 2016 the Central Bank of Argentina established that banks should offer immediate transfer of funds (online credit transfers and direct debits) through the "Mobile Payments Platform." By subscribing to the "Pago Electronico Inmediato (PEI)," merchants can receive payments initiated via a cell phone, tablet or laptop, with crediting to their accounts occurring in real-time. The client (buyer) can make daily transfers up to a total equivalent to the minimum wage (approximately USD 520), or higher subject to banks implementing supplementary security measures. Funds are credited with no charge to the merchant within a limit of about USD 18,800 per month, thus making PEI a cost-efficient payments acceptance solution.

A 2016 World Bank Group report[66] specifically looked at the issue of digitizing merchant payments, and identified six key obstacles as significant impediments to deepening these

[65] http://documents.worldbank.org/curated/en/765851467037506667/pdf/106633-WP-PUBLIC-Innovative-Solutions-Accelerate-Adoption-Electronic-Payments-Merchants-report-2016.pdf
[66] http://documents.worldbank.org/curated/en/765851467037506667/Innovation-in-electronic-payment-adoption-the-case-of-small-retailers

payments, especially in developing countries: i) An inadequate value proposition for merchants, including product design that does not adequately encourage them to migrate from cash to electronic payments; ii) Weak product and stakeholder economics in traditional card models; iii) Insufficient aggregate customer demand, needed to reach the "tipping point" that drives demand and supply towards a digital payments ecosystem; iv) Inconsistent technological infrastructure and regulatory environment in developing markets to support digital payments; v) Ineffective distribution models to serve hard-to-reach merchants in areas with limited economic capillarity (i.e. low density of micro, small and medium enterprises MSMEs and customer populations); and vi) Difficulty in formalizing enterprises and reluctance of merchants to pay full taxes on sales.

While industry will play an important role in addressing some of these obstacles, policymakers also have key roles to play in encouraging an enabling electronic payments environment, as is clear from some of these constraints. Examples of actions which have been taken by policy makers are:

- Streamline CDD requirements for merchants seeking to accept electronic payments; stimulate the formalization of merchants including through some degree of tax-related accommodations, particularly in the early stages, so as to not disincentivize smaller, and perhaps even larger, merchant adoption (one example of tax-related accommodations for formalizing small merchants can be found in Uruguay);[67]
- Create incentives for consumers and merchants to transact electronically (examples include tax rebates on digital transactions in Korea, or using receipts to enter into a digital lottery each time you transact electronically in Slovakia); and
- Accept electronic payments for government services (Modelo Peru has introduced a pilot to digitize a small merchant tax payment for small retail stores, for example).

<u>Public Goods Infrastructure Investment in Zambia and Peru</u>

In some cases, policymakers have decided to invest in broadband infrastructure themselves, often to extend services to rural areas that are not economically feasible for private players. One recent example is that of Peru, which in June 2016 announced[68] that the national fiber optic backbone network, RDFNO (Red Dorsal Nacional de Fibra óptica) was nearing completion, with plans to extend the benefits of the RDFNO to 195 district capitals, reaching about 625,000 people. The purpose of RDFNO is to bring connectivity to rural areas (in particular in Peru's highland and jungle areas), as well as providing high speed cable networks to more developed areas. Peru's Transport and Communications Ministry wants to encourage mobile network operators to extend their mobile networks into remote rural areas, by using RDFNO for backhaul.

The project includes both the expansion of the broadband network, built and operated under a PPP model, as well as digital content and skills development, including (i) the creation of a rural open data platform that will publish information regarding rural areas to the public; (ii) the creation of applications, content, and digital services that support public service delivery in rural areas; (iii) the development of prototypes for use of new technologies in areas critical to rural communities, such as early warning systems and disaster risk management; and (iv) training courses on digital technologies relevant to rural communities.

---

[67] https://www.itu.int/en/ITU-T/focusgroups/dfs/Documents/09_2016/FINAL%20ENDORSED%20Enabling%20Merchant%20Payments%20Acceptance%2030%20May%202016_formatted%20AM.pdf

[68] http://www.fomsn.com/fiber-optic-news/fiber/rdnfo-is-getting-ready-for-completion-in-peru/

Zambia went one step further in 2014,[69] setting up an initial 169 mobile towers through the Zambia Information and Communication Technology Authority (ZICTA) in rural areas of the country. The towers are owned by ZICTA and shared among the country's three mobile phone service providers.

3. Insights on Emerging Approaches to Digital Financial Inclusion

As is evident in the cases set out in this report, the increasing pace and complexity of innovation and adoption of digital technologies in the financial sector means that policymaker and regulator approaches must also evolve and be tailored to country contexts. Adding in the need to support efforts that are inclusive and help to reach those who are currently unserved by financial services adds to the challenge. While no two countries are identical in their approach or even in their particular market context, there are several insights which can be gleaned from the examples highlighted in this report. These include:

- Proactive leadership and political will are cross-cutting success factors, including through integration and coordination across national authorities, including Ministries of Finance, central banks and other regulators and overseers, and also social welfare agencies that interact with traditionally unbanked beneficiaries. Broad, cross-cutting programs involving government and industry are not easy to coordinate and can involve considerable effort, time and cost, but they can be effective in addressing the range of issues relevant to harnessing digital technology. As illustrated in the case of India, strong leadership and coordination across various government and non-government entities saw the development of a robust digital infrastructure (today dubbed the "India Stack"), coupled with rapid growth in access to digital transaction accounts. In China, the Government issued new Guidelines and rules to support the sound development of internet finance, which provided clarity to industry players and promoted the growth of non-bank internet finance companies.
- There needs to be more progress on digital tools to help regulators do their job. As digital innovation is rapidly redefining what it is to be a service provider, financial regulators are having to take a more proactive, data-driven approach to engagement with the industry, including the broad base of often informal SMEs that cater to the financially excluded. Many regulators are embracing a risk-based approach and looking for new ways to safely foster innovation, from test-and-learn programs to greater collaboration and information exchange with industry. In the case of the UK, the FCA's "Project Innovate" program has enabled the UK regulator to stay abreast of new financial technologies, while guiding the development of innovative financial services and ensuring consumers are adequately protected. Similarly, in Ghana, collaboration between the central bank, insurance regulator and telecommunications regulator, resulting in the issuance of risk-based rules to support the delivery of microinsurance services through mobile phones.
- Supervising digital financial service providers in an era of vast volumes of transactions (and increased use of fast or real time payment transactions) calls for more sophisticated and automated systems that can provide real-time monitoring and analysis. Some countries are developing such systems, but more effort is needed to design robust, flexible systems and provide the capacity-building support needed to fully implement them. As in the example of Rwanda, the central bank's implementation of the data warehouse project

[69] https://www.telegeography.com/products/commsupdate/articles/2014/11/13/zicta-confirms-147-of-169-planned-rural-communications-towers-are-up-and-running/

is expected to provide a more efficient and timely mechanism to obtain granular data to track progress on financial inclusion by gender, different target markets, and geographic locations.

- While regulators are making positive efforts to embrace new technologies and improve communications with industry, it can be effective to also clarify regulatory frameworks and supervisory expectations – to the degree possible – sufficiently early (and continually as needed), in order to guide and shape innovation in line with financial regulatory priorities, and to not be caught off guard by unforeseen developments.

- Promoting interoperable, open technology platforms for digital financial services helps establish a broad-based ecosystem for private and Government entities to better reach consumers and ultimately improve their financial lives. The means and timing of achieving interoperability can vary, but policymakers should make clear that it is an expectation. An important related element of open technology platforms is that they should make it (technically) easier for consumers to take ownership of their information and move it across service providers. In Tanzania, the industry-led development of scheme rules and arrangements for mobile money interoperability has seen rapid growth in cross-operator transactions. Schemes such as these, which build on existing infrastructure, have generally proven to be successful and enduring solutions to achieving interoperability.

- Digital identity forms an important foundation of public digital infrastructure and opens the door for access to services across the economy – including beyond financial services. National governments need to prioritize availability of robust and easily verifiable digital ID, whether biometric or other types of data-based forms, which can be used to facilitate access to digital financial services. There are valid concerns about privacy and civil liberties to be addressed. The need for universal identity programs increases the importance of addressing these concerns urgently. As seen in India and Pakistan, digital ID schemes with broad coverage have the potential to stimulate rapid access to digital financial services. In countries where full coverage of ID schemes is yet to be achieved, interim sectoral approaches can be incorporated into broader national ID solutions to ensure efficiency and sustainability.

- The rapid growth of digital services, of all kinds, raises concerns that financial policymakers and regulators have not traditionally needed to focus on increasingly important issues such as data protection[70], third-party access to data, quality of service and network reliability. Such concerns call for greater collaboration with authorities such as telecommunications, data protection, and consumer protection regulators. While regulators are rightly concerned with their respective remits and mandates, they is a clear case for working more closely through information sharing and agreement on areas of mutual interest and priority.

[70] The GPFI's separate work within the Responsible Finance Forum (RFF) focuses extensively on issues around data privacy and protection.

GPFI
Global Partnership
for Financial Inclusion

G20 GERMANY 2017

WORLD BANK GROUP

G20 Policy Guide

Digitisation and informality: harnessing digital financial inclusion for individuals and MSMEs in the informal economy

G20 ARGENTINA PRESIDENCY 2018

g20argentina.com

BUILDING CONSENSUS FOR FAIR AND SUSTAINABLE DEVELOPMENT

G20
Policy Guide

Digitisation and informality:
Harnessing digital financial inclusion for individuals and MSMEs in the informal economy

BUILDING
CONSENSUS FOR FAIR
AND SUSTAINABLE
DEVELOPMENT

Acknowledgments

The G20 Policy Guide has been prepared on behalf of the G20 Global Partnership for Financial Inclusion. This work builds on the input papers produced by Implementing Partners of the GPFI, namely the Better than Cash Alliance, the Consultative Group to Assist the Poor, the Organisation for Economic Co-operation and Development and the World Bank Group, as well as the International Committee of Credit Reporting. The input papers were developed for each of the GPFI Subgroups, namely the Regulation and Standard Setting Bodies, Markets and Payment System, SME Finance, and Financial Consumer Protection and Financial Literacy. The G20 Policy Guide has also benefited from peer review of representatives from GPFI members pursuant to the consultation process provided by the GPFI Terms of References. Finally, non-G20 countries, facilitated by the Alliance for Financial Inclusion, as well as the Bill and Melinda Gates Foundation, the SME Finance Forum and the UN Secretary-General's Special Advocate for Inclusive Finance for Development provided valuable contributions.

Acronyms

AFI: Alliance for Financial Inclusion
AML: Anti-Money Laundering
ARCO: Access, Rectification, Cancellation, Opposition rights
BTCA: Better than Cash Alliance
CDD: Customer Due Diligence
CFT: Countering Financing Terrorism
CGAP: Consultative Group to Assist the Poor
CRSP: Credit Reporting Service Provider
DFI: Digital Financial Inclusion
DFS: Digital Financial Services
DFSP: Digital Financial Service Provider
EU: European Union
FATF: Financial Action Task Force
G2P: Government to Person
GDPR: General Data Protection Regulation
GPCR: General Principles of Credit Reporting
GPFI: Global Partnership for Financial Inclusion
HLP: High-Level Principles
ICCR: International Committee on Credit Reporting
ID4D: Identification for Development
IP: Implementing Partner
LEI: Legal Entity Identification
MSME: Micro Small and Medium Enterprise
OECD: Organisation for Economic Co-operation and Development (OECD)
P2G: Person to Government
P2P: Person to Person
PSD2: Payment Services Directive
PSP: Payment Service Provider
QR-Code: Quick Response Code

Table of contents

Executive summary

Access to and use of financial services plays a critical role in supporting inclusive and sustainable development. Despite remarkable progress in the financial inclusion agenda, large segments of the population remain excluded from the formal financial system. Many financially-excluded individuals and firms are found in the informal economy.

Digitisation offers an unprecedented opportunity to address eligibility and affordability barriers to formal financial inclusion faced by informal individuals and firms. In particular, digitisation can (i) facilitate identity verification, (ii) promote digital payments and (iii) improve the information environment. However, to fulfil its potential digitisation also requires attention to (iv) financial consumer protection and financial literacy.

The G20 Policy Guide presents a set of key policies that support the delivery of interventions to facilitate financial inclusion of individuals and firms operating in the informal economy. It focuses on four key areas that can ease eligibility and affordability barriers.

The following table summarises the key recommendations for each policy area.

Digital on-boarding	Digital payments infrastructure
Improve the identification and verification of new customers 1) Ensure an integrated identity framework *A digital legal identity system could help recognition and authentication* 2) Adapt and upgrade the regulatory framework *A conducive regulatory framework should recognise the potential of digital identity* 3) Establish a robust and secure digital identity infrastructure in the financial sector *Digital identity systems could be built and used in the financial services industry* 4) Foster development of private sector-led services by leveraging legal identity infrastructure *The private sector could build innovative solutions* 5) Monitor new developments and approaches to identity *Regulators should keep abreast of technological developments*	*Build an open and inclusive payments ecosystem* 1) Prioritise development of interoperable payment systems enabling fast payments *Policymakers should establish a market-based, safe, efficient and interoperable payment system* 2) Create incentives for merchant payments acceptance *Business models should be sustainable while promoting use by merchants* 3) Create incentives for consumer use of digital financial services *Use by final consumers should be affordable* 4) Support cross-border payment systems *The development of cross-border approaches could be explored*

Use of alternative data for credit reporting	Financial consumer protection, financial literacy, and data protection
Leverage alternative data to enhance credit reporting 1) Improve availability and accuracy of information *The main categories of alternative and reliable data should be identified* 2) Expand credit information sharing *Credit information sharing could be extended to alternative data* 3) Enable responsible cross-border data exchanges *Regional cooperation could help improve consistency and comparability of data* 4) Balance market integrity, innovation and competition *Functional requirements should be applied to ensure quality of treatment*	*Increase opportunities while mitigating risks* Financial Consumer Protection 1) Adapt oversight arrangements and capability for financial consumer protection *Regulators should embrace technology while keeping high standards of consumer protection* 2) Enhance disclosure and transparency *Technology could be leveraged to adapt and strengthen disclosure and transparency standards* Financial Literacy 3) Foster data collection, coordination and identification of new core competencies on digital financial literacy. *New data should be used to identify competency frameworks in a coordinated manner* 4) Strengthen the delivery of financial education for digital financial services and support its evaluation *Digital technology could be leveraged for the provision and evaluation of financial education programmes* Data Protection 5) Enhance secure and effective consent models *Consent models to ensure data protection could be adopted* 6) Enhance access, rectification, cancellation and opposition rights *Consumers should be given options to access and change their own data.* 7) Address data security *Adoption of security measures could help protect against operational risks*

Author: **Moksumul Haque**

Digitisation and informality

Why it is important

Access to and use of financial services plays a critical role in supporting inclusive and sustainable development. Despite remarkable progress in the financial inclusion agenda, approximately 1.7 billion adults worldwide still do not have a basic account at a financial institution or at a mobile money provider.[1] More than half of the unbanked are women, with a gender gap estimated at 7 percentage points globally: whereas 72 percent of men had an account in 2017, only 65 percent of women did so.[2] Although account ownership increased in the past few years to 69 percent, adults reporting formal savings in the past 12 months remained at only 27 percent, while just 11 percent of adults worldwide formally borrowed.[3] Additionally, half of the 400 million micro, small and medium enterprises (MSMEs) in emerging markets lack adequate financing to thrive and grow, with a total credit gap estimated in the range of US$2.1-2.6 trillion.[4] As a result, many individuals and firms have no safe and reliable way to save, invest, make payments and insure against risk. This has negative repercussions for livelihood, productivity, growth and inequality.

Informality represents an important barrier to financial inclusion. For the purpose of the G20 Policy Guide, informality is broadly defined to encompass "all economic activities by workers and economic units that are in law or in practice not covered or insufficiently covered by formal arrangements".[5] While many factors contribute to financial exclusion, individuals and MSMEs operating in the informal economy find it particularly difficult to access and use formal financial services.[6] Around 80 percent of total MSMEs are informal,[7] and these firms consistently report access to finance as the biggest constrain they face.[8] Financial exclusion of both individuals and MSMEs is more widespread in countries where the size of the informal economy is greater.

Figure 1 shows that both account penetration and the share of small firms with a loan from a financial institution are lower in large informal economies, while use of cash and informal borrowing are more widespread when the informal economy represents a larger proportion of the total economy.

Women constitute the largest group in the informal economy. From street vendors and domestic workers to subsistence farmers and seasonal agricultural workers, women represent the main work force in the informal sector.[9] These women generate their own income and run businesses but often may not have available the benefits of the traditional financial system, lack collateral, credit records and, in the case of migrants, often documentation. Women who work in the informal economy need access to the full range of financial services to generate income, build assets, smooth consumption, and manage risks but these are rarely available to them. This highlights the importance of the gender dimension in the financial inclusion-informality nexus.[10]

Digitisation, or the adoption of digital technologies and approaches, offers a transformational solution to financial exclusion driven by informality. Rapid technological innovation is profoundly reshaping production and consumption of goods and services. One important area where the disruptive impact of new technologies, particularly digital technology, is already visible is financial inclusion. The use of mobile money and digital payments has increased heavily in the past few years, and this might have contributed to the inclusion of more people into the formal financial system.[11] Harnessing digitisation to financially include those in the informal economy and those that have new work arrangements lacking a stable and formal source of income, represents an enormous opportunity.

Digitisation can help address eligibility and affordability barriers, which are among the most salient barriers to financial inclusion faced by individuals and MSMEs operating in the informal economy.[12] Individuals and firms operating in the informal economy are sometimes unable to provide a reliable form of identification that can meet Customer Due Diligence (CDD) requirements to open a bank account. They cannot generally afford using payments services. When applying for a loan, MSMEs in the informal economy have limited collateral and cannot convincingly prove their repayment capacity because of information asymmetries.

FIGURE 1:

Financial exclusion and informality

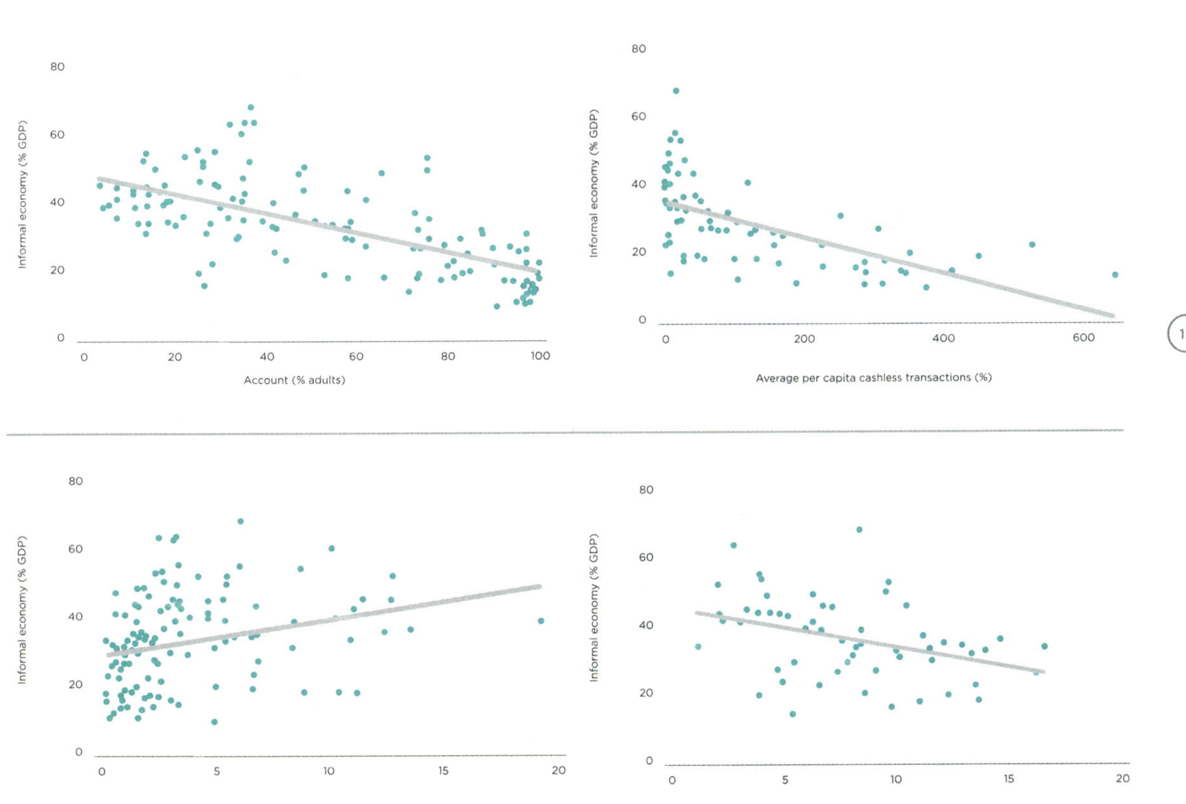

Source: Medina and Schneider (2017); G20 Global Financial Inclusion Indicators; World Bank Global Payment Systems Survey

To leverage the potential value of digitisation in the informal economy, widespread mobile connectivity and ownership are needed. This is an important precondition for unleashing the opportunities generated by digitisation. To enable broad access to digital financial services, individuals and firms in the informal economy must own a mobile phone and be able to use it wherever they are. Across countries, network coverage is generally high, and phone subscriptions and smartphone ownership are both growing fast. However, certain groups continue to have limited or no access to mobile phones. This is a particular challenge for women who, in most countries, are less likely to own their own phone. Women in low- and middle-income countries are, on average, 14 percent less likely to own a mobile phone than men, with important regional variations.[13] Therefore, it is essential that efforts continue to ensure broad and equal access to mobile technology.

The G20 Policy Guide focuses on how digitisation can help individual and firms operating in the informal economy access financial services to improve their lives or businesses. Digitisation is not a means to formalisation yet access to formal financial services can contribute to reduce informality in the long run. Access to formal financial services can increase the credibility of constrained individuals and firms, helping them overcome the entry cost into the formal sector.[14] It can also boost productivity, reducing the opportunistic informality and the number of individuals and MSMEs that choose to produce and trade in the informal sector.[15] However, informality remains a complex issue that may require policy action on several fronts, including in the areas of institutional development, employment regulations and tax, which are beyond the scope of the G20 Policy Guide.

This document outlines a set of key non-binding policies to financially include individuals and firms in the informal economy. It brings together evidence and consensus-based policy recommendations and guidance on four policy areas. These are deemed important to the fair and affordable inclusion of individuals and MSMEs operating in the informal economy into the formal financial sector (Figure 2). These areas include:

A. Digital on-boarding.
B. Digital payments infrastructure.

C. Use of alternative data for credit reporting.
D. Financial consumer protection, financial literacy, and data protection.

This work is in line with the G20 Financial Inclusion Action Plan and builds upon the work of previous G20 Presidencies, including most recently the G20 Chinese and German Presidencies, and supports the implementation of the G20 High Level Principles for Digital Financial Inclusion (HLP for DFI). The choice of policy areas also reflects technical relevance to address the financially excluded in the informal sector through digitisation. From this perspective, the G20 Policy Guide will contribute to move the GPFI agenda forward by focusing on specific topics that are important in the intersection between informality, financial inclusion and digitisation. However, policy recommendations may change over time, as new evidence on effective interventions is added. For this reason, the G20 Policy Guide should be seen as a living document.

The G20 Policy Guide targets policymakers in both G20 and non-G20 countries who are responsible for developing, implementing and evaluating financial inclusion strategies, plans and programmes, as well as those from sectors that influence financial inclusion outcomes, especially in the informal economy. In addition, a number of actors outside the government may play an important role in delivering digital financial services to the informal sector, including civil society organisations, professional associations and the broad private sector. Concerted efforts by the public and the private sector are therefore critical to capture the opportunity offered by digitisation.

This work aims to support policy dialogue, strategic planning, priority setting and implementation planning. However, the G20 Policy Guide is neither intended to inform nor interpret the work of the global financial sector standard-setting bodies. The G20 Policy Guide suggests key policy measures that could be considered in applicable national financial inclusion strategies and country level actions aiming at financial inclusion, always taking into account country contexts and national circumstances. The G20 Policy Guide includes key building blocks which need not be implemented in sequence, providing flexibility and an opportunity to be used as a check list, if desired. As a result of structural inequality, policy action has different implications for women and men. G20 and non-G20 policymakers and stakeholders are encouraged to undertake systematic analyses of their policies and programs to help eliminate the gender differences that exist in access to finance.

FIGURE 2:

Digitisation and informality

INCREASED ACCESS AND USE OF FINANCIAL SERVICES BY INDIVIDUALS AND MSMES IN THE INFORMAL ECONOMY
DRIVERS OF DIGITAL ACCESS AND USE
ELIGIBILITY
- Eased documentation requirements
- Enhanced credit risk analysis
AFFORDABILITY
- New products and services
- Reduced transaction costs
CRITICAL ENABLERS
DIGITAL ON-BOARDING
DIGITAL PAYMENTS INFRAESTRUCTURE
ALTERNATIVE DATA FOR CREDIT REPORTING
CONSUMER PROTECTION, FINANCIAL LITERACY AND DATA PROTECTION

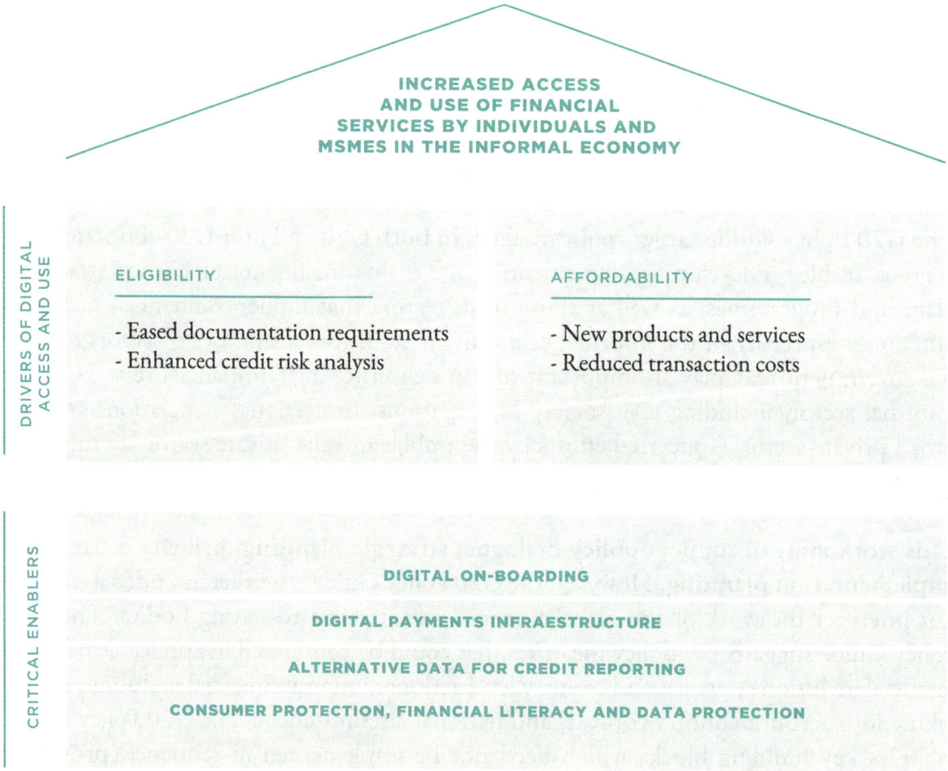

> *Millions of individuals and small businesses are relegated to the informal economy, getting by without access to the formal financial services they need to protect themselves against setbacks and create opportunities. So addressing informality is a priority in order to expand financial inclusion.*
>
> *The G20 Policy Guide on Digitisation and Informality is a good start to help us understand how digitisation has the potential to decrease informality. But we must address other elements as well—strengthening financial information infrastructure and data, and developing enabling legal and regulatory frameworks that can provide incentives for formalisation.*
>
> *I hope that the G20 Policy Guide will lead to more focused research on the contribution that financial inclusion can make specifically on reducing informality, including examples, as well as how informality hinders our progress on financial inclusion.*

— H.M. Queen Máxima of the Netherlands, United Nations Secretary-General's Special Advocate for Inclusive Finance for Development (UNSGSA)

Author: **Erin Rufledt**

Digitisation and informality

How to harness opportunities

A. Digital on-boarding[16]

Identification systems play a significant role in enabling financial inclusion. A unique and legal identity is necessary to allow all individuals to participate fully in the society and the economy. Identity verification is also important for MSMEs to establish the identities of the staff and directors authorised to setup, operate and instruct changes for the business. Verification of identity enables service providers to facilitate registration, minimising the risk of fraud and meeting the requirements of CDD regulations.[17] Yet approximately 1 billion people around the world are estimated to lack an officially-recognised proof of identity.[18] This is particularly the case for women and vulnerable groups such as forcibly displaced persons.[19] Where data are available, the female share of the unregistered population often represents more than 50 percent.[20] Progress in the development of identification schemes can therefore positively impact financial inclusion, especially of those individuals and MSMEs operating in the informal economy, given the pervasiveness of eligibility barriers for these segments of the society.

Technology could offer solutions to improve the identification and verification of new customers. The introduction of a digital identification system could potentially lead to more adoption of digital financial services by: a) making it easier for the unbanked to open a transaction account[21] in conjunction with simplifying documentation requirements; b) enabling more cost-effective customer on-boarding that can be conducted remotely; and c) contributing to facilitate the delivery of additional services to the individual. Digital identification systems can also enhance the security credentials and potentially make it a more secure process to enable financial inclusion among people while meeting regulatory requirements of Anti-

Money Laundering/Countering Financing Terrorism (AML/CFT).

The World Bank Principles on Identification for Sustainable Development provide guidance to advance the promotion of robust and inclusive identification systems, in particular digital ones.[22] As Principle 2 highlights, the emergence of new digital approaches, such as biometrics, allows individuals and small businesses to have access to identification services in a more effective way. National and local governments have a primary role in the registration and recognition of legal identity. As stated by Principle 7 of the HLP for DFI, in the financial sector the focus is on legal identity credentials provided by and/or recognised by governments for official purposes.

The legal framework is one of the most important aspects of the identification system, especially when it is scaled up to a variety of functional applications. The need for addressing the lack of identification of individuals and businesses in the legal framework is key to progress on financial inclusion. Approaches to scale up new technologies need to be evaluated, including exploring the role that the private sector can play in building out the digital identification layers. The constant emergence of new technologies and approaches to the identification process should also be monitored closely and policy framework should be adaptive towards these developments in order to take the ecosystem forward.

Based on experience to date and lessons learned from both government identity programs and private sector initiatives, the following policy recommendations are proposed:

1) Ensure an integrated identity framework.
2) Adapt and upgrade the regulatory framework.
3) Establish a robust and secure digital identity infrastructure in the financial sector.
4) Foster development of private sector-led services by leveraging legal identity infrastructure.
5) Monitor new developments and approaches to identity.

1) Ensure an integrated identity framework

A legal or foundational identity system is critical to reliably assign an identity recognised across governments and the private sector. During account opening, a customer is required to provide credentials to establish identity so that the financial service provider can carry out CDD procedures. These credentials then need to be validated and allow the financial service provider to access other sources of information such as credit bureaus to validate the information provided and assess the suitability of the product to the individual. Once complete, a transaction identifier is issued, to conduct the authentication for use in transactions. A legal or foundational identity system forms the legal basis for identity validation for critical services, including for establishing account relationships beyond a specific risk threshold. In the financial sector, once the identity validation is done, the subsequent interactions of the customer with the financial service provider can use other approaches for authentication and authorisation in the process of service delivery.

Policymakers could design a digital infrastructure appropriate for their context, including strategies to reach remote areas and ensure "last mile connectivity." Off-line solutions can complement the absence or loss of on-line connectivity. The development of robust procurement guidelines and open design standards to promote innovation and allow for greater flexibility, efficiency and functionality of the system both within and across borders could be also considered. In addition, the technical capacity of government agencies, private sector and other stakeholders in the digital identity ecosystem (including end-users) to operate and maintain new systems and devices should be ensured.

A biometric-based legal identity system can also potentially support authentication services while complying with AML/CFT regulations, upon which the service provider can further develop authorisation processes. However, wide-spread use of legal identity infrastructure for multiple phases of financial services provision has implications at several levels, including the cost of replacing existing infrastructure established for these processes; the pricing of these services; a liability framework for false-positives and false-negatives for biometric credentials; and the impossibility of replacing authentication credentials in a centralised legal identity database if there is a compromise of biometric information. Hence, there needs to be careful consideration around using national foundational identity infrastructure for on-going transactional authentication and authorisation, or whether to split the functions and isolate the foundational identity infrastructure from the rest if there exist well-established reliable, efficient and safe processes for these other functions.

2) Adapt and upgrade the regulatory framework

It is important that each country's financial services regulatory framework recognises the potential of digital identity services, and ensures that restrictions on how and where accounts are opened, and who opens them, are calibrated in line with the potential benefits of these technologies. At the same time, any such regulatory reform needs to be done in such a way as to remain aligned with FATF recommendations.

There are many specific areas which may need to be addressed in a conducive regulatory framework. These include (but are not limited to) the following: whether digital identity verification satisfies prevailing AML/CFT requirements; whether legal certainty and equivalence between digital signatures and physical signatures is guaranteed; whether private sector-managed third-party authentication services are recognised as legally equivalent to a bank doing the authentication itself; whether all bank customers should be required to provide a particular type of identity credential, for example one that is considered unique and has digital capabilities; and whether consumer interests are protected when new digital identity services are made mainstream, in particular ensuring that no segment of customers is placed at a disadvantage.

3) Establish a robust and secure digital identity infrastructure in the financial sector

Digital identity systems can introduce new challenges and risks, which need to be addressed by appropriate regulatory and oversight frameworks that apply to both traditionally regulated financial institutions and third parties. Notable risks include data security, which could be mitigated by ensuring robustness of the underlying technology, systems and processes used for digital identity; protection of privacy; and effective governance arrangements for the use of digital identity infrastructure in the financial sector, particularly as it applies to non-regulated entities.

Identity systems should be vested with security measures to protect the data. Given the nature of the data stored in the systems, security should follow a three-dimensional approach (logical, physical and organisational). It should include not only the system where the data is stored but also the network enabling its access, the back-up systems and any other system linked to the personal data of the individual, including those third parties that perform any task related to the personal data included in the identity system.

4) Foster development of private sector-led services by leveraging legal identity infrastructure

Legal identity infrastructures can provide a foundation on which the private sector can build solutions to meet the needs of the financial sector and beyond. This imposes requirements on the identity platform, in particular on areas of open interfaces and sustainable charging models, but can often allow for more rapid rollout of digital identities than the government may be able to achieve. Two of the Principles on Identification for Sustainable Development specifically call for creating interoperable platforms using open standards for this very reason.[23]

5) Monitor new developments and approaches to identity

There are a number of emerging technologies and new combinations of existing technologies that have the potential to leapfrog a unique national identity platform, digital or traditional. These methods include using distributed ledger technologies and social data. However, these are currently in very early stages of development and do not represent a viable alternative for a comprehensive build out of a foundational legal identity infrastructure. As with any innovation, the capabilities can dramatically increase and hence authorities need to closely monitor developments, use prevalent best practices and think in terms of open interfaces and modular approaches in the build out of legal identity platforms.

Box 1.
CDD requirements and biometrics

The **Reserve Bank of India** has permitted the entities regulated under it to accept Aadhaar identification number issued by the Government of India as proof of identity as well as address to meet the regulatory CDD requirements of opening accounts.

The Aadhaar Digital ID system has been unified with an electronic CDD (e-KYC) service to expedite the verification of a client's identity. The e-KYC enables an individual with an Aadhaar number to allow Unique Identification Authority of India (UIDAI) to disclose his/her personal information to service providers who wish to instantly activate services such as mobile connections and bank accounts.

The e-KYC is paperless, consent-based, private and instantaneous. As a result, accurate and reliable CDD data is shared with the reporting entity in real time. Furthermore, as the KYC data is released directly to service providers only upon the consent of the customer, his/her privacy remains protected. So far, a total of 5.9 billion e-KYC transactions have been completed through Aadhaar.

Banks and payment network operators have embedded Aadhaar authentication into micro-ATMs to provide branch-less banking anywhere in the country in a real-time, scalable and interoperable manner. From the financial services provider's view point, it offers tremendous benefits in terms of near elimination of paperwork and the consequential burden of keeping records and facilitating audit and forensics through the electronic storage of information.

In **Pakistan**, the national ID cards allowed registration of all SIM cards which re-

lied on the extensive agent network built by branchless banking providers. These ID cards enabled the opening of transaction accounts hence growing the branchless banking network.

Biometrics as the name insinuates is the metrics related to human characteristics that are unique and hence used as a means of proving one's identity. There is increasing interest around the world in exploring biometrics for authentication, as a response to (amongst other matters) AML and CFT concerns. Identity services in **India** and **Pakistan** are built on biometrics and **Bangladesh** is expected to follow suit.

Biometrics can be broadly divided into primary iris scans, fingerprints and face recognition and soft biometric- those that are more related to behavioural characteristics and mannerisms. Although they have both been considered for authentication, the former is by far the more prevalent while the latter is often used to understand patterns and trends and hence detect anomalies or unauthorised transactions.

The Payments Association of **South Africa** is working with Mastercard and Visa to design a solution that is interoperable in South Africa. The specification enables a range of biometric solutions, from fingerprint verification to palm, voice, iris, or facial biometrics. However there are concerns that the uptake of this by traders will be low due to the high cost of replacing point-of-sale (PoS) devices.

In 2015 **Nigeria**, began a biometric verification pilot for all civil servants in an effort to get an accurate record of the personnel and ensure 'ghost' salaries were not paid out. The Central Bank of Nigeria required that all customers enrol with their banks to get their unique Bank Verification Numbers (BVN) operated by the Nigeria Inter-Bank Settlement System (NIBSS). In early 2016 they announced the removal of 24,000 workers and that number has since doubled saving the tax payer equivalent of $74million USD.

B. Digital payments infrastructure[24]

Achieving greater access to and use of digital payments is essential for advancing the financial inclusion agenda, especially among individuals and MSMEs operating in the informal economy. The latest data reveal an increased use of digital payments all around the world.[25] Yet a gender gap remains: men are about 5 percent more likely to use digital payments than women.[26] Improving the payments infrastructure could dramatically boost financial inclusion and economic opportunities through increased use of formal payment services.[27] As stated in the HLP for DFI 4 ("Expand the Digital Financial Services Infrastructure Ecosystem"), the development of a payments infrastructure is one of the core enablers for a more inclusive and open digital payments ecosystem.[28]

Many governments recognise that an efficient, widely accessible and open, safe and inclusive digital payments infrastructure is an important enabler for an inclusive and growing economy. By way of general definition, an open payments infrastructure is one that can be accessed by Payment Service Providers (PSP)[29] within the regulated realm. An inclusive payments infrastructure results in payments services that can (ideally) reach any individual or MSME in the country. When the payment infrastructure is both open and inclusive it can drive digital payment volumes. This in turn can reduce unit costs and ultimately end-user fees. It can also enable competition among PSPs, leading to improved products and services and increased usage. But in addition to this, it is essential that individuals and MSMEs have the right incentives to accept those digital payments.[30]

A fully open payments infrastructure might not always be the immediately feasible or desired solution for countries. Joining such an infrastructure might not be viable or possible for some PSPs due to regulatory or financial requirements, e.g., to reduce financial stability risks, or due to existing operational issues. Moreover, some PSPs might abstain from joining the common infrastructure as they fear losing their innovative advantage when for example opening up their closed loop payments system. Those issues, among other specific circumstances like a country's infrastructure development, have to be considered in moving towards a more open and inclusive payments infrastructure. [31]

From the PSP perspective, progress towards a more open and inclusive payments ecosystem has, in some cases, been impeded by the perceived complexity associated with the participation to the existing payments infrastructures. As mentioned above, new PSPs have often not sought or been granted access to existing payments infrastructure. For example, mobile money was introduced in emerging economies as a way to encourage new classes of transaction account providers to serve unbanked populations. These have generally been introduced as closed loop systems, with limited success beyond domestic person-to-person transfer. The reasons can be found in a combination of factors, including the provider's business case, the cost and difficulty of complying with regulation, and the cost of managing agent networks and liquidity.

From the end-user's perspective, a main challenge to develop a more open and inclusive payments ecosystem has been the lack of interoperability, meaning that the customer of one PSP cannot easily transact or cash-out with a customer of another provider, and a mobile money customer cannot easily interact with a banked person or entity. Another issue, especially relevant for small merchants, has been the valuing of cash over electronic payments due to high cost of acceptance or delayed fund availability as a result of deferred clearing and settlement processes. Therefore, if countries move towards open and inclusive payments infrastructures, it may not only be critical to advance on the interoperability among digital payment services, but also to consider incentives to drive the use of these services vis-à-vis cash, and make formal financial services attractive for merchants and consumers operating in the informal economy. In this regard, utility, cost, security and trust play a major part in end-users' uptake.[32]

The following policy recommendations are intended to help move towards a more open and inclusive payments ecosystem and address the mentioned provider and end-user challenges. Further, recommendations aim to incentivise the system's use and acceptance among individuals and MSMEs, especially those operating in the informal economy. It goes without saying that an important precondition for the healthy development of a digital payments infrastructure is the establishment of widespread connectivity. Ensuring a widespread and affordable access to telecommunications networks might need to be encouraged. The main policy recommendations can be summarised as follows[33]:

1) Prioritise development of interoperable payment systems enabling fast payments.
2) Create incentives for merchant payments acceptance.
3) Create incentives for consumer use of digital financial services.
4) Support cross-border payment systems.

1) Prioritise development of interoperable payment systems enabling fast payments

The digital payment systems should allow for interoperability, providing an opportunity to connect all providers to the same system. Many countries have already pushed for their implementation, with the objective of improving efficiency over slow legacy systems and achieving financial inclusion goals. Interoperable digital payment systems need cooperation between all involved stakeholders and can provide lower-cost and lower-risk transactions, enabling greater participation in the payment system and increasing payment efficiencies, thereby contributing to more open and inclusive payment infrastructures. In addition, systems which enable Fast Payments are potentially able to take the adoption of digital payments for everyday use to new levels.

A defining characteristic of a fast payment system is the ability that the transmission of the payment message and the availability of "final" funds to the payee occur in real time or near-real time on as near to a 24-hour and seven-day (24/7) basis as possible, and are considered irrevocable. To achieve this outcome, certain activities associated with clearing have to occur in real time or near-real time and on a continuous basis for each payment order such that delays present in traditional payments do not arise. Settlement of funds between the Payment Service Providers (PSPs), however, does not necessarily need to occur immediately for each and every payment order. Payee funds availability and inter-PSP settlement can be either coupled (i.e. real-time settlement) or decoupled (i.e. deferred settlement).[34]

It may not be practical or feasible in many cases to move from the current reality to a future of ubiquitously available and accessible, interoperable and operationally robust and efficient in a single step. It is therefore important to plan the evolution of the payment system with a view towards phased implementation. There is no single best-practice route to establish this, but the following design elements should be considered:

• Use of international standards, especially in the exchange of information between systems, including transactional processing.

• The cost to the end-user is crucial. In the early phases this is not a simple matter to determine, but costing should be done on the basis of expected volume rather than short-term cost recovery. It is a matter of positioning the service for long-term benefit for all participants.

• Identify the system's components that are required and re-use, as far as possible, components already implemented by legacy systems. For example, if the settlement system is structured to handle multiple payment streams, this system could be used for new payment streams as well.

• To establish market acceptance and build trust, promote and secure the implementation of high-volume business cases. The role of payments emanating from government entities and due to such entities (G2P and G2B, as well as P2G and B2G payments) are crucial in this regard.

• Where feasible and where payment service providers do not already utilise a national ID system, it would be beneficial for interested stakeholders to have access to the national ID system in order to ascertain the identity of the real person or legal entity making a payment. This will increase utility and enable informed risk mitigation measures.

• Ensure that all regulated PSPs are able to, either directly or through some form of an aggregator, have access to the payment system. This does not imply that every payment service provider should be granted access, but rather that the criteria for use are based on the risk introduced by the PSP and the technical/operational ability to participate in the system only and does not exclude certain categories of PSPs.

The fast payments systems should be market-based, safe, efficient and low-cost. Participants could collaborate on the infrastructure level, e.g. by creating shared platforms and making their systems interoperable, and compete through innovation at the services level. This can provide space for competition and innovation while supporting openness and accessibility for providers. Further, this could contribute to levelling the playing field for providers while granting equal access to innovators and users alike. The shared infrastructure approach could ensure concentration of volumes and make "reach" (the ability of any payer to reach any payee) very simple, while keeping transaction costs low and affordable to enhance financial inclusion. At the same time, PSPs should be able to cover on-going costs and make profits.

For fast payments systems to exploit their full potential, settlement systems should be modernised to favour intra-day settlement, and consider real-time settlement and 7x24 hour settlement of transactions. As the number of participants within the payments eco-system increases as does the complexity of risk monitoring, regulators could develop additional capacity and use improved tools, particularly data management and analyses tools, to be able to perform their regulatory responses.

Policymakers could finally consider prioritising the rollout of large-scale use cases, which can demonstrate the utility, safety, and trustworthiness of fast payments systems. Focusing on priority use cases - such as transit, utility bills and marketplace/ street carts - can drive market awareness and volumes. The government itself could consider playing an active role in the payments ecosystem. For example, issuing social benefits or salaries via bulk Government to Person (G2P) payments, could enhance trust in the system, and could quickly drive uptake through its reach into a much larger proportion of households.

2) Create incentives for merchant payments acceptance

Fast payments systems need to be sustainable while investing in innovation, promotion and business development. This requires a robust business model, implying that pricing needs to be viable. At the same time, merchants or other payments acceptors such as billers should not be disincentivised by acceptance fees, while ensuring the commercial sustainability of the fast payment systems. This is particularly true for small businesses and informal retailers. With an acknowledgement that national context vary, policymakers should, where appropriate, consider a variety of incentive measures, including:

• Ensure that there is no "transaction extra charge" levied against Digital Financial Services Providers (DFSPs); such charges are often passed on to merchants and present a significant barrier to acceptance.

• Subsidising the cost of acceptance in the early stages of development. This could be considered by the private sector to reduce the initial cost of acceptance to the merchant and enable wider adoption.

• Consider the use of formal aggregators that connect to a clearing house and are able to group both formal and informal merchants. In this sense, merchants can accept payments regardless of their formalised status, significantly increasing the payment infrastructure.

• Ensure that merchant service providers, when fulfilling regulatory requirements, are given sufficient ability to act on financial and non-financial adjacencies.

• Increase transparency in the market, through the disclosure of exchange fees, discount rates and other commissions.

• Introduce financial incentives such as merchant exemptions, service charge reductions, reduced rates for merchant accounts, or government reimbursement of fees.

• Introduce thresholds for cash payments for a single transaction above which consumer cash payments are not allowed.[35]

• Where appropriate for national taxation schemes and oversight, authorities should consider incentivizing the use of the system for merchant supplier (B2B) transactions by providing tax incentives to merchants who purchase goods and services electronically. However, documentation on the impact of the incentives is scant mainly due to lack of impact evaluation embedded into the interventions and programs.[36]

• Non-financial incentives could be considered, e.g. automated reporting (fiscal, compliance), training and real-time support, etc.

Merchants should also be discouraged from relying on separate business agreements

or technology arrangements with different PSPs in order to accept payments from consumers. Public private partnerships could collaborate with DFSPs on the development of standardised technologies, for example Quick Response codes (QR codes) for merchant payments. Standardisation could support interoperability and improve usability and utility for merchants and customers.

3) Create incentives for consumer use of digital payments

Consumer fees for target use cases should be affordable for underserved populations. Consumer lottery schemes ("will your next bus ticket be free?") can also have an impact on both perceived cost and consumer awareness. For consumer/government interactions, discounts or other incentives for payments made electronically could be introduced. For consumer, financial incentives could include cash rebates, consumer rewards, loyalty programs or government-sponsored lotteries.

As recommended in HLP for DFI on Consumer Protection, it is important to establish clear and uniform regulations around the protection of consumer funds in accounts; the establishment of redress mechanisms, and access to consumer protection information. In addition, as recommended in HLP for DFI 6 on Financial Literacy, it is also important that policymakers consider market education initiatives, particularly with respect to newly implemented faster payments systems. This could be made easier where the providers involved have agreed on a common consumer brand.

4) Support cross-border payments systems

There are a number of initiatives underway or in planning stages to develop payments systems. Some of these are focused on cross-border transactions only, while others have a broader vision of supporting both domestic and cross-border transactions. Authorities in regional blocs are exploring the possibility of using approaches to processing domestic payments transactions, consistent with the principles outlined in the G20 Policy Guide and applicable regulatory frameworks. Cross-border infrastructure may be of benefit in the development of infrastructures used for financial inclusion purposes. Greater volumes through regionalisation of processing could sharply drive down costs, incentivising participation through affordability and ease of use.

Box 2.
Lotteries, loyalty programmes and POS subsidies

In **Mexico**, a 2004 presidential decree established FIMPE, a private trust fund to expand usage of electronic payment channels. Acquirers were free to opt-in and invest in this fund for a joint program to promote POS installation and use of digital payments. FIMPE was funded through acquirer contributions which were returned as fiscal exemptions. The resulting program had two main parts:

i. Demand generation (Boletazo): Lotteries were organized awarding cars to payment card users (more than 3,100 cars were awarded). According to FIMPE, transactions at POS increased 167% from 2003 to 2006 and 1 out of 5 surveyed said they increased their card usage.

ii. Supply generation: Through the trust fund, free POS were installed in merchants who did not have a POS machine and they were also offered a fixed monthly merchant fee up to certain transaction volume. The program also comprised national media campaign targeted to merchants on the benefits of payment card acceptance. According to FIMPE, the POS network increased 96.3% from 2003 to 2006.

According to an IDB report, under FIMPE, 205,000 POS were installed for free to the merchants who usually had to pay 6,000 - 7,000 MXN (approximately US$ 322 – 376). According to Banco de Mexico, POS transactions increased on average by 24 percent per year between 2005 and 2008; and stalled after FIMPE ended rising only 0.2 percent in 2009.

More recently, the Finance Ministry (SHCP) through the program Tablet para el Regimen de Incorporación Fiscal offered a subsidized tablet equipped with mPOS and accounting software for microenterprises registering for tax purposes.

In terms of cash payment caps, starting in 2014, according to article 55 of the Income Tax Law, financial sector institutions must report cash deposits made to taxpayers' accounts when the accumulated monthly amount of cash deposits exceeds 15,000 pesos (approximately US$ 806). Furthermore, Banco de Mexico issued a ceiling for checks payable to the bearer at 5,000 pesos (approximately US$ 268).

The Point-Based Incentive Loyalty Program was an innovation recognized by **Central Bank of Nigeria** (CBN) and Nigeria Inter-bank Settlement System (NISS) Efficiency Awards to "Recognize, Encourage, Reward and Appreciate" financial inclusion-geared innovations of payments industry players. The Points-Based Incentive Program aims to reward consumers for each card transaction conducted at the POS with loyalty "points" which can be accumulated and used to purchase gifts and goods from an online CBN Loyalty Portal.

Author: **Eakarin Ekartchariyawong**

C. Use of alternative data for credit reporting[37]

Around 80 percent of total MSMEs are informal. These firms face a number of challenges that can negatively impact their operations and growth, including limited public infrastructure and weak institutions.[38] However, according to the World Bank Group enterprise surveys, lack of access to finance is consistently reported as the biggest obstacle they face.[39] For self-employed people, and especially women, access to finance can also be an essential pre-condition for their work. For example, only 37 percent of women are able to use their own capital to start up their businesses, compared to 68 percent of men.[40] Informal firms report low use of loans and bank accounts, and a significant majority finance their operations through sources other than financial institutions, including internal funds, moneylenders, family, and friends.[41] Many of these firms would like to become formal (that is, to register), and report that the ease of access to finance would be the most important benefit they could obtain from registering.[42]

Recent evidence indicates that lowering initial registration costs and providing information on registration procedures have only small effects on firm formalisation. Variable costs associated with becoming formal, such as tax payments, may be comparatively more important for informal MSMEs.[43] Unless these firms grow and become sufficiently profitable to cover such costs, it would be difficult for them to enter the formal sector. Enhancing the financial inclusion of informal MSMEs can potentially help them grow and pave their path toward formalisation.[44] Considering that about two-thirds of full-time jobs in developing economies are provided by informal MSMEs, it is essential to step up efforts to improve access to finance for these firms, especially bank credit and other forms of financing.

Lack of credit data is a common cause of financial exclusion for informal MSMEs. Most informal firms do not have accounting systems to record their transactions and generate credible financial statements and projections. Very often, the only standard information that is available to assess their creditworthiness is the personal credit file or history of the owner of the firm. However, the latter often does not have a formal job and the informal business is the only source of income for her and her family. In this respect, technology can help.

In an increasingly digitised world, vast quantities of "alternative data" are being generated every day, which can complement or substitute for traditional financial data. It is estimated that the world's stock of digital data will double every two years through 2020, fuelled by the phenomenal intersection of and growth in mobile, cloud, big data, and electronic payments.[45] Financial systems are already generating many digitised data that is considered as alternative data. Such information includes online banking transactions, digital payments, and automated utility payments. In some instances, alternative data are being created outside the financial system. Every time MSMEs and their customers use cloud-based services, browse the internet, use their mobile phones, engage in social media, use ecommerce platforms, ship packages, or manage their receivables, payables, and recordkeeping online, they create digital footprints. Data collected through mobile phones and telecommunications (e.g. call data records, airtime top ups, Person to Person (P2P), Government to Person (G2P) and Person to Government (P2G) payment transactions) are also exponentially increasing data trails including for low income consumers in developing and emerging markets.

Traditional and non-traditional lenders have an option to mine this real-time, easy-to-access data, and use it for credit granting decision making. Lenders can use the alternative data to determine capacity and willingness to repay loans. Using alternative data to enhance credit reporting thus represents a large opportunity to expand access to finance to MSMEs, especially those operating in the informal economy. Lenders may leverage alternative data, such as information from utilities or retail lending, behavioural data, online platform and mobile applications to reach new customer segments including MSMEs. Beyond being used to provide access to credit, alternative data may offer valuable granularity on customer preferences and behaviours that can help to design new financial products and services, encourage positive financial behaviours and support the real sector by linking financing to energy, commerce, health or other sectors.

Notwithstanding these benefits, the use of new types of alternative data for financial and other sensitive decisions brings to the fore additional risks. Policymakers face the challenge of striking the right balance between promoting the benefits of the expanded use of alternative data while ensuring adequate data protection and attention to consumer protection, which is addressed in the next section. In this respect, the following policy recommendations are suggested:

1) Improve availability and accuracy of information.
2) Expand credit information sharing.
3) Enable responsible cross-border data exchanges.
4) Balance market integrity, innovation and competition.

1) Improve availability and accuracy of information

A first step would be to identify the main categories of alternative data. Alternative data in the context of credit reporting is information readily available in digitised form that is collected through technological platforms. Two categories of alternative data were identified: structured and unstructured data. The former is "information with a high degree of organisation, such that inclusion in a relational database is seamless and readily searchable by simple, straightforward search-engine algorithms or other search operations." The latter, which can be more useful in the case of first time borrowers, is "information that either does not have a pre-defined data model and/or is not organised in a predefined manner." In both cases, a unique identifier (ID, passport, financial ID, etc.) is necessary to uniquely link the data from all data providers related to the same individual or MSME. In order to improve the availability and accuracy of information, policymakers and regulators could, therefore, evaluate the implementation of unique identifiers such as Passport/ID for individuals, financial numbers that can be generated by regulators or financial institutions, Passport/ID of promoters or for unregistered MSMEs, or company/legal entity registration number for registered MSMEs.

In the case of MSMEs and individuals, policymakers could consider the importance of ensuring efficiency and consistency of national identification systems, where these exist. In countries where they do not exist, focus could be set on alternatives such as other identification documents issued by public agencies or consider working together with financial regulators to establish national financial identification numbers. For larger and established MSMEs, policymakers and regulators could examine the potential for establishing a Legal Entity Identification (LEI) framework that allows connecting data from different sources to improve accuracy of linked data. Additionally, relevant public-sector agencies in their role as other data sources, specifically to the extent they provide identification services, could therefore analyse the possibility to agree with Credit Reporting Services Providers (CRSP) a way in which the latter can access national ID databases for validation purposes.

Policymakers could also consider addressing data unavailability and poor quality by promoting automation in data collection, processing and ensuring that data is updated; developing and providing access to an open data system and data standards for MSME data, which captures public data such as corporate and financials; and providing guidance on the adoption and use of alternative data, including the circumstances on when structured and unstructured data can be used. Additionally, regulators and policymakers can amend laws and regulations to clarify how alternative data may be processed, taking into consideration data privacy and protection best practices.

The unavailability of data or the poor quality of data represents another impediment for financial inclusion. Governments could also consider digitising government services, such as tax filing, company registration and other government services, to encourage a digital footprint for MSMEs and individuals. Once digitised, consideration should be given to encourage governmental agencies to pro-actively ensure efficient and cost-effective access by CRSPs to datasets they manage, including but not limited to ID datasets, corporate registries, court of law systems data, and property and collateral registries. Therefore, promoting the digitisation of public information is fundamental.

Finally, consideration should be given to promote the use of digital platforms to address the limited footprints of MSME transactions through campaigns and awareness and by offering incentives to credit providers, MSMEs and consumers. Policymakers could encourage MSMEs to use as much as possible digital services to run their businesses since services that leave a digital record that can be accessed and combined with other information to be analysed for creditworthiness through offering incentive to credit providers, MSMEs and consumers; consumer awareness programmes; and digital financial literacy.

2) Expand credit information sharing

To expand credit information sharing, regulators and policymakers could analyse possible ways of addressing the limited coverage and incomplete data, by promoting open data platforms for CRSPs to interface with other data repository such as court records, company registry, collateral registry and other digitised information. They could make complete information sharing mandatory; expand the scope and list of mandatory data providers to include non-bank financial institutions, e-commerce, and utility companies; reduce or eliminate minimum reporting thresholds; promote information sharing between CRSPs; and open up the credit information sharing market by removing regulatory and financial barriers. Policymakers can assess the feasibility of establishing a Public Credit Registry/Databank when there is inadequate information sharing.

Regulators could also consider the possibility of amending regulations to require all PSPs, including non-bank financial institutions that are not regulated by a financial authority, to report credit data and other relevant information to CRSPs in their jurisdiction. Likewise, the oversight role of authorities such as the central banks over the regulated credit reporting systems and credit bureaus could be elaborated further to accommodate for the use of alternative data for assessing the capability of the MSMEs to get a loan.

Authorities could ensure that laws governing credit information sharing allow CRSPs to be able to offer services to their customers, including retail, corporate and MSMEs. Applicable laws could also allow CRSPs to collaborate, share information and consider joint products to avoid exclusion of MSMEs by CRSPs that usually focus on consumer or corporate lenders, which contributes to financial exclusion. There is a need to reduce or eliminate minimum thresholds for reporting credits/debtors to CRSPs. Additionally, commercial credit information companies and consumer credit bureaus should be encouraged to seek to collaborate, and to the extent permitted by law, share data among themselves that might be useful to each other and to their respective users. Eventually they could jointly develop certain credit reporting products.

3) Enable responsible cross-border data exchanges

There are no physical borders for most alternative data which are available through platforms that run in the internet and can be accessed from anywhere. However, cross-border data sharing may be hampered by, for example different: data collection; formats; country regulations; retention periods; unique IDs; and dispute handling process. Difficulties may also exist in identifying the source of inaccuracy. To enable responsible cross border data exchanges in the long-run, regulators and policymakers should coordinate and collaborate with relevant bodies to develop cross border data sharing standards and cross border information regulators; harmonise data privacy laws in relation to alternative data; and provide guidance on the processes of cross border sharing of information including the information that can be shared and possibility of evaluating the CRSPs. There is a need for further collaboration at the international level to improve the comparability and consistency of MSME credit data that is shared and eventually used across borders.

Authorities could finally coordinate to improve consistency and comparability of data that is collected and shared and assess the feasibility of implementing the Global Legal Entity Identifier or its variant such as the Identification for Development (ID4D) Initiative by the World Bank Group. There should be an agreement at an international level on a core set of data to be shared across borders on MSMEs covering both financial data and credit performance aspects.

4) Balance market integrity, innovation and competition

Since it is important to preserve market integrity while not unnecessarily inhibiting the access of individuals and businesses to innovative financial services, functional requirement should be consistently applied to ensure equality of treatment. In order to do so, policymakers and regulators could recommend enhanced risk management by CRSPs; increase the rigor and intensity of risk based assessments to operations to CRSPs; and collaborate on the development of principles of responsible innovation. To deal with the opaqueness over the use of alternative data, authorities should encourage transparency and disclosure of scoring methodologies of CRSPs that use alternative data. Authorities could also push for or participate in global surveys or similar tools performed periodically to obtain detailed, comprehensive and systematic information about credit reporting activities both in their jurisdictions and at the global level. Likewise, policymakers and regulators could consider the feasibility of implementing or utilising regulatory tools for enabling innovation to promote alternative data centric innovations, including alternative scoring techniques, in their own specific markets.

Box 3.
Global Legal Entity Identifier, open data system and APEC crossborder credit information sharing

The **Legal Entity Identifier (LEI)** is a 20-digit, alpha-numeric code based on the ISO 17442 standard to uniquely identify distinct entities that engage in financial transactions in the broadest definition. It connects to key reference information that enables clear and unique identification of legal entities participating in financial transactions. Simply put, the publicly available LEI data pool can be regarded as a global directory, which greatly enhances transparency in the global marketplace. The publicly available LEI data pool is a unique key to standardised information on legal entities globally. The data is registered and regularly verified according to protocols and procedures established by the LEI Regulatory Oversight Committee. In cooperation with its partners in the Global LEI System, the Global Legal Entity Identifier Foundation (GLEIF) continues to focus on further optimising the quality, reliability and usability of LEI data, empowering market participants to benefit from the wealth of information available with the LEI population.

Open data systems are platforms where some data is freely available to everyone to use and republish as they wish, without restrictions from copyright, patents or other mechanisms of control. Open data systems can either be private or government initiated. Some examples of open-data initiatives include **Data.gov, Data.gov.uk and Data.gov.in and open banking** (when banking data is shared be-

tween two or more unaffiliated parties, through APIs, to deliver enhanced capabilities to the marketplace).

Open banking is one of the drivers behind the **EU's revised Payment Service Directive (PSD2)**, which requires Financial institutions In the E.U. to release customer data to authorised third parties using open and standardised applied programming interfaces (APIs).A potential implication of open APIs could be the use of data and liquidity information to provide a very dynamic view of creditworthiness upon the client's specific consent. Some providers, such as bonify.de in Germany, are using transactional data (debit and credit movements on accounts, liquidity levels and historical changes) to create a creditworthiness score which is quite different from the static approach of the past. Instead of looking at long term statistical means they maintain an always up-to-date score based on both historical and current transactional data.

The International Finance Corporation and the Business Information Industry Association were invited by **Asia Pacific Economic Cooperation (APEC)** Business Advisory Council to conduct a pilot on the cross-border access of MSME credit information involving some CRSPs from five jurisdictions, Thailand, Cambodia, Lao, Vietnam and China, as part of the implementation of the credit information system elements of the APEC Financial Infrastructure Development Network (FIND). Efforts are currently underway to create a regional data dictionary to enable easier interpretation of cross border credit reports. These efforts will also include identification of any data elements (such as gender) that might be prohibited from being reported within a particular jurisdiction but which are commonly reported in other jurisdictions.

Author: Beuttah

D. Financial consumer protection, financial literacy, and data protection[47]

Digitisation can create opportunities to develop financial literacy competencies, confidence and experience with finance. The use of consumer and entrepreneurs' data, potentially including big data, by financial services providers can generate insights into individuals' spending habits, facilitating the offer of tailored products and supporting fraud detection. Under the appropriate data protection framework, these benefits can be substantial for consumers and entrepreneurs worldwide. They could also open up opportunities to integrate the low income and financially excluded groups in the formal financial sector by creating alternative indicators of behaviour that can be used to assess their risk as customers. For example, gender differences in financial literacy worldwide exist, with women 5 percent less literate than men, and technology offers an opportunity to close this gap.[48]

Digital technology can increase opportunities for fruitful interactions between financial services providers and consumers through digital interfaces. Such interactions can take advantage of behavioural insights, enhancing consumer and entrepreneurs' understanding of financial products and financial decisions. It can also contribute to broadening the range of providers. The digital revolution goes hand-in-hand with new providers entering the market and offering financial services directly to individuals through digital channels. These fintech companies, usually focusing on one product or service, can have an impact on the level of competition in the financial markets and contribute to lower costs, and offer improved experience to individuals and entrepreneurs.

At the same time, digitisation carries new risks for financial consumers. These risks can be:

• Market driven: this can include misuse of unfamiliar (or new types of) products or to uninformed consumers; new types of fraud, often taking advantage of consumers uncertainty in the digital environment; a lack of security, privacy and confidentiality of data; inappropriate or excessive use of digital profiling to identify potential customers and exclude unwanted groups; rapid access to high-cost/short-term credit or essentially speculative products (e.g. initial coin offerings), and other market practices that can reinforce behavioural biases.

• Regulation and supervision driven: this can encompass uneven levels of protection within (inadequate disclosure and redress mechanisms) and across countries (variety of providers, crossborder selling, regulatory arbitrage); consideration of data protection issues; a lack of coordination among authorities, for example with respect to new types of digital financial services.

• Consumer driven: the growing digitalisation of daily life and of financial decisions is not necessarily matched by increasing digital and financial literacy levels[48], and this is true even among the younger population.[49]

• Technology driven: the increasing use of algorithms, which can affect decisions about credit or insurance and can lead to denied access to certain services or inappropriate charges based on inaccurate or wrong correlations made without human interpretation; misuse of data including big data and small data; unreliability of mobile networks and digital finance platforms may lead to inability to carry out transactions; inaccessibility of funds or cybersecurity risks.

These risks can have a negative impact on consumers, and can result in a range of negative outcomes. They can perpetuate lack of, or uneven level of, trust in digital financial services, the financial system and technological innovation. Security measures must be ensured by financial providers to avoid fraudulent transactions and other security risks. Consumers should adopt security precautions when using digital channels. New types of exclusion for certain groups of the population (possibly including the elderly, women and entrepreneurs) can arise as a result of the use of big data and digital profiling for credit and insurance decisions. Low levels of financial and digital literacy and a lack of familiarity with the products available and new providers can increase self-exclusion. Finally, other unintended consequences such as over-indebtedness can surface, especially if consumers, particularly those who may be vulnerable, are tempted by immediate credit offers that play on preferences for instant gratification, or high-cost credit with limited checks on affordability are granted without proper monitoring (possibly including young people and students in particular, and low-income segments with limited access to more affordable credit).

Maximising the opportunities offered by digitisation requires a better understanding of consumers' behaviours and attitudes towards digital financial services, as well as of the financial and digital literacy needs and demands resulting from technological uptake. A sound financial consumer and data protection framework and increased digital and financial literacy are essential to the responsible and beneficial development of digitisation. Building trust and confidence in the acquisition and use of digital financial services for the financially excluded requires that regulation both promote innovation and incorporate financial consumer protection. In this sense, policies and approaches need to evolve and adapt in line with the environment.

In this context, the following policy recommendations are proposed:

Financial consumer protection

1) Adapt oversight arrangements and capability for financial consumer protection.
2) Enhance disclosure and transparency.

Financial literacy

3) Foster data collection, coordination and identification of new core competencies on digital financial literacy
4) Strengthen the delivery of financial education for DFS and support its evaluation.

Data protection

5) Enhance secure and effective consent models.
6) Enhance access, rectification, cancellation and opposition (ARCO) rights
7) Address data security.

Financial consumer protection

1) Adapt oversight arrangements and capability for financial consumer protection.

It is important to achieve the right balance between allowing technological innovations without undue limitations and ensuring that an appropriate level of financial consumer protection is maintained. Oversight arrangements and capability relates to the powers, structures and capabilities of the legal and institutional arrangements required to supervise and enforce financial consumer protection regimes. Technological developments present a range of challenges and opportunities for domestic public authorities responsible for the oversight of financial consumer protection, including balancing the development of fintech innovations while ensuring the appropriate level of consumer protection; and ensuring the adequacy of supervisory tools, resources and capabilities to oversee digital financial services.

Oversight bodies should ensure they have adequate knowledge of the financial services market, including by engaging with businesses, industry representatives and consumers to understand new digital products and services and identify market trends and issues. Oversight bodies should also ensure that regulatory and supervisory resources, tools and methods are appropriate and adapted to the digital environment, which includes having access to data and exploring the use of technology to assist in market supervision.

Oversight bodies should also be capable of dealing effectively with technological innovation issues while ensuring appropriate consumer protections are maintained. Depending on the circumstances, approaches may include establishing mechanisms such as "regulatory sandboxes" to allow new business models to be tested in a controlled environment, applying proportionate regulatory requirements and providing regulatory support, advice or guidance on the application of the regulatory framework.

Cross-border cooperation aimed at ensuring that financial consumers

remain protected through digital channels could facilitate cross-border transactions, contributing to promote consistency, reducing opportunities for regulatory arbitrage and supporting enforcement activity. This could be done through information sharing among oversight bodies from different jurisdictions. Given the provision of financial services through digital channels can facilitate cross-border transactions which can present particular risks, oversight bodies from different jurisdictions should cooperate, for example to support effective complaints handling or enforcement activity, to ensure consumers remain adequately protected.

2) Enhance disclosure and transparency

Requirements relating to disclosure and transparency are a fundamental part of most financial consumer protection regimes. Technological developments, including the availability of data, provides opportunities to improve disclosure approaches based on a better understanding of consumer decision-making (and an increasing recognition of the limitations of disclosure by itself) and to explore alternatives.

Approaches for consideration by policymakers include, *inter alia*:

- Evaluating existing disclosure requirements in the context of digital financial services to ensure they take account of disclosure via digital means.

- Embedding an understanding of consumer decision-making and the impact of behavioural biases to ensure a consumer centric approach.

- Encouraging financial services providers to test digital disclosure approaches to ensure their effectiveness, taking into account factors such as different screen sizes, communication formats, different local languages and dialects and the digital literacy of the target audience for the product.

Technological developments and the increasing availability of big data also have the potential to create opportunities to explore alternatives to traditional

forms of disclosure, for example, the publication of particular indicators relating to a financial product or service (e.g. consumer complaints) useful in decision-making, “smart defaults” where consumers are defaulted to the a particular option; or “personalised friction” which allows consumers to create steps which act as breaks in a financial transaction. In relation to the provision of advice, including digital advice, approaches for consideration by policymakers include ensuring that algorithms underlying the generation of digital advice are objective and consistent, and that the methodology underpinning digital advice services is clear and transparent, including options for recourse.

Financial literacy

3) Foster data collection, coordination and identification of new core competencies on digital financial literacy

Policymakers should as a priority collect and analyse data on the impact of digital financial services on consumers and entrepreneurs and identify key indicators both on the supply and demand side. On the supply side, data collection should focus on the products and services available, the distribution channels used by providers, and if relevant, the physical infrastructure required for a safe development of DFS and the technological requirements that enable it; on the demand side, policymakers should investigate the demand for and use of DFS, as well as the attitudes, behaviours, the digital and financial literacy of the population. This should also be instrumental in identifying the target groups that are most in need of specific financial education interventions.

In laying the groundwork for the development of these initiatives, policymakers should also ensure coordination with private and not-for-profit stakeholders involved in financial literacy and innovation, in a way that avoids conflicts of interest. This should begin with a mapping of the actors involved in the provision of DFS and of their online platforms and tools, with a view to understanding the message conveyed and possible risks for unaware consumers. It should also entail the involvement of relevant actors, those with expertise and carrying messages that are consistent with those of policy makers, in the design and development of digital financial literacy initiatives.

Policymakers should draw on available data and research to develop or fine-tune core competencies frameworks for the target groups identified, and develop appropriate financial education content. Building on existing core competencies frameworks on financial literacy, such as those developed at the international level, public authorities should consider additional core competencies required for a safe and beneficial use of DFS[50] that can contribute to:

- Build trust and promote beneficial use of DFS and related technological innovation.
- Protect consumers and small businesses from vulnerability to digital crime and misuse/mis-selling.
- Empower consumers to counter new types of exclusion due to the potential misuse of data sources, including data analytics and digital profiling.
- Support consumers at risk of over-reliance on easy access to online sources of credit.

4) Strengthen the delivery of financial education for DFS and support its evaluation

Based on these core competencies, the authorities responsible for financial education, in cooperation with relevant stakeholders, should support the effective delivery of financial education through digital and traditional means and address the needs of target audiences through tailored approaches. This should be undertaken in particular exploiting the advantages of digital delivery. Digital tools can first improve access to financial education by:

- Making it more affordable and accessible by wider audiences.

• Making it more palatable for all given the opportunity to depict information in a flexible, dynamic and graphic way more easily adapted to the target audience.

• Tailoring financial education to individual needs, through the possibility of setting up profiles or accounts on digital platforms and obtaining personalised information, instruction and advice.

Digital tools can also help reinforce core competencies, confidence and experience with DFS as they can allow to test financial concepts and products in real time, learn by trial and error, and experience failure in a controlled (and artificial) environment, thereby help shaping consumers' habits and attitudes to finance and strengthening the overall financial decision-making process. This can enhance money management skills and control over finances, and help to address consumers' personal biases, while incentivising positive financial behaviours through personal goal setting, feedback mechanisms and reminders. Policymakers should also consider that specific vulnerable target groups or entrepreneurs may still benefit from more traditional delivery tools, such as workshops, and that the needs of young people can be first and foremost met through the inclusion of financial education for DFS in the school curriculum.

Data protection

Policymakers should promote and support the evaluation of the impact and effectiveness of both financial education programmes addressing DFS and the digital tools chosen to achieve financial education outcomes. Consideration should be made to applying a standard framework for evaluation and reporting, to facilitate the comparison of results and to encourage further research on the data if possible. Ideally, such a framework will draw from existing tools developed at the international level.

5) Enhance secure and effective consent models

Consent is a fundamental principle concerning data privacy and financial consumer protection. Policymakers should enhance consent models and adopt—whenever necessary—mechanisms that are meaningful and pragmatic. Given the intrinsic limitations in the consent model, alternatives to the need for effective and informed consent, and innovative ways to obtain consent, should be implemented.

Regulators could encourage industry participants to adopt a "privacy by design" approach. Put simply, this concept envisages building privacy into all stages of the design and architecture of information systems, business processes, and networked infrastructure. The focus is on taking a proactive, preventive approach to the protection of privacy and the avoidance of privacy harms.[51] The concept rests on the following seven principles: (i) Proactive, not reactive; preventive, not remedial; (ii) Privacy as the default setting; (iii) Privacy embedded into design; (iv) Full functionality—positive-sum, not zero-sum; (v) End-to-end security—full life-cycle protection; (vi) Visibility and transparency—keep it open; and (vii) Respect for user privacy—keep it user-centric. This approach could be implemented through the adoption of a consent management system which would also allow for granularity of the choice to be made by consumers.

Minimisation of data collection should be considered. Regulators could identify key data items that are relevant for risk evaluation, identify those data items that should only be captured and used under specific circumstances or allow industry participants to evidence the relevancy of such data to the purpose of risk evaluation. This concept envisions that only the minimal amount of data should be collected. As an example, the General Data Protection Regulation (GDPR) covers this principle under its Article 5(1)(c), which states: "Personal data shall be... adequate, relevant and limited to what is necessary in relation to the purposes for which they are processed ('data minimisation')." In addition, the General Principles of Credit Reporting (GPCR) under GP1 establishes that "data collected should include all relevant information to enable any given user to adequately evaluate and manage credit risks on a continuous basis". The GPCR establishes a limit on the data that can be shared which is associated with the permissible purposes underlying information sharing or privacy considerations when dealing with sensitive issues such as ethno-demographic data".

It may be appropriate to introduce a concept of tiered consent by which consumers will be required to give different types of consent for the processing of certain types of data or for specific purposes. When adopting a consent model that enables consumers to decide the type of data that they choose to share and the service providers that they allow to access their information, regulators should bear in mind that there are certain circumstances and data items that do not allow for consent (e.g. us of default data on credit repayment). The adoption of a "privacy by design" approach would facilitate the choice of consumers regarding this layered consent.

A further alternative could be an expiry date for consents. Given that consents are virtually never reviewed or renewed, there should be a limitation period on the effectiveness of some forms of consent. It is, however, acknowledged that such an approach would not solve all the issues with informed consents. In the case of traditional data used to evaluate risk (i.e. credit repayment data) this solution might not apply at least until the obligation is fully performed.

Opt-in as opposed to opt-out consent could be a preferred option for regulators. For instance, the recitals to the GDPR state that "silence, pre-ticked boxes or inactivity should not [...] constitute consent." Industry participants could enable this feature by including clear processes to ensure that consumers receive all the relevant information to make their choice. Technological features and consent management systems could facilitate this process.

Industry participants (and data sources) should be responsible to record evidence of consent being collected from consumers. This is even more relevant when data is to be shared with third parties. For this process a consent management system would be useful. While many consumers care about giving meaningful consent, they often provide it without reading the terms and conditions of their consent. To address these issues, consideration could be given to developing tools that provide for simpler, more clearly expressed, and highlighted forms of consent. Such tools could well be technology-based. They could include a requirement for the use of standardised forms of consent, as well as the option of having verbal forms of consent that would be recorded by the financial services provider.

Policymakers and industry participants could adopt measures to ensure that the predictive ability of alternative data is tested and verified, that data is used fairly and scoring models developed using alternative data are neutral to minorities or protected groups. Consent is required when sensitive data (e.g. race, ethnic origin, sexual inclination, political or religious affiliation) is used in the evaluation of consumers' creditworthiness and when data included in the model is collected for a different non-compatible purpose. The use of alternative data that carries forward historical discrimination could either be prohibited or restricted, taking into account its ability to predict risk and the availability of alternative decision-making tools.

6) Enhance access, rectification, cancellation and opposition (ARCO) rights

ARCO rights are especially relevant in a digital financial services' context when an individual's data is held, or can be accessed, by multiple institutions and the data may be in many different forms. Consumers may not know who is holding, or has access to, their data, for what purpose it is being used, where it is being held or by whom, or the nature and scope of the data that is being held

At the minimum, allowing consumers to access their own data is a broadly accepted principle and practiced in countries where a data protection law is in place. It is also practiced in those countries where there is no data protection law but there are industries that collect, process and distribute data as part of their core business. Timeline to enable the access ranges from 1-7 days.

Consumers should be given options to correct their data. There is typically a timeline between the request by the consumer to the final resolution by the data controller. This timeline ranges from 7-25 days. However, for the use of alternative data from open sources as opposed to closed networks it is important to highlight the need to identify the data source and the person responsible for the accuracy of data as such person would also be the responsible to correct such data and respond to the consumer. The right to cancel (erase) data is linked to the right to be forgotten, the obsolescence of data and the usefulness of such data. In closed networks information is typically kept for a determined amount of time and consumers are also able to request the erasure of data when such data is not lawfully collected or has no legal grounds for its further processing.

Consumers should be given the right to make decisions regarding the use of their information for certain purposes. This is typically the case of such use as for marketing related purposes through the introduction of white lists for example. However, there are certain types of data and circumstances where the consumer cannot object the processing of such data (i.e. credit repayment data for credit risk evaluation when such repayment is in default). In closed networks there are certain data items considered mandatory and therefore not subject to this consumers choice. In open networks, the choice of consumers regarding the further use of data is broader.

7) Address data security

Data is becoming a key asset and personal data and identity theft become a major risk for consumers. Internationally agreed frameworks capture the need for safeguards to protect data against unauthorised access, loss, destruction, manipulation and data corruption. In this regard, policymakers should encourage the adoption of security measures to avoid data loss, corruption, destruction, unauthorised access, manipulation or misuse of such data and conduct cybersecurity risk assessments to also strengthen information technology systems, identifying potential threats, enabling mitigating measures and setting up prompt response to incidents would contribute to minimise the consequences of a cyber-incident. Policymakers could also set out rules and mechanisms enabling and encouraging reporting of incidents of criminal nature to law enforcement authorities and information exchange between public and private entities.

Regulators could encourage financial services providers the adoption of security measures to avoid data loss, corruption, destruction, unauthorized access, manipulation or misuse of such data. These measures could also include agreed protocols for incident response including the communication of data breaches. While the timeline for such communication varies from one country to another.

Cybersecurity assessments should be part of the overall risk management policies and

procedures of any service provider or data provider. In this context, identifying potential threats, enabling mitigating measures and setting up prompt response to incidents would contribute to minimise the consequences of a cyber-incident. Ideally, organisations should identify a person to act as Data Security Officer (DSO).

Authorities should continue to seek to leverage the benefits of cross-border data flows. All data flows –domestic and cross-border- should have mechanisms to ensure accountability of data controllers and industry participants and should put in place procedures and policies to allow consumers implement their rights regardless where the data is stored or has been transferred. Finally, cooperation agreements between authorities could facilitate achieving mutual objectives, including with respect to ensuring consistency with AML and privacy frameworks.

Box 4.
Advice provided to new entrants and innovation hubs

The **United Kingdom Financial Conduct Authority** operates an Advice Unit, which provides regulatory feedback, including individual guidance, informal steers and signposting to existing rules/guidance to firms developing automated models of lower cost financial advice to consumers.

The **Japan Financial Services Agency** supports fintech firms through a Fintech Support Desk and a FinTech PoC (proof of concept) Hub. The FinTech Support Desk responds to inquiries, mainly on the interpretation of the law, within 5 working days on average to address the concerns of fintech firms. The FinTech PoC Hub offers a venue for conducting trials with other relevant authorities, by forming special working teams within the FSA for each selected PoC project.

The **Bank of Italy** has recently launched its innovation hub (Fintech Channel), a dedicated space on its web site where operators propose projects with innovative features. The aim is to open up a channel of dialogue with operators and to support innovation processes.

Notes

[1] Demirgüç-Kunt, A., Klapper, L., Singer, D., Ansar, S. and Hess, J. (2018). The Global Findex Database 2017: Measuring Financial Inclusion and The Fintech Revolution. Washington DC: The World Bank Group.

[2] World Bank Group (2018). The Little Data Book on Financial Inclusion. Washington DC: The World Bank Group.

[3] Ibid.

[4] International Finance Corporation (2017). Alternative Data Transforming SME Finance. Washington DC: IFC.

[5] See International Labor Organisation (2013). Decent Work and the Informal Economy. Geneve: United Nations. See also ILO's 2002 International Labour Conference Resolution and Conclusions concerning decent work and the informal economy.

[6] International Labor Organisation (2014). Transitioning from the Informal to the Formal Economy. Geneve: United Nations.

[7] MSME Finance Gap Database. Washington DC: The World Bank Group.

[8] World Bank Enterprise Surveys (various years).

[9] International Labor Organisation (2014). Women and Men in the Informal Economy: A Statistical Picture. Geneve: United Nations.

[10] Promoting financial inclusion of women in the informal economy requires improvement in the quality of disaggregated data. See Co-Chairs' Summary of the Joint Development and Finance Ministers' Meeting of the G7 held in Canada on June 1st, 2018. See also Women Financial Inclusion Data Partnership (2018). The Way Forward: How Data Can Proper Full Financial Inclusion For Women.

[11] ibid.

[12] While physical access and connectivity are important barriers to financial inclusion, recent evidence points to the important role played by eligibility and affordability in the informal sector. See, for example, Honohan, P. and M. King (2012). Cause and Effect of Financial Access: Cross-country Evidence from the Finscope Surveys, in R. Cull, A. Demirguc-Kunt, and J. Morduch (eds.), Banking the World: Empirical Foundations of Financial Inclusion. MIT Press, Cambridge; King, M. (2012). The Unbanked Four-fifths: Informality and Barriers to Financial Services in Nigeria. IIIS Working Paper 411.

[13] GSMA (2018). The Mobile Gender Gap Report. February 2018.

[14] See Capasso, S. and T. Jappelli (2013). Financial Development and the Underground Economy. Journal of Development Economics, 101(C): 167-178.

[15] Beck, T. and M. Hoseini (2014). Informality and Access to Finance: Evidence from India. Centre Discussion Paper Series No. 2014-052.

[16] This section builds upon the input paper prepared by The World Bank: "G20 Digital Identity Onboarding Paper". Washington DC, 2018.

[17] CDD standards are set forth in the Recommendations of the Financial Action Task Force (FATF), the principal stan-

dard-setting body for preventing money laundering and terror financing. The G20 Policy Guide does not purport to interpret the FATF Recommendations or to summarise relevant FATF guidance.

[18] World Bank Identification for Development (ID4D) dataset.

[19] Global Partnership for Financial Inclusion (2017): GPFI Policy Paper – Financial Inclusion of Forcibly Displaced Persons.

[20] Ibid.

[21] A transaction account is broadly defined as an account held with a bank or other authorised and/or regulated service provider (including a non-bank), which can be used to make and receive payments. Transaction accounts can be further differentiated into deposit transaction accounts and e-money accounts. See Committee on Payments and Market Infrastructures and World Bank Group (2016). Payment aspects of financial inclusion. Bank for International Settlements and World Bank Group, 2016.

[22] World Bank Group (2017). Principles on Identification for Sustainable Development: Toward the Digital Age. Washington DC: The World Bank Group.

23 Ibid.

[24] This section builds upon the input paper prepared by Better than Cash Alliance (2018): "Achieving Development and Acceptance of an Open and Inclusive Digital Payments Infrastructure. A Guidance Note for the G20/GPFI Markets and Payment Systems Subgroup". New York, 2018.

[25] World Bank Group (2018): The Little Data Book on Financial Inclusion. Washington DC: The World Bank Group.

[26] Demirgüç-Kunt et al. (2018), op. cit.

[27] When the Mexican government digitised and centralised payments, the cost to distribute wages, pensions, and social welfare dropped by 3.3 percent—or nearly US $1.27 billion. See Better than Cash Alliance (2013). Sustained Effort, Saving Billions: Lessons from the Mexican Government's Shift to Electronic Payments. New York.

[28] Global Partnership for Financial Inclusion (2016). Guidance Note on Building Inclusive Digital Payments Ecosystems.

[29] A payment service provider is an entity that provides payment services, including remittances. Payment service providers include banks and other deposit-taking institutions, as well as specialised entities such as money transfer operators and e-money issuers. See Committee on Payments and Market Infrastructures and World Bank Group (2016), op. cit.

[30] Better than Cash Alliance (2018), op. cit.

[31] Committee on Payments and Market Infrastructures and World Bank Group (2016), op. cit.; CPMI (2014). Non-Banks in Retail Payments. Bank for International Settlements; and International Telecommunication Union (2016). ITU-T Focus Group Digital Financial Services. Access to Payment Infrastructures. Geneve.

[32] World Bank Group and World Economic Forum (2016). Innovation in Electronic Payment Adoption: The Case of Small Retailers. Washington DC.; and BTCA (2018), op. cit.

[33] Better than Cash Alliance (2018), op. cit.

[34] Committee on Payments and Market Infrastructures (2016). Fast Payments – Enhancing the Speed and Availability of Retail Payments. Bank for International Settlements.

[35] Ernst & Young and Master Card (2017). Reducing the Shadow Economy through Electronic Payments.

[36] World Bank Group (2016). Supporting Payment Sector Development: B2B Corporate Payments Requirements in the Traditional Retail Sector". Washington DC: The World Bank Group.

[37] This section builds upon the input paper prepared by the International Committee on Credit Reporting and Global Partnership for Financial Inclusion: "Policy Guidance Note on the Use of Alternative Data to Enhance Credit Reporting". Washington DC, 2018.

[38] MSME Finance Gap Database. Washington DC: The World Bank Group.

[39] World Bank Enterprise Surveys.

[40] UN Women (2015). Progress of the World's Women 2015–2016: Transforming Economies, Realizing Rights. New York: United Nations.

[41] Farazi, S. (2014). Informal firms and financial inclusion: Status and determinants. Policy Research Working Paper No. 6778. Washington, DC: The World Bank Group.

[42] Ibid.

[43] Bruhn, M. (2013). A Tale of Two Species: Revisiting the Effect of Registration Reform on Informal Business Owners in Mexico. Journal of Development Economics (103): 275–83.; de Andrade, G., M. Bruhn and D. McKenzie (2013). A Helping Hand or the Long Arm of the Law? Experimental Evidence on What Governments Can Do to Formalize Firms. Policy Research Working Paper 6435. Washington, DC: The World Bank Group; De Giorgi, G. and A. Rahman (2013). SME's Registration: Evidence from an RCT in Bangladesh. Economics Letters 120 (3): 573–78; Campos, F., M. Goldstein and D. McKenzie (2013). Business Registration Impact Evaluation in Malawi. Unpublished paper. Washington, DC: The World Bank Group.

[44] Ibid.

[45] Global Partnership for Financial Inclusion and International Finance Corporation (2017). Alternative data transforming SME finance. Washington, DC.

[46] This section builds upon the input paper prepared by the Organisation for Economic Co-operation and Development through the G20 OECD Task Force on Financial Consumer Protection: "Policy Guidance Note – Financial Consumer Protection Approaches in the Digital Age". Paris, 2018, for the Consumer Protection sub-section; the Organisation for Economic Co-operation and Development through OECD International Network on Financial Education: "Policy Guidance Note on Digitalization and Financial Literacy". Paris, 2018, for the Financial Literacy sub-section; and The World Bank and Consultative Group to Assist the Poor: "Data Protection and Privacy for Alternative Data". Washington DC, 2018, for the Data Protection sub-section.

[47] Hasler, A. and A. Lusardi (2018). The Gender Gap in Financial Literacy: A Global Perspective. Global Financial Literacy Excellence Center. The George Washington University School of Business.

[48] See OECD/INFE (2016). International Survey of Adult Financial Literacy Competencies. Paris: OECD; G20/OECD INFE (2017). Report On Adult Financial Literacy in G20 Countries. Paris: OECD.

[49] See OECD (2014). PISA 2012 Results: Students and Money: Financial Literacy Skills for the 21st Century (Volume VI). Paris: PISA, OECD Publishing; OECD (2017). PISA 2015 Results: Students' Financial Literacy (Volume IV). Paris: PISA, OECD Publishing.

[50] For further details see OECD/INFE Policy Guidance Note on Digitalisation and Financial Literacy. Paris: OECD.

[51] See, for example, Deutsche Gesellschaft für Internationale Zusammenarbeit (2017). Selected Regulatory Frameworks on Data Protection for Digital Financial Inclusion. Bonn: Germany.

后　记

为向读者介绍国际数字普惠金融领域的最新研究成果、进展与实践，我们决定翻译出版由二十国集团（G20）普惠金融全球合作伙伴（GPFI）组织撰写的系列报告——普惠金融全球合作伙伴（GPFI）数字普惠金融系列文献。本书由《G20数字普惠金融高级原则》《数字普惠金融：新兴政策与方法》《G20政策指引：数字化与非正规经济》三部分共同组成。本书由中国人民银行金融消费权益保护局组织翻译，是全系统集体劳动的成果。

《G20数字普惠金融高级原则》，系在余文建、孙天琦的指导下，由白当伟、汪天都、杨佩、周蕾和谢霓于2016年执笔翻译完成。为了与公开发布的翻译版本保持一致，本次出版除极个别地方外，未对2016年的译本加以改动。

2017年春，基于GPFI向各成员的报告征求意见稿，我们组织人员对《数字普惠金融：新兴政策与方法》进行了初译。当时译者分工如下：汪天都（第1、3节），周蕾、李思颖（第2.1节），张丽康、吴晓艳（第2.2节），蒋智渊、陈飞（第2.3节）、谢霓、赵鑫（第2.4节）。2018年，在初译的基础上，白当伟对照报告正式发布稿补译了概要和报告其他部分，并对翻译初稿进行了修改和校对。余文建、马绍刚最后对全文进行了审定。

《G20政策指引：数字化与非正规经济》于2018年完成。承担翻译任务的译者有：汪天都（开头部分），赵鑫（A小节），冯丝卉、陈飞、魏莹（B小节），李思颖、张丽康、张晓梦（C小节），蒋智渊、周蕾、谢霓（D小节）。在此基础上，李潇潇初校了译文，白当伟对译文作了最终校对。余文建、马绍刚最后对全文进行了审定。

本书能够出版，首先要感谢东北财经大学出版社国际合作部对普惠金融事业的热情关注和大力支持。本书的翻译、出版得到了中国人民银行金融消费权益保护局及分支行金融消费权益保护处（办公室）领导、同事的支持，有许多来自分支行的同事参与了翻译，金融消费权益保护局蒋润东、茹中昊也参与了部分工作，在此一并致谢！

对于本书翻译中存在的不足之处，欢迎读者批评指正。

译　者

2018年10月